P9-EEC-522

Other Voices
Works in Progress

Other Voices
Works in Progress

Edited by
Norbert Blei

CROSS+ROADS PRESS

2007

Publisher/Editor N. Blei
Layout Editor: Jan Mielke
Cover Art: Tom Becker
    front cover, The Poet; back cover, Morning
Copyright: © 2007
ISBN: 1-889460-15-X
Printed in Canada

CROSS ✚ ROADS PRESS
P.O. Box 33, Ellison Bay, WI 54210
www.norbertblei.com
www.bleidoorcountytimes.com

Once upon a Time. . .

large publishing houses had more faith in showcasing the work you find in these pages: a lively assortment of talented writers and artists, mostly unknown, mostly dedicated to pursuing and perfecting their art, anxious to share what it is they are doing in the hope of creating greater interest, wider publication and distribution of their work.

Writers and artists spend their entire lives seeking confirmation. They need to know they are being taken seriously, for their own good, for the satisfaction of others (friends, loved ones, parents), many of whom fail to understand how a person can turn away from everything and lead an isolated life of work and dedication with no guarantee of success or financial gain. *"You want to do what? Go find a job."* It's all about money of course, given our culture.

Well, no one in this book is going to make any money for his efforts. Including me, who hopes that the financial loss in publishing OTHER VOICES won't be so severe that it might put me and the press under for good. I've come close before. But not *this* close, given the size and scope of the project. Not that I expect to keep on doing this forever. It's about time for me to bid adieu. Time for others to carry on the mission of small press publishing—the conscience of American literature.

The manufacture of best sellers may be important to the book biz in this country, but *real* writing is what we need to know ourselves. You cannot estimate the cost of that, create the product by committee, manipulate the masses so they will purchase what they see and hear on talk shows. What we need are good readers who will acknowledge and support writing that matters, wherever it appears. Writers who give readers *more* than what they paid for. Longer lasting.

I started a small press in 1994 to acknowledge those writers/publishers who extended a hand to me years ago when I sought and needed confirmation. It seemed (then and now) *my* time to see what I could do. And what I did, what my intentions were, remain the same: Support new writers—primarily those with solid publication credits but no first book to their name. And, whenever possible, help those writers who have faded into oblivion and refuse to remain silent.

That's pretty much it for me: a literary search and rescue mission.

Art matters. Good writing can change lives. These voices deserve our attention.

—*Norbert Blei*

Cross Roads by Kari Anderson

Contents

Laurie Kahn

Listening to the Untold Stories

As a therapist I listen to the untold story. I am the midwife to a narrative that needs to be constructed, told or infused with compassion and new meaning.

The loss of the ability to make meaning is crippling. Therapy not only touches the lives of our clients but also transforms the experience of the therapist. It is a cliché to say our clients are our teachers but it remains a truth. One of my clients remarked once that "therapy was going great, it was just the rest of her life that she was worried about." How a therapist lives life has everything to do with the capacities of a therapist. I have had the opportunity to train and mentor many therapists. I say to them "live life more fully and your work will follow." So therapy changes lives and life changes us. My writing is about moments that have changed my life and lives I have had the privilege to touch. It is also about the spaces in-between where meanings emerge.

Traumas are often wordless. I have learned that words are a gift. If you were allowed to name it, describe it , teach it, you could master it or at least tame it. When it remains wordless; the horror and shame takes over and limits people lives and potential.

The walls of the counseling room are constraining, although filled with people's truths and confidences. The moments are profound yet, secretive and private. The lessons, I believe, need to be shared integrated back into community. Words give voice. Abuse silences.

So I began to write. Write through the lenses that my work had provided. My willingness to companion my clients as they face the sometimes-unimaginable horrors changed me. So my writing is about moving from wordlessness to words and making meaning out of the traumatic and the ordinary.

***

The first section of essays, "Witnessing," is about the work of being a trauma therapist. How I chose working with trauma for my life's work, or how it chose me, eludes me. One of my students once said she was "called" to do this work but she didn't hear the phone ring. I have never felt called to help people. I felt called to make a difference. Working with the traumatized is humbling. The work changes us, as it should. To be unchanged would mean we had not fully paid homage to the magnitude of the traumas. We stand on a similar precipice as our clients, vulnerable to the curse of indifference and in danger of becoming numb, of being swallowed by the horror that so often renders us helpless. It is a challenge as a clinician and in the poetics of being human not to fall over that precipice. With these essays I hope to provide a small window into the experience.

"Making a Difference" is about social conscience, friendship, and rituals, about constructs that sustain meaning. "Traumatic events undermine the belief systems that give meaning to human experience" (Judith Herman) . The trauma therapist follows in the dust behind our clients in a parallel path creating, reflecting and examining constructs of meaning. Deliberate attention to what matters stokes the resilience of trauma therapists.

The next section of essays, "Love," attempts to untangle love and abuse. How do we learn about love when those who "love" hurt us and jeopardize our well-being? The scars of child abuse invade longings for intimacy and love. Bessel van der Kolk reminds us "withdrawal from intimacy is one of the most enduring effects of (childhood) trauma." I am a relational therapist. I believe that when one is damaged in the context of a relationship it is best repaired in the context of a relationship.

"My Untold Stories" are some snapshots of moments and relationships that have informed my development. It is not the job of a therapist to share her history or stories. It is however misleading (and may be unkind) to allow the therapist to be perceived as other, untouched by his own human struggles.

"Sacred Moments" surround the therapeutic process and life itself. Sacred is the opposite of abuse. It is respectful, filled with meaning. It is neither dogmatic nor prescriptive. Mine will differ from yours. It is found in the quiet spaces, the spaces in between.

Listening

"It takes two to speak the truth: one to speak and another to hear." – Henry David Thoreau

Girls not yet in their women bodies are sold into the sex industry; mass graves from ethnic cleansing are filled with the corpses of men, women and children; freedom fighters are tortured, stripped of their humanity and humiliated by their captors in prison. How can our ears bear to listen to such stories of atrocities. The list grows longer: rape, incest, commonplace atrocities that happen just down the street or next door; natural disasters, such as hurricanes and tsunamis, where lives, towns, memories, mothers, fathers, and children lost to nature's fury.

The witness and the bystander stand side by side, the witness with an open heart, willing to be disturbed, the bystander hiding or immobilized, unwilling to look or to act. Each one lives inside of us. They take turns hiding and appearing. If we turn away from what demands witness, our humanity is compromised, yet our willingness to witness can pull us down into deep water as if we are drowning as we are inundated with stories, each of which is enough to break a heart. A companionate heart can be numbed with too much exposure to horror. It is not a simple task to bear witness or to companion those who have been left in the wake of trauma. It is a natural instinct to want to turn away from the knowledge of random violence, cruelty and evil.

I am not a stranger to condolences or to violence, or to the impact of trauma on family and friends of victims. Actually, I am considered somewhat of an expert by my colleagues. I have a friend whose father was stabbed to death. He was found with his blood covering the sidewalk where he was attacked. I avoided calling her. I found myself rehearsing what I would say. "Sorry about the loss of your father." I know not to collude with denial or to act as if this was an ordinary loss. I know it is one of those losses where the world will never be the same. I try again: "I heard your father was murdered, I am so sorry." Closer, but still lacking in appropriate outrage, empathy for the assault, the onslaught of violent pictures that will haunt her before sleep. So I avoid a little longer, not wanting to fall short in my desire to comfort and pay my respects.

Avoidance is a familiar strategy, not too difficult to rationalize in my busy life. I have patients to help, staff meetings to attend, children to take to the dentist. I try to imagine, just take a glimpse: what if my father, the man I believed till the ripe age of adolescence was invincible, all knowing, funny and kind, was murdered. Before the perspiration on my hands becomes too noticeable I distract myself. My avoidance and my desire to provide comfort to my colleague are temporarily at war. I know this war. I know the way out because I have chosen to find the way many times. I do call my friend. She is back at work at the university. I express my sorrow about the murder of her father. I acknowledge my avoidance and wonder out loud if others who care deeply about her may be having the same difficulties. I speak to the loss of her father, the traumatic experience of his violent death, and to her isolation, when it is hard for friends to find words for the experience and not easy for her to find people who can listen. We talk about the murder, the ordeal of an upcoming trial, her exhaustion and her loneliness in the midst of friends and family. She thanks me for calling.

Listening: every beginning therapist learns the craft. Companioning, as some refer to it. One confiding relationship has been found to be the best buffer for psychological difficulties in times of distress. All the theories point to the centrality of human connection for healing. In the study of psychological trauma we speak of bearing witness. Bearing witness is the opposite of being prohibited from speaking, from hearing and seeing no evil. It is the willingness to know intimately the cruelty of interpersonal violence, of human atrocities, and of their imprint on the lives of victims.

In my work I have become all too familiar with the words like "rape,", "incest," "human atrocity," "brutality," "shattering," "violation," "betrayal," "berserk," "murderous," "speechless," "shame,", "disgust," "repulsive," "cruelty," "psychopath," "crimes against humanity." These words roll off my tongue with more
frequency than I wish to admit. They are relevant to the stories

12

of abuse and trauma I am to witness to as a therapist. But am I listening? To really listen I have to stop squirming or choking or numbing myself, and be present. I have to open a door inside of myself to let in a universe, a universe that does not allow for rose-colored glasses. In my work with those who have survived child-hoods where abuse was the norm, and neglect more common an experience than the support and loving care of a parent, I become an insider, privileged to hear the first-hand accounts of cruelty. I am a witness to the recounting of the stories of children's trust destroyed by betrayals. I am a witness, for example, when Mary trembles as she tells of the nighttime terrors that began at age five as her bedroom door opened; or when I hear of Alice's piercing emptiness from neglect, never having experienced a birthday party or words of love; or when I know Jessica's rage at the betrayal by her mother when she refused to believe that her uncle raped her at family gatherings. I have to be willing to fall short, as language does, in the face of these and many other unbearable losses and betrayals.

Silence can be sacred and respectful. Trust is built slowly by not pushing for a response or relationship when someone is hesitant to speak and wants to be the one for once who sets the pace. Silence can reflect a desire not to trivialize an atrocity with insufficient words. Elie Wiesel remained silent for ten years after being freed from a concentration camp. The terror of the death camps, he believed was beyond words and comprehension. Speaking, he feared, could betray the dead, trivializing what he knew and had seen in death camps.

Sometimes I talk when silence would be respectful because I can not tolerate feeling helpless in the face of someone's pain. Silence can also be the horrific sound of indifference, causing humiliation for the one who had the courage to speak the unspeakable. Never be silent, I remind myself, in the face of abuse or brutality. Neutrality supports the oppressor, never the victim.

My resolve and courage ebb and flow. There are days I feel inspired, moved by the courage, strength, and resolve of those who have been so deeply injured. I know that there is hope for repair. My friends and colleagues in South Africa taught me that you can dance with your pain and it will be transformed to joy. They taught me of communities where truth-telling is encouraged, and begins to heal the deepest wounds. That is the good news. But, on the other side, my spirit gets weary. I remember a four-year-old girl who had just witnessed her mother's bruised body and disfigured face after being raped. She turned to her Dad and asked. "Does this happen to people a lot or a little?" In moments of despair, I wonder, as did she, what kind of a world this is when the average age of children who are sexually abused in this country is five. That is intolerable.

There are days I am reluctant to go into my basement to wash my laundry. I have heard too many stories where bad things happen in basements. I check my door three times before leaving for work as pictures of invasion and rape flash in front of my eyes. I have been changed by this listening and I want at that moment to return to who I was before: more innocent, optimistic, carefree. There are nights when I am awakened haunted by images of children being injured. Yet I am strangely reassured that I have not been moved into indifference. There are times, I remind myself, that we must be willing not to sleep well at night.

So listening is no easy craft. It is a state of being willing to be deeply disturbed and not flinch or turn away. It is the willingness to struggle with your own faith in goodness, deities, or a divine order.

The Untold

You cannot tell a story when you have no words. You can't tell, if there is no one who will listen or believe you. You cannot tell a story if it is devoid of meaning, just filled with sensations, scars that suggest injury but no story line. It cannot be told if you are too young to know that this was your story, not just the way it goes for all children. It remains untold if telling threatens precarious ties with the parent who is also your sole source of care. It is untold when you have no memory, because knowing was more than you could bear. It stays untold because you were silenced through fear. It is untold because you never thought of yourself as a teller of stories.

Telling is the act of engaging someone so the story lives both inside and outside. It can then become textured with color and shades. It can begin to evoke emotions in the teller and listener such as passion, fear, regret. Left untold it remains a secret, a story filled with shame, confusion and fear.

Most people who venture into my office do not begin with a story of childhood abuse, detailed with shape and form. If they do have a story it is often two dimensional, lacking the stirrings of emotions they believe to be too dangerous to express.

The story is always in the room, however. It is in the life that is led and the life not led. It is in the startle response when the door bell rings. It rests in night terrors and the nightmares. How, for example, did Ellen grow up believing she is disgusting? "I am not like others," she would insist without flinching. "I have often wondered if I am from another planet, resembling humans but different on the inside. I feel nothing. Sex is nauseating to me. My body never responds."

Over time, her thoughts and sensations become understood as reasonable responses to a childhood filled with abuse and humiliation, a childhood without care and comfort to buffer the assaults to her body and spirit.

Amy tells me that as a child she ate as much spinach as she could, hoping she would become like Popeye. "I wanted his super strength so I too could beat the bad guys and escape from their clutches. "And why did Susan beg me as her therapist not to like her or care about her? Being cared about elicited terror, not soothing. There sits her untold story.

The untold stories live in the cells, in one's relationship choices, in our bodies. I have learned to be the midwife to the untold story. I witness the words, pictures and sensations that are stored in the mind and body when a voice claims or explores a narrative that was once forbidden and too dangerous to speak . These are the moments of transformation.

So yes, I listen with a different kind of ear because I know some stories are too difficult to tell.

The Story

Cindy was sexually abused by her father. She came to see me because she was filled with guilt and shame. At age twelve, she had taken her younger sister to her father, as he demanded, to show her what to do. Her sister's abuse began and hers stopped. In her adult years, her sister was still enraged with Cindy and blamed her for the abuse. Her mother also saw Cindy's behavior as sinful and also believed that Cindy was responsible for her sister's abuse. There was no narrative of Cindy's victimization. This is the upside-down world where victims are responsible for the sins of their fathers. Cindy carried the twisted narratives of a disturbed mother, an injured sister and a sociopathic father who believed he was entitled to the young bodies of his daughters and who still had no remorse.

The child's story is different than an adult's story. The child does not have the luxury of truth-telling if truth threatens the bonds that keep her alive. She may invent stories of fairy tales and monsters that further challenge her credibility as a truth teller. When unencumbered by fear, or when fear subsides, memory is more reliable.

The narrator determines everything. The narrator determines the voice, the perspective, the psychological landscape of the story, the intentions of the characters. It is the narrator's eyes through which the story unfolds. Switch narrators and the story changes.

As I continued to expressed compassion for her childhood horrors, Cindy became able to develop a narrative of her own making, one in which she was no longer just a character in a story, one where she became the narrator. She no longer carried the shame of the family. She held her parents accountable. She could see her and her sister as victims. She came to understand that abusers ask their victims to participate in the abuse of others to ensure their silence. She claimed her rage, rage at her father for robbing her of her innocence, for violating her body, for assaulting her sense of her own goodness. She grieved the losses of a child whose mother could not nurture her or protect her. She and her sister are now united in compassion and determined to live lives free of abuse and fear. Cindy has married a kind, respectful and loving man. The narrator has changed and so has the story. This is my work.

Julie C. Eger

The Secrets of Arbishaw County

The Secrets of Arbishaw County is a fictional tale about young Gypsy Rose. Her mission is to complete Princess Lei Lei's challenges in order to earn a more suitable name and avenge Beggar's death, but Tetta's superstitions crop up at every turn. When the crow caws five times, it is a long wait to see if five people will die before the year is over. Will she ever be able to identify the Lincoln Hat Man who murdered Mrs. Tiffit? Who will break her heart in that seemingly innocent town of Vedisville in the heart of Arbishaw County where superstitions are sucked into the people, the soil, the graves? In a place where murder and the Lincoln Hat Man co-exist, it is a surprise to find out that someone she is very close to is an actual descendant of the town's legendary grave robber. Gypsy Rose must choose quickly when faced with a life or death decision. In the end, held up to the light, Gypsy Rose sees through innocence, love, and loss as she unwinds the dark secrets of Arbishaw County, and witnesses the true power of a person's name.

Chapter One

These things I knew for sure on the day of the naming ceremony. I knew the chicken coop was in Arbishaw County, and Arbishaw County made Grampa's brain twitch even when he wasn't full of whiskey. I knew I liked Gator a lot, well okay, more than a lot. I knew I needed to be worried about what Princess Lei Lei would say when I saw her glance at the floor. She had been acting very strange toward me lately.

These things I didn't know. I didn't know about the Lincoln Hat Man of Arbishaw County. I didn't know that what he did to Mrs. Tiffit would affect me for the rest of my life. From the moment I found out, I was never sure whether I should leave a door open or closed. Up until then, I didn't know what scared meant, and that scared has a tendency to repeat itself.

It was two weeks since school let out, and with naked arms glistening, bare toes kneading the dust, they stood in a wide circle surrounding me as I breathed hard from the back of my throat. Wisps of smoke, left over from the barn fire that killed Beggar, stung my green eyes. My jaw worked hard like the broken hinge on the sawed-off door that creaked in the heat. Just once, I wanted to get the best even if I wasn't first.

Princess Lei Lei waved the hockey stick over my head, *"May don doe cas condo."* She tied a beaded leather band around my wrist, and then placed five keys in my hand. I knew the rule. If I removed the band, a penalty awaited me.

I held my breath as Princess Lei Lei glanced at the white flower poking up through the dried chicken shit that covered the floor. No-o-o! The word slammed through my brain, ricocheting inside my head, but my lips stayed pressed tight. Princess Lei Lei's voice thrummed, "Wilamena Rae, you are to be known— as Gypsy Rose."

The sun teased its way through the dirty glass windows that were up so high I couldn't see out of them even if I stood on my toes. Dust hung in the light beams, forcing the watchers to breathe in ragged little sips.

Cast through the air, the name sifted down through the dust in Tetta's old chicken coop, and landed on my shoulders like pieces of misplaced confetti. Fate, that relentless old friend, forced me to reel it in as the dreaded name pulled itself together, and snuggled in tight around my shoulders. *Gypsy Rose. I can't believe Princess Lei Lei chose that name.* Disappointment shuffled in and would not leave. The back of my throat made a clicking sound as I swallowed. *Princess Lei Lei is testing me. I'm a tomboy for Christ's sake. I can't go around with a pansy-ass name like Gypsy Rose. Should I contest it? Do I dare?*

Princess Lei Lei pulled the gunnysack over my head, the musty burlap clawing at my arms as I poked them through the slits on each side. She ripped two holes in the top of the sack, and I tugged the whole thing sideways, positioning it so I could peek through the hole on the left.

A hush attempted to calm the dust as Princess Lei Lei chanted, "You will follow the guiding principles of the Haunted Horse Club without fault or be prepared to pay a sacrifice. Your purpose is to keep the secrets of Arbishaw County. Expect to answer questions you thought had no answers."

She bent to scoop up a handful of powdery chicken dust, and then let it trickle through her open fingers until it settled on her toes. "You will honor the forces that are More Than We so the spirits can make their wishes known."

My throat clicked again as I stepped center and bowed to the three sacred directions, Down—Keeper of Witnesses, Up—Keeper of Spirits, and Within—Keeper of Souls. My brain spun fast and crazy as a tornado, the skin around my eyes puckered as I hunted through thirteen years of murky recollections; furiously scanning the files of my mind for any information regarding the cost of things. *Could I afford to contest the awful name Princess Lei Lei had given me? I was sure the price would be high, but how high would she go?*

My eyes skipped around the room, daring any of them to look at me. Those who had already received their names, decent names, stared at their feet, the corners of their eyes crinkling as they peered through their jagged holes, pretending to be safe behind the thin shield of their gunnysacks.

Sweat rolled down my forehead, stinging and causing tears. It sliced a river down each side of my face, joining at my neck to form a noose that glistened. I was glad no one could see the sweat rolling down into the valley between my breasts, rolling down my belly.

"I want to contest my name," the words erupted from my lips, and my throat would not stop making that clicking sound, but I didn't care. I would do anything to get my name changed, no matter what the cost.

"Are you sure you want to do that?" Princess Lei Lei challenged.

"Yes."

"Very well, then," she said. "There are three tasks you must complete before I will consider changing your name." Her eyes pierced mine. "You must plant a tree in a rock, tell me the name printed on the red light that blinks at the top of the radio tower, and tell me where Mrs. Tiffit hides her keys."

My jaw dropped. I could not imagine how to plant a tree in a rock. It was against the law to climb the radio tower, not to mention dangerous, and Mrs. Tiffit never allowed anyone in her house, except for Miss Pruddie, who helped polish her handed down silver.

Princess Lei Lei paused. I hesitated. Her voice cracked with impatience. "Do you accept?"

I nodded. Even though the tasks were impossible, I could not make myself say no.

The other nine had already received their names, and Princess Lei Lei skimmed each set of eyes in the circle, "Is there anyone else who would like to contest their name?" Bare feet shuffled in the dust, but no one spoke.

She turned to my little brother, Ronny Ray. His cheeks glowed red, blond hair cropped short to reveal wood ticks burrowing into the skin of his scalp. He would stand still just long enough to let us pull them out before he took off running free through the summer. His slingshot dangled from his neck and it would click against his chest as he hurtled himself through the day. He smelled of frogs, marble dust, sticks and stones, moldy leaves, and yesterday's dirt. His pockets spewed trails of tangled ropes, ready to string a thing up at a moment's notice.

He propped his BB gun in the corner, and then stepped forward, standing straight as one of Grandpa's hard-driven posts, his chin high, lips mashed tight. It was a high honor to be included in a sacred ceremony with the big kids. We taught him that even though pennies were bigger, dimes were worth more; and that if he was quick enough, and got his hands behind his butt, it didn't hurt near so much when Tetta went to spank him with the old leather strap.

Princess Lei Lei pulled the gunnysack over his shaved head and it hung all the way to the floor, covering his grubby feet. Scraped shins boasting angry red welts from running barefoot through the raspberry patch, flat feet, calloused heels, an array of toes, round and brown, some tipped black and blue peeked out from under the other gunnysacks.

Out of the whole lot of us, Gator was the tallest, and the fringed edge of his gunnysack scratched against his sixteen-year-old thighs. I could see his knees poking out through the holes in his jeans. I knew he didn't have a shirt on under that old sack marked with blue and orange letters, NORTHERN BEAN OF MICHIGAN. I imagined sweat shimmering down his tan bare back. I made myself pinch my toes in as hard as I could, scrunching them so tight, I heard them squeak as I coaxed my mind away from the naked part of him and back to the matter at hand.

Ronny held out his left arm and Princess Lei Lei tied a band around his wrist. She laid six keys in his gritty palm, and he gripped them so tight his fingers turned white. In a climactic finish, Princess Lei Lei spun until I was dizzy watching her, and then, "You are to be known as — Knot." My little brother accepted the rules, took his sacred bows, and the last spoke of the sacred wheel was locked in place.

The sun was still burning hot at six o'clock on that dry summer evening, and when we stood like that, all of us in our designated places in the sacred circle, holding the wrist of the person next to us, a cold wind blew over me. It blew right through my gunnysack, drying the sweat on my forehead. I shivered and tried to shake off the prickly feeling going down the back of my legs. I wondered if the others felt the chill. I knew it had nothing to do with the fact that the sun had, just a short time ago, begun its turn toward the western horizon. The ice that slid in on that wind disturbed me.

We stood for what seemed an eternity, holding each other's wrists. My shiver melted away. The prickle left my legs. I stared at the miserable flower poking up through the dust on the floor, hating it.

Princess Lei Lei broke contact, and stepped to the center of the ring. Even though the rooster feather poking through the top of her gunnysack hung lopsided, her voice was sure and even, "You are to discover the meaning of your names. When you're ready, you'll have a chance to stand here, in the sacred circle, to report what you've learned. "

She searched our eyes. "You have one week to solve the following riddle or you will pay a sacrifice. If your answer is correct, there won't be a penalty. If your answer is wrong, be prepared to face your penalty. Have no answer, and the penalty doubles." She passed us each a slip of paper.

The riddle went like this:

> One points east, one points west
> One points north for it's the best.
> One point each, not quite south,
> You'll see the light once figured out.

I groaned. *Here we go again.* Growing up with Princess Lei Lei, I knew she rarely finished what she started. She was the queen of mystery, making up games, chasing wild ideas, whispering, "Let's go here, no here, this looks better, or better yet, here…" and we followed. We followed because Tetta said we had to, because Princess Lei Lei, at seventeen, was the oldest. The neighbor kids followed because they didn't have anything better to do during the summer. Boys followed because she was pretty.

Her bossiness was frustrating, full of sass and sarcasm, but I followed her because the girl with the 4.0 grade point average fascinated me. She was the only junior to secure the lead in the Sankton High senior play, who defeated the longstanding school record in the one hundred yard dash by three full seconds, held by a Victor Tropinski since 1932.

I envied her long brown hair, how it draped over her tan brown shoulders like satin ribbons. I watched the way her fiery brown eyes melted the inquisitive boys. I tried to look away, but I saw the pulse of their veins throbbing in their necks, in their arms, hard pulses that made me believe their blood pumped through their bodies like hot syrup. I watched as they rubbed their hands down the front of their jeans trying to wipe away the sticky sweat that seeped into their palms. I had ideas about what was going on. I'd heard things.

Crouching quietly under the porch boards one night I had strained to hear what Aunt Noxeema had to say about Princess Lei Lei. I heard her whisper to Tetta, "That girl is going to get burned. Talk about an alley cat! And the way she bosses them kids around, you'd think she cast a spell over the whole lot of them."

Princess Lei Lei interrupted my thoughts, "Meet here every Wednesday at four o'clock sharp. Miss a meeting and you will receive a penalty. You'll receive one strike for each miss; three strikes and you're banished from the club."

We finished the ceremony by suppertime. Gator jumped in

his blue two-tone Cutlass, and with a squeal of back tires throwing a spray of gravel across the black top, he hurried home to milk cows that couldn't wait.

After supper, Mouse and I sat on Tetta's porch steps. The kitchen doors were propped open to let the heat out, and Mouse had to whisper so Tetta wouldn't hear, "I already know the answer to the riddle. Want me to tell you?" Mouse was a year and a half younger than I was.

I grunted, still stewing over my awful name. "What do you mean you already know?"

Mouse stretched her neck and rolled her eyes as her lips made a popping sound.

"Fine, then tell me what it is if you think you're so smart."

]"It's star," Mouse said as she cocked her head to the side and smiled.

I glanced at my sister, and then went back to picking at my fingernails. We sat for a while in the heat, and then I asked, "What do you think your name means?"

"I'm not sure. I want to be sure before I give my report."

"I'm not going to give a report in front of everybody."

"Yes you will, because you'll want status," she taunted.

]"I hate my name. It's a sissy name," I flicked a sliver of fingernail into the dirt between the cracks of the stone sidewalk.

"Gypsy Rose? It's not that bad. Could have been Dip or Shit," Mouse smiled. She aimed her chin toward the pump house. "Just look at them. They came back strong this year. They weren't there last year."

"They look more like frigging daisies. Their leaves are all spidery. Roses should be red, or pink, those don't look like roses at all."

"Neither do you," she teased. "But remember what Tetta said, if it has just a whisper of thorns, then you can call it a rose."

I ignored her. "I think Gator got the best name, a good hard name. Charlotte got a good name even though she's an idiot. Who would have thought Princess Lei

Lei would give her a name like Bee Jaws?"

I picked up a stone and threw it hard and far so it landed over in Arbishaw County on the other side of the driveway. I watched the stone roll to a stop in the dust. "Coon and Woodtick are good names for Eddie and Donnie. Cat Claws is perfect for Carol. I don't know what Pinion means for Carlee Rae. That one's beyond me, but I like the sound of it."

I shifted my weight to my other hip. "Swisher is an interesting name for Les, and Knot fits Ronny because he's always tying things up in knots and being naughty. Knotty. Get it? Trompin Johnny is a good name for Johnny Bilscoe. Running is all he likes to do. I like your name, too. It suits you." I was glad Mouse got a good name. I was sad that I got such a crappy one. Then I asked, "Do you think I'll be able to complete the tasks Princess Lei Lei gave me so I can get my name changed?"

"I don't know. She really nailed you. What did you do to piss her off?

"Could be that I found out why she calls herself Princess Lei Lei."

"You did?"

"Uh huh, but I can't tell." I waited until Mouse stopped glaring at me. "Do you know why she called us The Haunted Horse Club?"

"No, do you?"

"I was thinking it had to do with the barn fire. Somebody set that fire so Beggar couldn't get out, burning all his legs off. She's still not over it. I bet he's coming back to her in a dream, searching for her so he can give her instructions on how to avenge his death. Tetta told me that when things die in a terrible way, their spirit will come back, looking for something to help them avenge the guilty. I don't think it matters that he was a horse and not a person." I slid my feet out in front of me. "I don't think Princess Lei Lei started the fire even if the sheriff thinks it was an accident."

We sat in the quiet heat and watched as the shadows stepped out from behind the trees. I scratched at Storm's scruffy neck as he leaned into me. Suddenly a low growl rumbled through his chest. His head came up fast as his tail stiffened, his gaze locked on the side of the house. A crow, black as the shadows, ambled around the corner. It stopped and stared at us. It didn't flinch, not even when Storm rolled to his feet. Storm growled, but he wouldn't go close, and the hair along the line of his back stood straight up.

Then the crow hopped and flapped its wings, shrieking and cawing, making the hair on my arms prickle. It stood for a minute, and then flew away.

"Did you see that?" Mouse whispered.

"How many caws did it caw?"

"Five."

"Tetta said that means five people we know will die within a year from this time."

It was a long walk home that night from Tetta's house, the severity of the prediction sinking in as we pondered which five would die. When we reached Broken Edge Ridge we saw long silver poles of light flash in the sky, disappear, and then flash again. We had never seen spaceships before. One omen was bad enough, but now there were two. Two sad girls went to bed that night, and I dreamed of omens I could not ignore.

Chapter Two

One hot afternoon in July of 1939, Tetyanna Shimter faced an angry mob of women. They pressed toward her, arms crossed tight over a patchwork of colors covering their heaving breasts, as she came out of the Danville Grocery with her arms full of milk, sugar, and flour. The largest of the Mississippi River hillbilly women, Ester Hoboken, stepped forward, and unfolded her arms. Chin leading her tight jaw, hands clenching and unclenching at her sides, she backed Tetyanna up against the red door of the grocery store.

"We warned you to keep your skirt down and stay away from our men. It appears you didn't hear us the first time. We've decided you should leave Danville. If we have to tell you again, we won't be this polite."

Tetyanna looked Ester in the eye, and saw that her days in Danville were over. She hurried over to Clayburn's Sawmill to wink at Alvin Garretson, and show him a bit of knee. She laughed as she leaned against him as they snuck down to the edge of Carver's Creek, where she reached under the bank, and pulled up a bottle of dandelion wine. When they reached the dregs at the bottom of the bottle, Alvin asked her to marry him, and they ran down to the Justice of the Peace that very day. Then she took out a map, closed her eyes, and spun the bottle. Wherever it pointed, that's where they'd go.

The bottle rocked to a stop, pointing to Edgarton over in Arbishaw County. As far as towns went, the best it could boast regarding work involved filling feed sacks which created a halo of dust that constantly circled the silos down at the feed mill a half mile north of town.

Ralph's Grocery Store headed a row of two story buildings, crowned with run-down apartments, lining the east side of County Line Road that doubled as main-street. Don't blink, they said, or you'll miss Edgarton.

If the grocery store toppled to the east during a storm, it would knock over the post office, which would tumble into the hardware store, which would tumble down onto the elbow-polished bar of Cee Cee's tavern. Old Mr. Gavinski's barbershop would tumble down last, falling into a gully that pointed to what should have been the other side of the street, but the west side of County Line Road held only stubbly clumps of grass and scattered rocks. The people of Edgarton traveled to Sankton or Vedisville to deposit their meager checks in the bank or have a doctor hold a cold stethoscope to their congested chest.

Tetyanna suffered nine pregnancies, producing eight children, first a boy, Richard Lee, followed by five girls, who grew up, and then ran away to get married. Robert was next, and Tetyanna closed her eyes and pressed her hand against Alvin's chest as they buried their stillborn child in the empty space that no one else would claim in Cemetery Number Two over in Vedisville, next to Manny Dean, the grave robber's grave. Pauline was born ten years after they laid Robert in his grave. Eddie entered their world a year later.

Their first born, Richard Lee, my father, was a dark-skinned, handsome man. His starched white shirt, sleeves rolled up, collar turned high, tail tucked into the waistband of creased pants made of fine material cuffed at just the right height above the ankle of his black boots marked him as the city-slicker in the family. "Brown boots are for the poor," he said. "A man wearing a red shirt conjures up bad luck," he said. He combed his dark hair in the manner of Elvis, and possessed the bluest eyes people said they'd ever seen. His teeth flashed white as winter moonlight, though I heard that no one ever saw him brush his teeth, not once. Some questioned whether he really was Alvin's boy.

In 1955, sparks ignited when Jack Parker introduced Richard Lee to his hot-tempered, hard as a whip sister, Vesta Lynn, who claimed her name meant fire. Richard and Vesta Lynn married within six months of their first kiss, her fire consumed him, and she tried to keep afloat in his deep blue eyes.

Blessed with five beautiful children, no steady work, or a home of their own, Richard watched his exhausted wife pull the ropes that would make ends meet as she watched her father die a year after her mother, leaving her to raise six younger brothers along with her own children. Her brothers, except for Uncle Jack, drifted away to follow a God that didn't allow them to associate with the likes of her, and she never saw them again.

Be it needle and thread, spoon and bowl, hoe and dirt, or too many children tugging at her sleeve, Vesta Lynn covered more ground in a day than most men did in a week. Tetyanna held the other end of the rope as often as she could, rocking with a baby in one hand and a home brew in the other, breathing her hot breath onto dimpled little cheeks, declaring it an honor to watch her grandchildren wobble through their first steps, and struggle to say their first words.

During the early years, in a tangled attempt to pronounce Grandma Tetyanna's name, four-year old Lester Ray spit out the word Tetta. The name stuck like a pitchfork in a stack of hay, and the old woman who lived on the Arbishaw-Lelton County line soon realized she would carry the name Tetta for the rest of her life. In 1963, when I was two years old, I graced my mother with a nickname of her own after discovering the word momma didn't come out the way I intended, and Vesta Lynn, momma, faded as Old Ma was born.

For six years Old Ma watched my father lay on the couch after he came home from lazing around at the factory in Vedisville, watched him get up in time to go to bed. "He lacks character, he's got no gumption," she fussed. "Doesn't even look at his kids."

She waited for him to come home one night, and when he

didn't, she stopped waiting, and filed for what Tetta called the dee-vorce, just after conceiving Ronny. Just after convincing Richard Lee to buy her a new house over in Vedisville where they could raise their family instead of living in the old rundown shack behind Grampa and Tetta's house, but it turned out that wasn't what he wanted or he would have stayed. Storm, ever-faithful to every member of the family, head resting on his white paws, eyebrows raising up at the sound of crunching gravel, tail held still, continued to wait for him to come home, but he, nor I or my brothers and sisters, ever saw the city-slicker again.

Since Tetta and Grampa Alvin lived on the county line, with half their property in Lelton, and the other half in Arbishaw County, the county representatives allowed Tetta to choose where Pauline and Eddie went to school. She chose Sankton over in Lelton County because she liked the colors of their mascot, the double-fisted purple and yellow hornet of the Sankton Stingers. The red and black helmets of the Vedisville Vikings did not impress her. Grampa Alvin said it was a good thing, too, because of the signs that set his brain to twitching, the signs that lead a person to believe they were welcome, but unless they had enough jingle in their pockets, a person wasn't welcome in Vedisville, no matter what the signs on the doors said. To Grampa's dismay, after father moved us out of the run down shack, away from the family farm, Carlee, Lester, and I had to go to school in Vedisville, welcome or not.

Chapter Three

The wind blew in from the south the first day of spring in 1974, which meant the summer would be long and hot, an uncommon occurrence for Arbishaw County. The month of May kicked off the yearly growing contests to see who would produce the first ready-to-eat vegetables.

Grampa Alvin always won the first-cucumber-of-the-year contest. He was the winner going on ten years in a row, which secretly pleased Tetta. She believed it was because he kept a firefly in a jar in the house to bring him good luck with his crops.

The neighbors, Mr. Huston who tooted the horn of his black Ford LTD three times every morning at 6:15 as he headed for the feed mill, and Miss Pruddie who flew the American flag proudly next door, raised their eyebrows when they first learned of it. Regardless of their skepticism, there was no denying Grampa had the best vegetables in the county, and most often, the first.

I was sure Crow Man, whose neighboring yard was speckled with a million crows, kept a jar of fireflies in his cellar in an attempt to steal Grampa's fame. I turned my face away every time I saw all those crows pecking around in his yard.

Grampa's ramshackle sheds curtsied awkwardly behind the house, spines swayed, with red slivers of paint clinging to the slapped-up gray boards. Doors battled to hold back an onslaught of junk, but surrendered in despair as the junk spilled over into the pasture and yard in such disarray, it looked as though they'd retched on their skirts.

I loved the fact that the rickety chicken coop was empty and still had all its windows, though I wondered how long it would stay that way. "Goddamn it Alvin, the shed's full," was something Grampa didn't understand, as his whiskey helped him fill one shed after another. He would stumble from building to building, looking in cautiously past the edges of doors, his eyes blinking fast, looking for empty spaces to fill. I believed he was trying to fill something inside himself that he couldn't even name. I don't know how the chicken coop dodged his ferreting eyes, but for now, it was empty.

Grampa amazed the people of Arbishaw County by charming and cajoling vegetables from his section of barren land. We watched Grampa as he went round and round, scratching the dry earth with the one-bottom plow or the four-foot disk dragging behind his 320 John Deere. We attempted to climb aboard and putt around in circles with him, but he swiped at us, shooing us down, down and away.

His promise to get a cultivator evaporated as the whiskey bottle inched toward empty, so with bare feet smoldering in the hot dry soil, and nostrils caked with dust, each with a hoe of our own, we hacked weeds from adolescent beans, cucumbers, corn, and potatoes. Eddie had the hardest time mastering the art of keeping one eye trained on the tiny plants, while the other eye scanned the horizon for the cloud of dust that announced the arrival of Tetta coming to take us home.

Discipline was not something we took seriously, and Grandpa's patience wore as thin as his threadbare cover-alls. "I'm not paying them to stir up anthills," he mumbled as he watched us stir colonies into confusion with the handles of our hoes, watched us forget that the money we could earn working in the fields could pay for our school clothes or roller skates. He shook his head as he watched us neglect the rows of tiny plants that struggled to survive in the tangle of weeds, watched us piss away time that could have bought each of us a new bike, as the ants scurried for cover, carrying their eggs to safer places.

He hired any man showing the least bit of interest in handling a hoe, digging a row, picking some more, or trucking a load. This lead to a menagerie of colorful characters hanging around the farm pretending to be dedicated, backs bent over the dirt just so they could collect a dollar or sneak a peek at Pauline.

The appearance of the evening star was the signal to stop work for the day. After tucking us in, Tetta and Grampa hurried to the porch, Grampa clutching the neck of the whiskey bottle, Tetta with a jug of precious home brew to help loosen her jaw so her stories would flow more fluently. She didn't know we climbed out of bed, snuck under the porch, hid among the fireflies and peeling lattice slats, listening to the stories she told until the skeeters chased us back to our rooms.

Some of her stories were so funny; we held our faces in our hands, trying to stifle the laughter that struggled to spurt out. The best stories dripped with superstition, which I believed soaked through Grampa's skin and into his brain while he rocked toward oblivion. My cheeks turned red one night as I sat under the boards alone. I heard Tetta recall the time she and Grampa drove all the way from Wayburg to Canada, drove buck-naked during the coldest part of winter. I never told a soul, because that time Grampa shushed Tetta, telling her to be quiet about their secret lest the neighbors hear. If only I had known then, it wasn't the only secret kept in Arbishaw County.

With the city-slicker gone, there was one less mouth to feed, but still Old Ma had to force the ends to meet, and she managed with a little help from Tetta and Grampa. During the summer, we often stayed with them as Old Ma slaved at her new job, polishing toilets for the richest folks in Vedisville while we walked across country to Tetta's house.

Tetta's rules governed our trek from Vedisville to Edgarton through the woods, across Old Hwy 84, and then through the valley winding up to Loxy Liggnan's apple orchard. We walked softly past Mirror Lake whose water lay magical and still, and if you were fortunate and possessed 'the gift', you could see your own soul rolling across the water that quietly bubbled up from the northern tip of Broken Edge Ridge. Then we would run laughing and rolling down the backside of the hill, and then sprint across the railroad tracks that marked the southwest border of the home farm to rest our weary feet on Tetta's porch by nine o'clock. If we were late she threatened to tie us to a tree with ants under it, or worse, she would sell us to a nigger. She insisted that the oldest children watch out for the youngest. If the hired hands failed to show up, we had to do the fieldwork.

Most important of all, Tetta would not allow us to ride in the truck with Grampa. In the summer, the locals dodged out of the way when they saw him weaving down the road with Old Blue Bessie heaped full of vegetables destined for the cargo cars of the Missouri Pacific that chugged into the feed mill each day at two-twenty-nine. In winter, he drove an old red Chevy van loaded with carpenter's tools clunking and clanging so loud folks said they could hear him coming a mile away. He called that van Old Red Bessie. Tetta called it Clatter Trap.

Charlie Abraham, who used to run Ralph's Grocery, insisted that Grampa Alvin have his eyes examined, said it would straighten out his driving, but Tetta said she knew the truth. Every time Grampa's whiskey skimmed the bottom of the last bottle, he stopped at Cee Cee's to pick up a fresh one. She complained about Charlie, sitting at the end of the bar, offering to buy one more drink just as Grampa was ready to make his way out the door. After the tenth time, Charlie would aim his taunt at Grampa's shoulder blades, "Get your eyes examined," and then Grampa would bounce Old Blue Bessie in and out of the ditches on his way home.

Old Ma sadly accepted meager wages, earning just enough to put a few dollars in the utility envelopes she kept hidden in the egg money drawer. "Struggle," she said, "and its cousin, scarce, seem born to my family. I do my best to make the ends meet but I can't hold them together much longer. The bank is demanding more money than I can supply."

I watched as she put the for sale sign in the yard between the garden and the rabbit cages. "This is one of the hardest things I've ever had to do. This house, this acre of land is my hero. It rescued me from the poor side of town ever since that city-slicker left nine years ago. It's the first place I've been happy to call home, but Arlene down at the grocery told me about a better job over in Theinsville. I'm thinking of applying for it." I didn't say anything when she told me that. Theinsville was miles away from here, clear on the other side of Lelton County.

I had grown accustomed to our neighborhood. Trompin Johnny, who was Swisher's best friend, lived just down the road from us with his Armenian mother, Corra, whom everyone adored as she doled out mysterious sweet and nutty mamouls, jars of rechel, or sticks of simit to each neighbor within shouting distance. Everyone smiled when they heard the echo of her voice, "Jah-nee, you come home dis minute!" Corra's voice bounced off the hill behind Mrs. Tiffit's creaky old house, all the way over the fence that corralled the gray bull that looked longingly at the black and white cows that filled the green barn on the farm where Gator lived with his Pa over on Anydown Road. It bounced on through Mrs. Thank-You-Then's yard, and then boomeranged back to Corra, quiet like a whisper, *dis minute, dis minute.*

I believed more than one heart would break if we had to move away. Our house was good, better than the shack behind Grampa's house. Our piece of land was beautiful. It would make me sad if we had to leave even if I didn't have a friend of my own. I didn't want to think about going to another place, a place that might be worse.

I, with my long blond hair and tomboy grin, (all knees and elbows, secretly pleased I had not blossomed small, much to the aggravation of my older sister with the princess necklines that outlined her small breasts) set out to help pull the ends together by making sure I did all my chores. It was a major concern of mine, as doing chores was no easy task for me. I never knew what Old Ma was thinking when she said, "Now you three oldest ones get your butts out there, and pick up those potatoes!" and in the next breath, "You three youngest ones get the dishes done before the sun goes down!"

It was easy for me to be confused, as there were only five children, but Old Ma had jobs for six, and it was true, I was one of three oldest, but I was also one of the three youngest. We often wondered if there was a baby born somewhere in the midst of us that Old Ma never told us about, one that wouldn't let go. We'd heard Tetta say that could happen. The spirit of the baby would hang onto the mother, afraid to let go until the mother let it know that it was okay, and gave it final permission to go on to the next world. Nevertheless, I did my best and didn't complain because I didn't want to move to Theinsville.

Swisher was determined to help, and his fifteen-year-old hands mixed mud for a local bricklayer earning him three dollars a day. Mouse and Knot helped by agreeing not to knock each other silly causing the kind of ruckus that drove Old Ma mad. Pinion was no help at all, for she lived alone in a world inside her head. She was a hummer, and she hummed; all through the house and into the yard, her high heeled shoes poking holes in the grass as she twirled her skirts at the edge of the woods. Rabbits snuck out of their brush piles and came to watch, and birds perched atop her wide brimmed hats, hopping down onto her shoulders to whistle new melodies into her ear.

Even at the age of sixteen, she kneeled each night with fingers steepled in front of closed eyes, and whispered prayers of salvation, for herself, and the people she loved. Old Ma told her to pray harder for the food and clothes denied us by the church, denied us when we so desperately needed them after the city-slicker left, denied them because Old Ma would not agree to teach Sunday school when she didn't even have time to turn around. "That is the last time I ask for help," I heard her say. "No more depending on anyone but me." However, that changed when Old Ma found herself face to face with a serious suitor.

Oh, she'd had suitors from time to time. They took her fishing on Bass Lake, out to dinner at Silver Shores Supper Club, or to O'Mally's theater to see the latest picture show. Inevitably, the romances fizzled when they introduced her to their weekend children. She soon came to know what kind of men they were, not so much looking for a place to park their affections, but a place to park their children so they could go fishing undisturbed. With five children of her own, she said, "Another man's kids just aren't an option."

Then Arel came in over the fence of our lives, unlike anyone we'd ever met. He didn't even get mad when Knot called him Scarel because of the jagged scar that twisted down the corner of his left eye. His dark hair was so long he braided it into a beard that brushed all the way down to the fourth button on his shirt. He could hide the scar under the brim of his cap, but not the twinkle in his deep blue eyes.

Decked out in a chambray shirt under a leather vest covering the back pockets of faded denim jeans patched clear from his thigh to his ankle, Old Ma said the clothes he wore marked him as a man who worked hard. Leather moccasins snaked down from his knees and stopped at his steel tipped toes. Fringes brushed softly down the length of his calf as he said, "I learned the hard way about steel tips when I dropped an anvil that showed no mercy to my toes." Arel, it seemed, came with no intention of leaving after he'd arrived.

We, except for Swisher, fell in love with him the very first day, pulling at him, looking for the carving of old father time he said was sleeping inside one of his pockets. I secretly longed for a father figure in my life after having been without one for more than nine years. He took delight in showing us how to reach under the crankiest hens to sneak out the brown eggs without them pecking us. He taught us short-cuts concerning such mundane tasks as washing dishes, to not smoking up a room when opening the door on the woodstove, to washing the bathtub, (if it's not clean when you get in it, you won't be clean when you get out). He amused himself by teaching us his "common sense lessons of life."

Everyone teased me about having to attend more of those classes because even though I was book smart, I had the least amount of common sense. Knot said I didn't have any common sense because I had boobs, and he'd heard Grampa say that would only lead to trouble, though he wasn't sure why.

I loved sitting next to Arel, learning the art of carving. Sometimes I would look at him, and wonder about the scar. Even though it pulled down the side of his face and gave him a somber look, he had sparkle in his eyes. That was something new to me as I compared him to the men I'd known so far. The men I knew slipped into my heart and then snuck out again through the back door, silent as smoke. They were serious and mean, tired and angry. They could not give without expecting something in return. If I wasn't quick enough, and usually I wasn't, it would cost me a piece of hide off my backside or a broken heart. I wished it was different, but that's how it was. I'd learned to keep away from men, as far from them as I could. However, Arel was different. Arel, he had... well, as far as I was concerned, he had shine.

Sometimes Arel would leave for a day or two with no mention of where he was going or when he would return. I didn't care, because after all, it wasn't as if Old Ma and Arel were married or anything. He had his own place and I wondered why he never invited us to go there. When I asked Old Ma about it she just said, "It's not important. I prefer my own home. That way, if a man wants to see me, he can come here. I don't have time to go chasing a man around trying to figure out what he's going to do. I've got enough on my mind as it is."

However, after a day or two, Arel would slip back into our lives, back from wherever it was he had gone, and Old Ma would smile and give me a knowing wink as if she was saying, "I told you so."

As far as I was concerned, it didn't matter where he went. All I cared about was the fact that he was good to Old Ma. He was good for her because he made her smile. Good because he made her cheeks blush red as he did the dishes wearing Tetta's old apron, and he made her heart flutter as he teetered on the ladder while he tacked up the end of the gutter that had come down during the storm. Good because she looked content as he taught us girls the art of whipping an egg or took the time to show Knot how to clean the dirt out from underneath his fingernails with the edge of a knife.

Spruced up is what we became. He lifted the lid off the box we had been living in, pretty much tore the lid right off its hinges. Light scraped against the side of that box like a match to a zipper, kindling the wick that sparked our spirits. Arel was the weight on the opposite end, bringing a balance to our lives that had been missing since the city-slicker left.

Kristin Thacher

The Drought Poems

The Drought Poems are a collection of verses about the unforeseen changes in the land during a long drought and the unexpected changes in the human landscape during times of spiritual drought.

Drinking in the Drought

No one could believe it.
All those little fish
died,
white bellies reflecting the pale dry sky.
The scale tipped
The balance of acid to alkali
in the shrinking lake,
changed to poison and
all those little fish
suffocated
in the thick water.

Bird Bath

In the early morning
I skim small moths
Littering the surface
Of the bird bath.
Their wings are spread flat
On that last long flight
On water

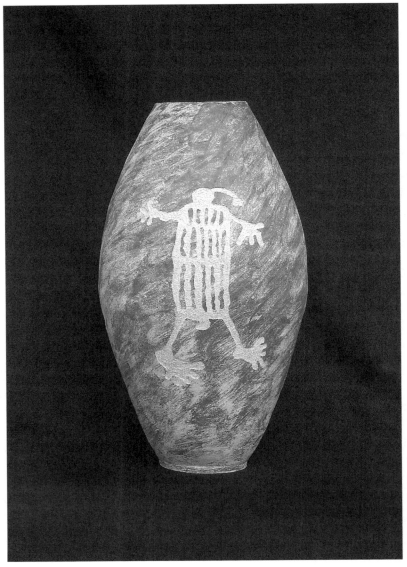

Pottery, Kristin Thacher

Sky Father

Fallen from the night air.
At noon
In the hot silence
I replenish the water
And hear
Hundreds of small ears
Listening to the splash.

In the late afternoon
I take one hard dry oak leaf
And rescue wasps and wild bees
Seduced over the edge
Into the shallow water
Where their contorted swimming
Carries them round and round.

In the silent dusk
Thousands of flies
Make a dark fringe
Around the damp rim
Of the clay bird bath
And suck down the water.

In the morning
I pour another gallon of water
Into the clay bowl.

How much water
Can a fly drink in a day?
How much water
Do a thousand flies drink?
A million?

As much as a new golf course?
As much as a new adobe house?
As much as a tourist?
As much as I?

Lucky for the lizards.

They don't drink water.
They get their moisture
from eating flies.

Fighting the Drought

I smear on
    invisible war paint
    sunscreen
    eye defense gel
    age defying créme
    skin therapy
    sheer body oil
    radiant hands cream
    all natural moisturizing formulas
    rich in aloe and vitamin e
    secret luxurious softness
    long-lasting texture improvers
    blemish bleaching
    wrinkle removers
and walk out over the hill
into the desert
of old age.

The Mystery at Night With You

It is evening.

We are watching TV.
We are watching a mystery
    about a police detective whose wife was murdered.
    The detective is obsessed with finding her killer.
    He has photos of the crime scene
    taped all over the back wall of his garage.
    It looks like a stalker's sacrificial alter.

I say it looks like he killed her.
You say, No, it doesn't.
    If someone murdered you,
    I would do that,
    assemble all the clues
    become obsessed
    with finding the killer.
I think
you have missed all the clues.
We are watching TV.
We are watching a mystery.

It is evening.

In the First Year of the Drought

In the first year
Of the drought,
The Rain became
The Land's teenage daughter,
Full of broken promises.

"Believe me, It will rain on Wednesday!"
    but on Wednesday, another scorcher.
    Heat waves cursed their way
    out of angry rocks.

"I'll be there-early in the afternoon…"
    but after a smirking sundown,
    another hot black night
    sniggered behind the tepid moon.

"I promise, I'll be back by dark!"
    but late winds emptied the evening sky.
    Is that the sound of rain on the roof?
    No, just a dust devil hurling sticks and stones.

"I'll be there on time. Don't worry!"
    but after five months of damp excuses
    the Land stopped listening
    and locked the door.

Spring's wise flowers refused to uncoil
Or rise from the spurned Land
Shamed by the Rain's lies
And the dishonor of Drought.

The Food of Love

At the end of the day
she wanted to ask him
if they would ever
fuck again.

He tramped in the kitchen
with the mail, just more bills,
and the bag of groceries,
just more chicken.

He was getting bald,
love handles and a belly,
but who was she
to talk.

She began to baste the chicken thighs
with Hawaiian barbeque sauce,
sweet and tangy, hint of oranges,
just enough sugar, just enough sass.
Before she replaced the cap
her tongue mindlessly licked
dripping spicy sauce running thick
down the twisting ridges of the bottle neck.

She licked her lips.

He said, Don't do that. It's disgusting.
If you do that again,
I'll get my own bottle of sauce.

She stopped and looked up.
She put the bottle down.
She wiped it clean with soapy water,
rinsed, dried, replaced it on the shelf in the fridge.

The answer was
No.
They weren't.
The chicken was done.

In the Fourth Year of the Drought

106° in the shade
The cats ironed out flat on the tile floor
Today's thin newspaper crackles open
To a warning centered on page one

The Forest Fire Danger is Extreme.
Residents Should Prepare To Evacuate.
Remove All Valuables

I try to sort it out.
    What size storage unit will I need
    For 20 acres of pinyon forest,
    How tall, for ponderosas and white fir,
    How deep, for thick groves of Gambel oak,
        How wide for alligator junipers, 500 years old?

How do I pack up blue flocks of scrub jays, kettles of ravens,
Choirs of coyotes, barking foxes, twitching deer, desperate bears,
Round-eyed ringtails and sleight-handed raccoons,
Lizards, lacewings, crowds of moths, tiny green acorns, lichens,
moss,

The soil, the rocks, the clear bright air?

I try to sort it out.
    What can I leave and what may I keep?
    A lifetime's possessions
    Some I hold dear, some that hold me,
    Tokens of journeys, keys to doorways,
        Objects through which prayers have passed

How many boxes will I need to pack up 25 years?
That's 9,000 sunrises, 300 full moons, more or less.
Our old wooden house on South Mountain
Just one big box, a tinder-dry vault,
    And Fire, that thief, knows the combination.

Will I forget where I came from
Without my antiques
Great Aunt Sarann's table, Mary's chairs,
Grandma Belle's locket, Frederick's watch?
    Sepia, black and white, Polaroid, color- their
faces look out at me.

Will I forfeit my heart
without your love letters,
weightless roses, short sweet notes,
silver promises, golden rings,
    Love's song played over and over again?

Will I lose my knowledge
without all my books,
truth or fiction, bibles and myths, dictionaries, almanacs,
history, maps, geography, philosophy, cookbooks and
poems,
    words on paper released to the air?
Will I lose my vision
without all my art,
pottery, paintings, sculptures, and prints,
mirrors into dreams, metaphors into light,
    hands turning mind inside out?

To the East
Dingy smoke fingers lace the sky
above a thousand-acre fire
burning down the pines
    60 miles off in the Pecos.

To the South
Smoke scents prowl the air
like a lost coyote hunting ghost quail
flushed from the scorched bosque
    50 miles down near Isleta.

To the North
Drifting shadows veil the sun
Burning white above Santo Domingo,
Laid out in a pale smoke shroud
    40 miles across the Rio Grande.

To the West:
Thunder growls in empty clouds;
Lightning strikes our captive mountain.
I blow out the candle, as if fire might call fire,
    and answer my questions with ash.

Earth Mother

The Last Year

It's happening
everywhere.
There are so many of us
we appear
in strangers' dreams.
I can hear your heartbeat
across the borders.
Distance is not far enough
for separation.

Fix it and limp on.
End it and jump out.
I won't know just who I am
until I do
without you.

Should I leave or should I stay?
Should I go back to where I began
or out beyond some other beginning?
If I'm never lost,
can I be found?

How I will travel
depends on what matters most,
the destination or the journey.

In what space can I stand
and take up no one else's place?

Dry Run

My bags are packed.
Full boxes stand
Against the wall
At the front door.

The rooms are still filled
With the things I will
Abandon.

When the forest fire comes
You have just a few minutes
To get out.

I practiced
Getting out,
Had a fire drill
For the cats, into their carrying cases,
For the dog, into the back seat,
For the bags and boxes, into the back of the truck,
For myself, into the front seat,
Key in the ignition,
Done in fifteen minutes.
Everything important packed in tight.

All that was left was
To leave.

Sun Shaman

Rain Dreams

Late in the night,
just past the edge
of that weightless freefall
through the depthless sky
of deep dreaming,
the telephone rings.

The body returns first.
Tentative, the arm stretches out of the blankets,
The hand on the end opens and grabs the receiver.
The mouth halts the ringing noise with a question,
"What?"
You whisper the secret password,
"It's me."
The mind catches up,
runs back down the path
through the inner landscape
stands at the frontier,
lifts the barrier,
and listens.

You are standing in a doorway, a thousand miles away,
listening to the rainfall
hitting hard on the porch roof.
I hear the rush of rain streaming off the eaves.
I hear the water shadows streaking down the window glass,
hear into the silent corners of the room behind your back,
hear you are alone, late in the night,
hear the drop in your voice saying,
"I love you."
a thousand dreams away.

Never give me something
you don't want back.

Jim Roseberry

All of Us Went to Vietnam

This excerpt describes the author's experiences of the war in Vietnam—before, during and after the war. All of Us Went to Vietnam *is written non-chronologically, weaving together many elements including the experience of a convoy during the war, letters written from Vietnam and disparate vignettes drawn from the author's life before and after the war. Everyone experienced the war, whether they went to Vietnam or not, and they continue to struggle with the meaning of this experience.*

October, 1969

The Meher Baba wrote, "Don't Worry. Be Happy." Why worry? Like sated jocks, Hutch and I cruised up highway four to Long Binh. Olive drab on the outside and even drabber on the inside, the ton truck carried our weary asses through the Mekong Delta. "Light My Fire" was accompanying vital rhythms deep inside, inciting my nerves to create a semi-conscious Fillmore-like reverie while the chatter in the cab divulged cynicism in a raw GI dialect. Fuck this. Fuck that. It don't mean nothin. What is mama san doing? Shit, that fuckin dink almost hit us.

We left Can Tho in the dark; it was 5:30 a.m. We had to wait two hours to catch the Can Tho ferry to cross one of the branches of the Mekong River. From where we parked, I had a good view of farmers fishing in a rice paddy. The rice paddies are like small lakes. Life revolves around them: plowing, planting, harvesting, eating, shitting, talking, fishing, hiding, burying relatives and honoring ancestors. It took centuries for Vietnamese life to settle into these patterns and it took a few seconds for Lt. Nickeldick to break into my rice paddy daydream with his third query in ten minutes about the exact location of Vinh Long.

51

I said that I did not know how far it was to Vinh Long. Hutch mumbled, "lifinmotherfucker," referring to Nickeldick. Since I was the radio man on this adventure, Nickeldick kept calling me in the pursuit of information that I did not possess. Hutch and I were tired of his questions. We were tired of the Army. We were tired of being in Vietnam away from home. We were getting tired of an America that sent us to Vietnam.

We were not too tired to pick up a boy who was hitchhiking to visit his grandmother in Vinh Long. Now we had a companion with local knowledge. Communicating in the hybrid dialect created by the interaction of GIs and the Vietnamese, we talked about the weather, the distance to Vinh Long and local food. The boy said it was "buku hot." He said that the distance to Vinh Long was "titi." He said that the Nuoc Mam was "number one."

When we reached Vinh Long at 11:00, I could agree with his first two assertions, but having not eaten the local fish sauce, I had to take his word on the third one.

When we boarded the Vinh Long ferry, he exited the truck. With an exuberant goodbye infused with apparent joy, he walked the rest of the way to his grandmother's. After a short wait Hutch and I crossed the Mekong amid a menagerie of craft distinguished by their garish styles and multiple uses from housing to shipping. It felt like a circus parade. It was delightful. Why worry?

Where was the music? Hutch liked country. He was from Florida, divorced with one kid. His ex-wife wrote about getting back together. Just a little country tune about recovered love and the pain of separation would have shortened the trip across the Mekong at Vinh Long. He might have fantasized about a reunion with his ex-wife and erased the unpleasant images of the reality of being in the Army in Vietnam. Maybe it was all fantasy, the whole fucking thing.

I wanted the Fillmore Auditorium. Give me the Jefferson Airplane. I would have settled for Jimi Hendrix or Janis Joplin. Just a faint wisp of irreverence seasoned with fluid guitar riffs and lyrics about love, that's all I needed. The good fairy was too exhausted to rescue me; maybe this music and images of my girlfriend, Elinor, would take me away from the dreary state of the Army in Vietnam.

She was my connection to home. I wrote her almost every

day and she wrote me scores of letters, too. We searched for an adult persona together in the mess of Vietnam and Berkeley. She was working on her academic career and I was working on my sanity. Even though they did not intend to do it, Local Board #11 drafted her when they drafted me. Music, ideas and the worries that accompany young souls were the text of our communication. Fretting about one's state of mind and professions of love were the substance of this communication. We may not have known where we were going, but we tried to help each other along the way. It was an heroic effort, the closest I came to heroism in Vietnam.

Hutch wanted to go home. I wanted to go home. Home was not far away in the music. For me it was still 270 days to DEROS*.....making home seem very far away in reality.

*Date of Estimated Return from Overseas

October, 1966

For a while home was 1755 LeRoy on the north side of campus. Elinor and I met here on the porch overlooking the north branch of Strawberry Creek which ran through the property from east to west. Looking south and drinking beer, we inhaled the essence of Eucalyptus trees. Establishing that I was a junior from the valley and she was a freshman from San Francisco, our conversation roamed to the edges of our conceits, flirting with our insecurities and igniting our passions. I inhaled her smile. Acquaintance became love; I was in love by next summer when I moved to San Francisco.

We loved ideas. We read books, changed majors, went to City Lights, walked on the beach and were marked by the buzz of campus life. We wanted to live our lives some distance from the conventions of American middle class life. Comforted by the bonds of family, we did not know the exact distance. We were worried about Vietnam. We were angry about Vietnam. And then ....I was in Vietnam.

I wrote her. She wrote me. I described the Army. She described her classes at Cal. I explained how the system was crushing me. She described how the system was running amuck because of the war. I read Dostoevsky. She read Goethe. I agonized *Date of Estimated Return from Over Seas about the government. She agonized over papers and tests. I said that I was depressed. She said that she was depressed. I said that I loved her and it gave me joy. She said that she loved me.

Eventually I came home, but I did not leave Vietnam behind. Years later I discovered that no one left it behind, despite pretending to overcome it.

Vietnam kept coming up. Everyone had her/his own story; usually it seemed like a generic tale. With pride some said they avoided service. Expressing guilt others apologized for not serving. Some said that the war could have been won. Others were still outraged at McNamara for causing it. Vietnam did not go away.

All of us went to Vietnam. It is in our collective consciousness, whether we actually traveled to Southeast Asia or not. With stories of the Iraq war bombarding our senses, images of Vietnam resurface—images that shape the public dialogue and haunt the private sphere. Are there any regrets?

October, 2005

What did the Joseph Conrad write about regrets? How can we die in peace if we are overcome with regrets? Regrets may come in peculiar forms.

Ned and I were sitting on the porch. It was an unusually warm day for late October. We were talking about our children when Ned's thoughts took a different tack, as if he was the skipper and the winds had shifted abruptly. Reminiscing about his Army days, Ned collected his thoughts and tossed a salad seasoned with pride and regret.

"I got out of the army in 1965. I have buddies who went to Vietnam, but I did not go, although I regret having missed the experience."

I said, "You didn't miss anything."

"Where were you in Vietnam?"

"I was in a trance."

Ned said, "What? I know you guys wanted to win over there. They wouldn't let you win."

"The Presidents wanted to win, but we knew better. What could we win? At what cost?"

"Right, maybe if they had let you invade North Vietnam and take Hanoi, things would have been different," Ned said paraphrasing Rush Limbaugh.

"My wife, my youngest son and I went to Hanoi in March. Things were definitely different. My favorite stop was the Temple of Literature. We witnessed a ceremony honoring teachers."

"Hanoi, Hanoi that reminds me of Jane Fonda. She really let you guys down."

"Jane Fonda has been given far too much importance. If anyone let us down, it was the U. S. government."

"Well, I'm glad I served and I'm sure that you feel the same way."

"The military was a form of detention to me—minimum security detention.

It was not at all like the WWII stories I heard in the 1950s. Military service must have a legitimate purpose. Lacking that, the military is exposed as an authoritarian institution similar to prisons."

Content with his own take on the war Ned said, "What? You want a beer? I'm going to have one."

Robert McNamara had regrets.

June, 1970

With less than a month to go before DEROS, I took an afternoon off to drive to the Michelin Rubber Plantation. My tour in Vietnam was almost over and I was bored out of my skull. Sick and tired of the Army and increasingly bitter about the face that my government had given to America, I mused about the POW camp I had seen next to the base at Can Tho when I was stationed in the delta.

I watched the prisoners and they looked at me. Some were strolling, holding hands, as if they were on the Seine enjoying a

Sunday afternoon. I sat like an overripe pumpkin in a November patch waiting to be picked and with no place to go. We watched each other like humans at zoos. Did the same question arise in their minds that crossed mine? Who was the prisoner in this picture?

Then my mind drifted to LBJ. Not the President but the Long Binh Jail. It was the post prison for the base at Long Binh. Woodrow had been sent there for being AWOL. He would leave the base to get drunk in town and then get caught by the MPs.

It was a ritual rooted in mindless authority responding to human compulsion. Mike almost served time at LBJ for possessing marijuana. Why didn't Thieu and Ky do some time? Wasn't their government financing some of its operations with drug money?

Cascading thoughts leading to dead ends awakened my curiosity. Where was LBJ? I had seen the POW camps at Can Tho, but I had never seen LBJ.

Just then a black GI came by and I asked him if he knew. His reply was crisp and very cogent. "Hell, I don't really know, but it doesn't really matter. This whole base is a prison." He said "that the Army should take down the fence at LBJ, remove the prison sign and place it on the gate to the whole fucking base."

Homilies about American foreign policy delivered by elites in comfortable settings had no meaning in this context. Pedantic references to national security and serving one's country seemed hollow.

The official name for the post prison was USARVIS (United States Army, Vietnam, Installation and Stockade.) Imagine doing time at USARVIS. LBJ was fine.

Elbie Jay (the pres not the prison) was vilified by the students at Berkeley, placing fourth on a list of "dangerous men." He was considered less dangerous than Reagan, Hershey and someone or something I can't decipher. Was it Westmoreland?

Poor LBJ, he was not the only person responsible for this fiasco and he was tormented by it. The whole damn country went to war whether they wanted to admit it or not and whether they wanted to share the sacrifice. I expected more of America in 1960 in Chico, California. But then, I was very naïve in 1960.

May, 2006

NYT, May 12, 2006, p. A1 PFC Mathew Scarano described the Physical Training and Rehabilitation Program at Fort Sill, Oklahoma in bold language. "I am an inmate. I sometimes ask those friends of mine with jailhouse tattoos if they'd rather be back in jail, or here. So far they are unanimous—jail."

July 13, 1969

With a man just about to land on the moon and a generation just about to gather at Woodstock, I arrived in Vietnam. It was insufferably hot. Burning shit assaulted my nostrils. Medics plied me with anti-malaria drugs. Vietnam was no longer an abstraction.

The cover of the July 11 edition of *Time* announced "The Sex Explosion."

Lee Trevino said that one should play a "lively ball." It was an ad for some golf ball.

America was becoming an abstraction.

How did I get to Vietnam? Why?

Why was I in Vietnam?

Johnson said it was to defend South Vietnam from North Vietnam. Nixon said it was to achieve "peace with honor." John McNaughton said it was to "avoid a humiliating defeat." The draft board did not give a reason; they did not even respond to my letter opposing the war. Drill sergeants had us chant "I wanna go to Vietnam" without asking us if that was how we felt or telling us why Americans should feel that way in the first place. If the President said we need to fight, then the chain of command simply followed the order. They didn't ask why.

We were following the benighted attempt the unworthy with the wisdom of a stone and the empathy of a drill sergeant.

War starts to get old when the first person dies. By 1969, the American war in Vietnam was putrid. No amount of army propaganda could hide that fact. The military added toxic substances to what was already a fetid mix.

People need reasons.

Excerpts of Letters Written in Vietnam in 1969

July 17

I'm sitting on a thin mattress. It is 4:00 a.m. and 85 degrees. I can hear the artillery. No need to worry now. Vietnam is no longer an abstraction.

I hope that you can find a good job.

July 20

I'm sitting on my ass in Binh Thuy. So this is the Mekong Delta, ain't been here before. It is hot, humid and the stench is overpowering. Once I get to Can Tho, the routine is pretty simple. We work during the day and perform guard duty two or three nights a week. Eventually, we will be assigned to convoy duty.

Two VC prison camps are nearby. The area is quilted with rice paddies. Hoa is our hootch maid. A lot of the GIs are "heads."

Jagger said that "time is on my side."

July 23

The unit is full of southerners. C&W is popular. Pot is potent and pervasive. Alcohol is consumed in large quantities. The morale is pathetic. Everyone has a fuckit attitude. The DelMonte cannery was heaven compared to this.

I miss you.

July 24

I'm depressed again. It is such a waste of one's life to be in military in this war and no one seems to understand this, at least no one who could do anything about changing the situation.

July 25

I can see a Vietnamese graveyard from here. It has trapezoidal headstones that are white. Grass is planted between the headstones. We lived near a cemetery in Chico, but none of my ancestors was buried in it. It was a place to take a walk, but not a place to honor the ancestors like the Vietnamese honor theirs.

July 26

The racism is rampant and nauseating. This war is an obscenity.

August 6

I am sorry that you are depressed. I hope that my depression is not infecting you. Please send John Wesley Harding, Country Joe and the Jefferson Airplane.

August 20

About the fighting—we are on condition yellow which means that we might get hit. I don't know what in the fuck that means. Don't worry.

August 26

We were mortared last night. I don't think anyone was hurt. Art is 19 and madly in love with Mindy.

Gene is from the Bay Area. He is good guy who is being transferred to Vinh Long unfortunately. He will give me some of his shit. I feel like I did when I was 13. Bryan Shelton, a very good friend, moved to Idaho and gave me his baseball mitt and baseball cards.

Hoagie and Williams are black. We play a lot of basketball.

JIM ROSEBERRY

September 3

I watched a guy shoot up. I felt like a med student watching a
nurse taking her own blood. It's ugly, but one way for guys to escape this madness temporarily.

Your mother sent some cookies. mmmmmmgood...

(Some argue that the GI heroin epidemic may have started in
the fall of 1969 and clearly began to grow in early 1970, especially after the invasion of Cambodia opened up shipments from
Phnom Penh to Saigon. Was I lucky to be there?)

September 20

Today, I accompanied the local garbage men. They found a
half cooked ham and were very happy.

Someone said that the VC got within 50 yards of the base last
night. Nothing happened.

September 23

I visited a Buddhist temple yesterday.

Mike is high on opium all the time. I feel like his therapist.
We talk a lot, mostly about home.

I had dinner in Can Tho with an ex-ARVN and his mother. It
was very pleasant despite language problems. They are very
proud of Can Tho. Their ancestors have lived in the delta for
many generations. Vietnam is very beautiful. I can appreciate
their sentiments.

I told them that I did not agree with my government's policy
and did not want to be in Vietnam in the Army. They asked me
why America chose to fight and I launched into a pedantic discourse that bored me more than them. What did I know?

September, 1969

Slade was nineteen. He was from Oklahoma. He arrived in Vietnam about the same time that I arrived. We had not talked about much so I was surprised when he interrupted me one evening.

"You read a lot. Tell me, why are we in Vietnam?"

"I think I know, but it's a complicated story. Are you sure you want to hear the details?"

Slade did not want to listen to my lecture so he offered his own view, "I think I know and it's not so complicated."

"Tell me."

"We're here to defeat the communists."

"What is a communist?" Words spoken with a Socratic tone. Nonplussed, Slade said, "I don't know."

286 days to DEROS

Letters

Oct. 2, 1969

Dear Elinor,

Dan Crowe wrote about the protest at Berkeley. Although he does not like some of the rhetoric of activists, he is persuaded, like I was, that this war is a big mistake. The government's arguments make no sense. He has been talking to guys from the Progressive Labor Party. They advocate organizing in the Army. I think Dan should stay out.

Vietnam is a beautiful country. It is nothing like I have ever seen. Since I can't speak the language, cultural nuance is beyond my grasp. I recognize some universal traits like devotion to family, self-interest, obedience to social norms and willingness to work hard. The rest of it is beyond me. How a whole nation can be objectified as gooks or dinks disgusts me. I'm sure there is something like Vietnamese ignorance, but I feel responsible for American ignorance. There is no excuse for it, especially when it is promoted and reinforced by our leaders.

I'm rambling. I miss you. I love you. I hope that school is going well.

> Love, Jim

1970

The hootch was our temporary home. It was a common space like a room in a hippie commune, but persons came and went without ideological commitment and little was really shared except a desire to get out of Vietnam.

The bed was modest; no doubt it was made by some military contractor to specifications that seemed to fit 19th c. Russian military standards. I read and slept there.

The hootch had one female daytime occupant—a Vietnamese woman who cleaned and did our laundry. Called a hootch maid, she served us in order to support her family. In the context of the economic chaos spawned by the war, it was a good job.

Hoa was our maid. Her family had moved south in the 1950s. She was Catholic, but clearly a Vietnamese Catholic. Confucian ethics were evident in her devotion to her family.

We talked a lot. Since I did not speak Vietnamese, our conversations were limited by her grasp of English which was good. Once she asked me if I had a girlfriend and I said, "Yes."

"Do you plan to marry and start a family?"

"I would like to do that some day, but I feel incapable of it right now."

"Why?"

"I am too angry. I don't like American culture and I have not settled on a new one. It is unfair to have children in that state of mind. What will I tell them? How can I show them enough love?"

"We don't think about these things. Marriage, family and commitment are our duty."

"It's not that simple in America."

"You would be a good father and husband."

"Hoa, you are a good daughter and mother."

Confucian principles endured the chaos of war better than suburban middle class values. She had a better grounding than I did. My anger about the war had hemorrhaged into an indictment of American culture including work, family and religion.

Hoa treated me with kindness. I wondered about how Dean Rusk would have talked to me.

Imaginary Conversation

Dean Rusk was adamant. We did the right thing in Vietnam. We were fighting the communists. I *fantasized* the following exchange:

I said, "What is a communist?"

Rusk answered, "It is a person who acts according to communist principles which are antithetical to freedom and the American way of life."

"Who were we fighting in Vietnam?"

"Communists"

"Who were these communists?"

"North Vietnamese regulars and the Viet Cong."

"Were they all communists?"

"No, but communists ran the show."

"What did these communists in charge really want?"

"An independent, unified Vietnam with a communist government and a socialist economy."

"What did we want?"

"An independent, noncommunist South Vietnam."

"How long, how hard and against whom had our enemy fought for the goal of a unified, independent Vietnam?"

"A long time during which many of them served decades in prison and suffered a lot of torture trying to defeat the French, the Japanese, the South Vietnamese and the Americans."

"I can see how our goal conflicted with theirs. How did their goal of a communist, unified and independent Vietnam threaten the U. S?"

Rusk was losing his patience. "It didn't, but you have to understand one thing, *young man*, when an American President gets into a war, he's got to win it."

"What if the war's political goals are unachievable and the costs are very high?"

"It doesn't matter. American pride is on the line. We must win."

Nixon/Johnson: "I don't want to be the first President to lose a war."

90th Replacement Battalion—July, 1969

The military tried to explain our purpose in Vietnam simply, very simply using the language and graphics aimed at a person with a fourth grade education. They gave us handouts when we arrived in Vietnam.

One handout entitled "The Soldier in Vietnam" made four bullet points using the typical code words for fear like aggression and terror and the code words for our honorable cause like lasting peace and viable nation.

Of course words like these are absolutely meaningless without defining them and illustrating how your actions are consistent with those definitions. If you knew some Vietnamese history, the words were hopelessly off the mark. Is aggressor an apt description of any side in a civil war? Was a strong viable South Vietnam possible?

Another handout described our "...Diplomatic Mission." It described a few Vietnamese customs and suggested that one of the most important aspects of Buddhism is that one's head is sacred. How about the sacred nature of nonviolent conflict resolution?

It said that we are guests of the Vietnamese. Who asked us to come? Ho in 1945? The French in 1946? Diem in 1954? Diem in 1963? Any one of the eight governments between 1963 and 1965?

Maybe we asked ourselves when McGeorge Bundy became an instant warrior at Pleiku on Feb. 7, 1965?

Letters: October, 1969

October 4

A Korean tried to sell me a Bible. He asked me about California because he is going there next month. How is the surfing? Where is Disneyland?

October 16

Tomorrow is the 104th day in Vietnam. I have 261 to go. Some of the children beg for food saying, "you GI give me chop chop."

October, 1969—The Convoy

Lt. Nickeldick addressed us before we left Can Tho. He tried to act like John Wayne and we appeared to listen. Lt. Nickeldick told us to be careful. He sounded earnest. He said that good soldiers keep their shit together. My mind strayed to "The Good Soldier Schweik"—an antiwar film/book that exposed the idiocy of the military in WWI. The smell of burning shit accompanied Nickeldick's lecture, too. Was this scripted?

I appeared to listen intently, but my mind drifted to the image of Elinor and the Jefferson Airplane on the Panhandle in the summer of 1967 when I lived at 2179A Grove St. and shopped for my groceries on Haight St. That was the summer of love; this was the winter of war. In my mind, the world was seamless. Music, politics, feminism, civil rights—all that stuff—coexisted with the war in the war. You could take me out of America, but images of America remained in my consciousness. Back to Nickeldick.

Was Nickeldick improvising or were his words drawn from some USARV manual? The military had a manual, pamphlet or stick on label explaining everything from loading your weapon to unloading your bowels.(USARV stood for United States Army, Republic of Vietnam.)

I kept a copy of USARV label 31 entitled "A Good Dozer Operator." Ending with the exhortation "I am the best dozer operator in USARV," the label was a list of 21 characteristics of a good bulldozer operator. Most of them related to being careful. He "does not have accidents." He "has and uses his operator's manual." He "checks his dozer before starting." And so on.....

I wondered if the guys who drove the Rome plows in Operation Cedar Falls in early 1967 were careful when they leveled the terrain, attempting to make it uninhabitable. Joni Mitchell's lyrics could go something like this: "they paved Vietnam and put up a parking lot." Focusing on an area north and west of Saigon called the Iron Triangle, Army units forced villagers to leave and turned 2700 acres of jungle into a flat, denuded landscape in order to make this hotbed of VC activity "secure." Huge Rome plows were used: plows large enough to cut swaths in the jungle like my lawnmower beheads the grass in my front yard. By depriving the VC of cover, the Army expected to drive them out of this area. It didn't work; the VC returned. The war continued. But as long as the dozer operators were careful, why complain?

Being careful is an invitation to worry, that's why. Adults had been cautioning me to be careful most of my life. My baseball coach cautioned me to lay off the high fastball. My football coach told me to put my pants on one leg at a time. My high school history/civics teacher told me to be very wary of the communists. A worried Johnson reminded McNamara to manage the troop escalation in 1965 so as to not worry the American public. My father worried about taxes. My mother worried about oddballs on the freeway.

Now I was expected to worry about my bulldozer.

Bruce Hodder

Some or all of the poems featured here will be included in Death Row Dog, a collection of shorter poetry and prose writings which I am assembling for future publication.

Death Row Dog

this woman who i work with is a major beauty

however many blocks you've been around,
your breath catches every time you look at her.
and when she comes up close to you, which
she does when she wants to ask a question—
eyes wide, breasts pushed against your arm—
it's like gazing into heaven, you could almost cry
that something so divine exists on earth.
she's a perfect work of art, God's first masterpiece
since He sat down after creating rain.
yesterday she walked through in leather coat
and boots, with plaited hair, belly half-exposed,
and five men stopped talking all at once,
like wild birds silenced by a pistol shot.

***

it wanted poets.
Instead the moon
found the new May leaf.

a flash of blue brassiere
on peach-like shoulder: ah!—
forget my white beard, honey!

too much inner dialogue
to enjoy the band—
we're really over this time

the golden glow
around those people—
autumn evening

ripe as a new apple
picking hair out of her eyes
waiting to collect her kid from school

the bare trees
have bird villages
on top

chasing peaches round a bowl
old man and son both laughing"
now come on, dad, one more."

my neighbor's gate
bangs in the wind—
the remembrance of you

* * *

ENGLAND

your england, kingsley amis
england of dirk bogarde in the "doctor" films
england of sidecars attached to motorcycles
england of clipped accents
england using "wretched" as a swear word
england watching elvis and dreaming of america
england baking sponge pudding inside a tea towel
the england that listened to "the archers"
england that went to tangiers and wouldn't take its trunks off

england watching fellini and dreaming of sophisticated europe
tony hancock's england
england meeting at the corner coffee house, sitting with the boys
imitating the sucking noise of the chrome espresso maker
england in a tie
england letting its hair grow out a little
england whose dad wore cardigan and slippers
england whose dad smoked a pipe and stunk the house out every
day
england going to a bloody war to find the nation great comedians
england's great comedians talking over radio to children sitting in
the dark
england driving ford cortinas
england that did the pools and 'spot the ball' and never won a
penny
england of brylcreem in the bathroom cabinet and dentures on
the sink
england with a hank of greasy hair falling in its eye at breakfast
england that said "the pictures"
england riding bicycles with clips
your england, billy cotton,
wakey-wakey england
england of norman wisdom falling over all the time like he had an
inner ear infection
england that dreamed of overthrowing england
england that finally succeeded
england that was eaten by america and regurgitated as a burger
chain
england whose amiable ghost now stalks its crumbling architecture
nettles growing on abandoned tracks,
paint peeling on old business signs hanging over empty yards
where children aimlessly throw bottles and smoke stolen cigarettes

To Pat, your energy & zest for life inspires me to reach for challenging goals. Friends always, Catherine 8/5/07

Catherine Hovis

Unfolding

Memoir, Unfolding, *examines the fear and confusion of grow-ing up with an alcoholic father and two older schizophrenic broth-ers—both committed suicide—and their impact on my actions.*

Journal Notes

Endless Searching and Scratching for Words and Structure

November 6, 2007: Last week I jumped into the start of my book, wrote sixty-seven pages. It's a memoir—well, something bigger than a memoir—but not as detailed as an autobiography; —I'm not sure what to call it—I just know I want to write it.

I envision a three-part structure: youth/innocence, vulner-ability/being used, gaining control/maturation. The middle, a turning point when I realized I had to make changes. It happened while my angry, inebriated husband sped down an unlit two-lane highway. I huddled against the driver's side door with my fingers wrapped around the chrome door handle and envisioned myself flying free of his alcohol-induced abuse. Then images of my three children with their father pierced my despair. I saw them asleep while his cigarette smoldered in his mattress. I heard my daugh-ter wheeze while he continued to puff on his cigarette. I heard them scream while he swerved out of a drainage ditch into the path of an oncoming semi. I removed my hand from the handle.

My children's needs drove me to create a plan to change our lives. I didn't know how I would do it; I only knew I would. I've thought of them as the audience of my book, but perhaps their faces would censor my words. A couple of days ago I thought of my cousin Sister St. Jean as my audience—a woman twenty-five years older than me who encouraged me when I didn't believe in myself—with her in mind I would strive to tell how things were, to fill in the parts she didn't know; I'd create full images.

The first sixty-seven pages haven't even scratched the surface but they will help me to crack the ice of the story to be told. To tell how I felt shabby when I compared myself with the other children in the neighborhood. I believed their parents would not allow them to come to my house because my parents weren't there—my father drank too much; my mother worked to support us—and, my oldest brother lived in a mental hospital. I felt guilty of something, I didn't know what, but my mother always cross-examined me when I came home. I did not understand her concern. I never knew what made her so angry. Perhaps because she had to work long hours she felt frustrated that she couldn't keep a close eye on me, realized people might be cruel to me or take advantage of me, knew she wanted to protect me; knew she never could.

No one could have protected me from myself. I wanted something more. I wanted something better. I wanted to feel the way I did in sixth grade or so while wearing a brand new dress I bought with the insurance man's money; my eyes sparkled as I reveled in the compliments of how pretty I looked. I wanted to have music inside of me. To have it stir my limbs, increase my height and send my body into that place where I joined each note with precision and grace—thanks to years of dance training. I tasted that pleasure once, when I danced at the Wooden Shoe—a place my mother most certainly tried to protect me from, where people called me a Go-Go Dancer; a secret I thought I'd never tell—the applause healed my broken spirit.

This is what I need—this time away to write—time without distractions so ideas push through and materialize. Will I ever create disciplined time to fly with ideas and words across the page, or am I a dilettante—do I dabble but never really succeed? Do I ever finish what I start or do I merely play around the fringes? I know that time like this is how I will create depth in what I write, and, just possibly, discover a gem or two of polished words.

***

The Wooden Shoe

I found it after a day of job-hunting, a restaurant-lounge recommended to me by a friend. I paused before entering the long, thin downtown building; held my hand out to open the door and felt a tingle of hesitation. *No, this isn't one of Dad's haunts.*

The door opened in and music filtered out. The sound lured me to a table at the edge of a scarred, polished dance floor. I sat and scanned the length of the room past a mahogany bar backed by mirrors, sparkling glasses and paper-labeled bottles. I fidgeted a bit in my chair...*No, my husband won't find me here.*

Has he even figured out where I've gone? Will Mom tell him about the old woman who gave me shelter after he battered me about? Does he know I'm trying to *develop a plan? I need a job. I need a divorce. I need my son back in my arms.*

I tapped my feet. Moved my fingers across invisible piano keys. Lyrics swirled in

"Would you like to dance?"

My eyes moved up to his face. Tall, young, dressed in a business suit. The stranger extended his hand.

"I couldn't help but notice you're almost dancing in your chair." His smile bent toward my feet.

"Okay...sure." *Somewhere My Love* transported me while he circled my waist, took tentative steps, found fluid response, and led me around the floor.

My years of dance training held me captive to all the music as it changed. I didn't want to sit down. He obliged. The pace increased. The music swirled around and hugged me in until applause drug me back, and I found myself dancing alone while the stranger watched. Red spread up my neck, past my freckles, around my glowing eyes, to my auburn hair while I caught up with what I'd done.

"I'm sorry."

"You're an excellent dancer; a treat to watch."

That's how it started. Every day I looked for work and every evening I found refuge at *The Wooden Shoe.*

The Employment Office arranged for me to take a skills test—coordination really—where I assembled parts and puzzles to a timer along with other people sitting around a long table. "You did exceptionally well," I'd been told. Yet, no job had presented itself.

One evening the manager asked me if I wanted to work at *The Shoe.*

"What would I do?"

"Wait tables and what you're already doing. Dancing. Only it'd be up there in a cage."

He flipped on a light and nodded in the direction of a small stage with an apron floor, surrounded by bars that flared up like umbrella spines to a wood canopy attached to the wall. It hung up above the heads of seated patrons.

"How can I dance in a cage? What do I have to wear?"

"I don't care what you wear."

The cage had its attraction. The prospect of money would allow me to implement my plan. I left *The Shoe* and returned in a short tan skirt, yellow, sleeveless scooped neck-top, nylons and white, high-heeled shoes.

Small steps led up to my new perch. I mounted them, grabbed a bar with my left hand and palmed the other against the red brick wall. I stepped into the cage, jumped slightly—testing its ability to hold my size six frame—paused, looked out and felt the poles close in; I fixed my eyes on a distant wall.

Music moved in, my arms arced up and out, my body turned, my hips swayed—I pretended to be on a real stage. *Downtown* allowed me to *forget all my troubles, forget all my cares* and *Do You Believe in Magic* inspired me to dream.

Each day it became easier to climb into my cage. I nodded to people, responded to their suggestions for particular songs, often slipped out of my cage and moved onto the floor; closer to their applause. More and more customers filled *The Wooden Shoe.* I earned great tips while I waited tables between dancing stints.

I hired a lawyer, bought a costume—a satin elastic-strapped red leotard, circled at the hips with knee-length silk fringe—and ignored my mother's pleas to find a different job.

I dashed up the stairs to my cage, felt the music flow while fringe caressed my legs. Cheers went up. Customers enjoyed my new look. My head lifted higher.

My eyes grew brighter, my hips moved faster. *You Can't*

Hurry Love, These Boots are Made for Walking, and, *Wipe Out* connected with heightened energy.

One day I received a message from my employment counselor concerning a job at General Electric assembling TV's, radios and record players. The same day, my lawyer confronted me.

"Your husband's attorney is delighted. Not only are you a runaway mother, you're a Go-Go Dancer in a bar."

"I didn't run away," I sputtered out. "He beat me, shoved me out the door and down the stairs, tossed a wet washcloth at me and told me to clean up the blood.

I had to get away to save my life!" "And I'm not a Go-Go Dancer. I'm a waitress. And a dancer!"

"It's a choice you have to make."

Within days I stood putting wires, tubes and tape into cabinet TVs.

An Image of Mother

In the warm summer darkness, Mother and I sat on a concrete step with our backs to the front door of our two-story asphalt-shingled house.

Our feet—mine bare, hers in long black slippers—rested side-by-side on the sidewalk next to a vacant street. She raised a lit cigarette, inhaled for an instant, then brought her hand down. I had never seen her smoke. *Had she smoked before?* She curled forward and drew her legs up under the draped red plaid skirt of her dress below the thick black plastic belt that cinched her waist. Two pearl buttons of her bodice lay undone beneath a Peter Pan collar and revealed a plain gold cross in the hollow of her throat. I wondered, *Will I grow up to be as beautiful as you? No, probably not,* while I looked at my eight-year-old skinned elbows and knees hanging out of my shorts and white T-shirt. I also wondered; *Why are you so sad?*

A distant street lamp etched her silhouette. I saw the line of her long nose, the edge of her widow's peak and the shape her black hair pulled back into a careless bun at the nape of her neck. We sat without talking. She stared off as if seeing someone out beyond the darkness—perhaps, Junior? He'd been in a mental institution for a year now. I'd told my oldest brother not to pray all the time, "...just cause you're a priest," I'd said, "doesn't mean you have to be perfect."

Mom's fingers formed a V while she held her cigarette away, at the end of the extension of her arm, out from where it lay across her lap. An orange ember hung in the darkness. It didn't blink like the lightning bugs I caught and put into glass jars or pinched their "lights" off to wear as rings on my fingers. The ashes fell to the ground. The smoke rose in a gray wafting line, like the flutter of silk spreading apart in the dormant air. She clasped her bodice and pulled it in and out to cool her skin. Unsatisfied, she took the edge of her skirt and waved it like a fan up toward her face. "Is anything wrong?" I ventured.

"No, Sweetheart, why?"

"You look so sad."

"Oh, no, Sweetheart, there's nothing to worry about. Everything will be alright." She tossed the cigarette away and pulled me into her arms.

Hatto Fischer

Love Beyond Images
—on a Journey of the Soul—

No search, no journey is possible without thinking about Greece, Homer and those many other souls having gone on a trip but never to return. In modern terms Greeks call it their diaspora. Others have similar names when leaving the place of birth becomes a journey never finding again Ithaca. To return to the same place demands apparently something more than just luck or favorable winds; Homer said it is faithfulness in love and in friendship while culturally speaking it is the ability to anticipate. Clearly that is one of the greatest failings of recent times as if humanity needs disasters to know what is going to happen once war has started, namely to rob the others of their dignity and most important their intangible heritage: memory. That is why cast in the sunlight of Athens, Greece, these poems reflect a few shadows while seeking to understand a world at war and in which love seems to make no difference, or even to succumb to what can be described as a 'permanent war of feelings'. It leaves all those involved unable to cope. These poems reflect then a bit of that search for answers where often the most important questions are not heard since a terrible silence prevails against which even the winds cannot speak up.

Footsteps

Often we seek the astonishment of a poem,
As if we need the birds in the trees to tell us
What time it is, morning no longer asleep
And a day as of yet not gone with the winds,
Forever a sign of doubt etched into the pillar
Against which would lean the Goddess

Contemplating what to do next in her universe
Of bright dresses and fields filled with flowers
While animals and men would scurry over hills
To face their foe, and behold their woes, for fight
They did until no one had any rest, freedom gone,
So that the price has to be paid when flowers mourn
While graves are still, bells ringing so often
Like silent tear drops remembering the past,
The day when no courage was shown on fields
Of battles not meant for voices to be heard,
Just footsteps......

On the Horizon of Ancient Times

On the horizon
I see the boats
Entering the twilight
Before darkness
Illuminates the night
To let knowledge of blind people
Go with the winds
Till they smell the grass
So often forgotten
By ancient warriors like Achilles,
Says Homer,
For war and fighting
Makes men blind
But blindness of another kind,
The one so close
To the rubbish heaps of history.

As gentle the landscape appears
So encapsulated are still the ancient thoughts
Speaking about those times
When men did not listen
But ran instead the ships aground
Even though they had found once

There the protection they needed
Against burning arrows
Of the Persian army.
It was the oracle of Delphi
That saved the citizens of Athens
But they did not go at first willingly
For they felt to leave the city behind
Was just an act of betrayal
Hence they even stoned to death
The wives and children
Of their leaders who decided
To accept that interpretation
To be safe behind wooden boards
Meant to be on ships
And not at home
So as to escape the burning arrows.
Marx added to this story
The further going thought,
Indeed the city was destroyed by the Persians
But not the memories of the people
So that upon returning they could rebuild the city
And therefore helped to achieve despite their mortality
Something standing out in time, an immortality
Called the Parthenon on the Acropolis
With Piraeus being that close to Athens
Like the practice of survival
By analogy as to what we see and interpret
So as to listen to words of wisdom
Before it is too late.

Ancient Times are never forgotten.
The dialog of the present with the past
Is ongoing. Step by step a sense of time
Is made to compose some music.
Tunes float through the air.
A whisper of a thought, found there,
Where future becomes reality
In the significant bow like ships and harps
Entering the harbor and therefore back home.

The magical wish is written on the door
Behind which life begins as no return
Can ever be the same, for forgotten is the love
By which she went that morning when the breeze
Swept over the still water as if to caress its innocence
Into some ripples of laughter or was it pain?

Here then the hieroglyphic substance
Has yet to be written in the sand
And no matter what end is envisioned
Ancient Times remain the burial grounds of history
If not merely forgotten, but left aside
Out of preference to remember merely the pain,
The poisonous substance or disbelief
He will never leave nor come even if favorable winds
Could let any sailing ship find its harbor.

On the horizon behold the sea gulls
And at a distance the islands
Emerging out of the waters like whales
To witness the birth of the earth again.

What makes wonder akin to the universe
If questions asked are not responded to?
These then are trailing thoughts, lingering
Like the seagulls near the gush of waves
The boat leaves behind when sailing out
Into the open sea always there, and reflected
In the blue horizon of the Aegean light.

The Father

Strong is the grip of his hand
But weak his heart
Since unsure what he is doing
Exactly all the time
Within a family

He has abandoned
A long time ago
And maybe even before he was born
Since the way children
Are conceived
Is often arbitrary
And who knows why
Mothers begin to resent a child
From early stages on
As if the relationship to the man
Depends upon counting fingers
While running to work
To keep up the image of the family
When he goes drinking
And talks with other men
About women they desire
And not the one who is waiting
For them at home
Since that place is a mere refuge
From the street
In which all signs
Point skyward
To the omnipresence
Of a still greater father
Sure to squash any hope
For feeling anger
He lets the fist
Come down hard
In rage to smash
The tableau of rules
Meant to be broken
And not the stone
On which they are written on
For only then
They cast their spirit
In the air
With father
Becoming a man
Who does sue life

For what he has lost
In the job he is doing
And so he threatens
Love withdrawal
As a way to force
Especially his daughter
Into subtle submission.
Hence lighting a candle
In the Orthodox Church
On Athinasstreet
Near the central market
In his memory
Is like a request
To let her go free
From this self suppressing guilt
Of having betrayed him
When not caring enough
About the troubles
He could not put behind
But slipped instead
Into depression
Till his death.
If only love could do away
With such guilty feelings
Bearing down on her
Forever so hard
That even tears
Will not soften
The ground dried out
Since the beginning
Of the end of the father
As a man to be loved.

Open Window

Drafting the letter
Is like letting clothes
Breathe the fresh air
The wind brings in from the sea.

Someone shouts over there, over there,
Do you see the rainbow colours lift the eyes to the sky?

Children search and run,
While adults look on.

A man climbs up the stairs,
The stairs of nothingness
For they do not lead to heaven
Nor to the darker abyss men fear.

Darkness descends at times
Like a weeping shadow
Of the day sweeping through the streets
What has been left behind.

Turquoise colours show signs of relief
In geometrical forms
That hold the colours of someone dreams
Provided the light of the candle
Is held against that evanescent porcelain
To show what Pre-Columbian art could do
To keep the human warmth alight.

Aspects of thoughts in the middle of a city
Show up like unexpected guests
Even though around the corner awaits a familiar tone
Making no other noises but for the songs of the birds.

In pavements are inscribed the written stories
Of feet rushing home whenever there is an expectation
Someone is there awaiting the return of the man

From the blue moon with the shadows of the day.

Once no one dares to speak out against silence, so listens silence
To what every heart beat has to say when fear goes away
And instead there remains behind at least an open window.

Poem about Love in a World Divided

I would not know
Where to put my love poem
If not underneath the pillow
For when I sleep and dream
There comes a world to your threshold
Of consciousness
In vivid colors, all alive
As if only philosophers could walk that terrain
In-between city walls and historic routes
Which poets used to take
And now beggars sweep with bare hands
Since their daily loan
Are the metal chunks
Caravans left behind
Many centuries ago
But now the air is filled with other scents
As if rose petals float above the roofs
And give to the sunlight a shade of dust
Not known in the Western world until now
When overwhelmed by all these challenges
From the Islamic side articulating new sounds
Which many no longer understand as call of love
When compared to someone as close as far away
Not in distant lands but down by the river washing the feet
Of those who have carried out of the city
All day long the rubbish and used up sentiments
To free those stranded in the city from the anxiety
That this night they need not fear sickness
Or the laughter of death stalking ever closer in

For love resonates within city walls
And cools the forehead of the body shaken by temperatures
Soaring up to near forty degrees
To elongate the wild fantasies
Created when men view women veiled
As if only eyes could talk in darkness
About to descend when sleep puts to rest
Those wild dreams about love.

Stones and Sand

Along the curvatures of the earth
There is a universe
Of love
While ships pass by coastlines
Remembering the loneliness of sailors
Having left their ports
To find never again
Back home despite favorable winds
For as the myth of Homer suggests
Only those return whose wives remain faithful
Through years of waiting all alone
While surrounded by friars and fearful wishes
The man they love will not return
To challenge them to love again and again
Till midnight passes and then there is no escape
For the wild goose
To fly away
From North to South.

Bonnie T. Summers

Inside Out

The following chapters are from Inside Out, *a memoir-in-progress about coming to terms with long-term trauma. This visceral account is part of my experience of what I believe it is for all of us to be human—to be born both vulnerable and miraculously able to hope and to heal.*

RED

I don't like to handle raw meat. I cook it, if at all, as quickly as possible, clean up its wrappings and juices fast, and wash my hands with more hot water and more soap than is necessary. I don't keep it in the refrigerator long enough for blood to pool in Styrofoam trays or drip onto glass shelves. I am picky about where I buy meat and am glad to pay a premium to get it boned, trimmed, pre-sliced, even cooked. I eat out often and order meat well done. I try not to think about how meat gets to my plate.

I am about five years old when my dad and I follow the grocer in his long white apron into the cold meat locker. We walk along the rows of sides of deer, skinless red flesh hanging from the ceiling from hooks. Some time later, I tour the Armour meat packing plant during a family vacation, where I see slabs hanging again, beef instead of venison. Meat hanging in vertical rows, animals without life, skin, feet or face. I feel somehow superior and happy, being able to walk through these rows. I'm glad I'm a good girl, not an animal. Look what can happen to you.

RED
I choose wallpaper for my newly remodeled kitchen with a red background. In the next home, I paint my dining room deep

red. I buy artwork bold with red, matted in red. I wear dark red to cheer myself up in the winter. I draw and paint, over and over breaking red crayons, wearing down red pencils, running out of red paint, using up the red markers while the other colors wait, hardly touched. Red is a fact of my life. I need to see it clearly and truly, not watered down or muddied. But not too much. I love my new red cotton rug until suddenly one day I see it differently. I've placed it at the foot of my bed, where today it looks to me like a pool of blood. Immediately, I give the rug away.

RED

Our family drives everywhere we go, across broad states with long distances between the few places to stop. I am good at pouring coffee from the thermos for the driver. I never spill a drop. I drink some, too, steaming hot from the red plastic cup. We cross plains and mountains on those trips. Late at night, lights emerge out of the darkness. Blue, white and red ones form patterns on small rural airfields to signal pilots, tall flames rise openly at refineries, yard lights from ranches dot expanses of land, and constellations are clearly visible. My father, who is a minister and is studying to be a school psychologist, says that coming into a town after hours of following truck drivers' tail-lights on the highway, he has to remind himself not to keep moving right through the traffic lights. Red lights. Stop signs. Stoplights. He ignores the signals with me, too. I can't stop him. He goes wherever he wants. Does whatever he wants.

RED

I am twenty-five and wish I were pregnant like so many other women my age. It just isn't happening. Blood and its absence have new meanings for me now, and I'm overwhelmed when my period shows up on time, as always. I don't fit in. Again.

I feel compelled to paint with the color red. Now. With the most available and inexpensive materials I can find—tempera paint, a large wide paintbrush (the kind used on house exteriors) and a large cardboard box cut into affordable canvases. I sit down on the basement floor with the cardboard propped up against the washing machine and let loose. I cover one big surface after another completely in red, using straight-up-and-down motions, then swirls and strokes coming out from the bottom center of the paper, like a fountain. Immediately I feel release and fear, because of my intense drive to do this. Because of the frenzy in my arms to make red cover something completely. Because I have no idea why I must make these red paintings now.

RED

The unofficial symbol of my women's group is Red Shoes. Those who wear them report that their power is seductive and energizing. The rest of us try them out and concur—something happens to a woman when she looks down at her feet and sees Red Shoes. She can't help but wiggle them, smile inside, even laugh out loud. They make a statement of strength, daring, and passion. They say, "Look out!" They're dancing shoes, like the fairy tale. They become a reminder that I'm one many women who love to kick up their heels. Years after I have left this circle, when I see a pair of red ballet slippers or strappy, glittery evening sandals, I'm reminded that the feminine spirit is alive and well. I realize that don't own a pair of my own now, and add to my shopping list: Red Shoes.

RED

As an adult, I visit the rabbit cages at the state fair. Each has different colored fur—white, black, brown, mixed—and they all look incredibly soft. I'd like to touch them, but not the ones with red eyes. The rabbits are so quiet. I wish they would make noise. Their silent, alert, trusting presence saddens and frightens me.

I am nine years old. My father and I are sitting in a shed alone while visiting someone else's farm. No one else is around. He gives me a small rabbit to hold, a young, smooth warm creature dependent on me at this moment. I have let it down, my father says. He tells me that I have to sacrifice it for my sins. I must either cut the rabbit or be cut. He says this is the consequence of my behavior—that next time I will not have a choice. He takes out his pocketknife. The rabbit goes limp, never making a sound. I don't see any color.

RED

I wear deep red lipstick, and keep re-applying it so it doesn't fade. I learn that when I feel a memory resurfacing, it becomes clearer sometimes when I draw the feelings or images I'm experiencing. I draw an oval leaf shape—the same shape of the space between my legs. I remember pain in this place, but not the reason why. I color the shape red with a marker, over and over until sometimes the paper wears away. I can't get my drawings red enough.

RED

My upper chest below the neckline reddens like a rash. I don't itch. But I have just said more than I intended, exposed myself by saying my true feelings before thinking. The person with me notices and comments on my skin. I am aware that I am suddenly having trouble breathing and speaking, feel anxious, want to change the subject, but have no idea about my rash until it is brought to my attention. My skin returns to normal, quickly. I wonder why I turned red like that. I wonder what secret I think I have almost given away.

RED

I didn't go to my high school prom. I wasn't asked, although in the late sixties it wasn't "relevant" and few of my classmates went anyway. I make up for this one winter many years later when I am married and a mother. My then-husband graciously goes along with the idea to reconstruct a belated special evening. We plan a formal celebration on the town, just the two of us. I spend weeks shopping, trying on beautiful formal dresses in exclusive stores. I buy my first one, a sequined red dress. The skirt is chiffon, the top and thin straps sparkling. The day arrives. I luxuriate that afternoon at the Eve Arden Red Door Salon. I hardly recognize myself in styled hair and evening makeup. I'm wearing new red heels. We stay in a downtown hotel, go to dinner and a night club, kiss in a horse drawn carriage, and talk happily about our adventures to the man in the hotel elevator on the way back to our room. He wishes us a good night as the doors open for his floor, one stop below ours. I see myself in the hallway mirror as the elevator door opens, shocked. The man in the elevator never lets on that my lipstick, red to match my dress, is now smeared all over my face. I wonder why my husband didn't say anything, either. Or the carriage driver.

RED

I try never to miss communion, observed on the first Sunday of the month in my small evangelical church. But this ritual becomes more and more difficult for me. As a deaconess, I help serve, barely breathing, standing with others flanking the altar that is covered with an embroidered white cloth. It is like the one my father laid me across when I was two, where he raped me there in the empty church one Sunday after the people he had led in worship had gone home. The key words of the sacraments haven't changed. "This is the blood of Christ. Drink ye all of it." I can hardly bring myself to swallow the juice, remembering the times later on when he forced me to taste my own blood as part of his private version of ritualistic abuse. Still, I do it. I drink from the communion cup to know that it is really grape juice, swallow the fact that I am safe here, now, in this church that is not his. Then I slip the little glass into my pocket, take it later to the street outside the church and stomp on it. Shatter the pretense under my feet.

RED

That summer we all pick peaches to earn money and to help a farmer friend. In the afternoons we take breaks, cooling our feet in ice-cold irrigation pools. My dad's red Swiss Army pocketknife peels the skins from ready fruit in 110-degree heat. The soil is sandy, and grit gets into the knife, but it still works. We have handled these reddened peaches all day, their fuzz irritating our skin, their weight in long sacks a burden. Their outsides so different from their insides. Sweet, fragrant juice drips down our hands and faces, quenching our thirst as we rest in the shade.

RED

I am eleven. The Kotex pad feels bulky between my thin legs and irritates my skin. The metal grips of the sanitary belt poke into my stomach and tailbone. I sit with my friends in their backyard shade, all of us about the same age. We make tiny pads out of cotton strips for our new Barbie dolls. We sew tiny snaps on the ends of the strips and on wide pieces of elastic to hold them in place. We make red spots on some of the cotton pads with markers and great care. Our dolls are complete and we are pleased. We don't let our mothers know, or anyone else.

RED

I hate the color orange. I don't have orange things in my home, and I don't wear it. I don't even like orange fall leaves.

Red mixes with yellow in the toilet bowl and makes the water orange. I stand in the bathroom, my stomach cramping. Did the cramping come after the color, or before? A little red form, slippery and warm, falls to the floor. I am eleven years old, frightened and dizzy. I don't dare call for either parent. I don't know what to do about this tiny person on the floor. I don't understand how it came out of me. I don't know how to stop reeling or how to stop cramping. I must have killed it, how? Somehow there is bad inside of me, death, and it has fallen out. My father must be right. A little lump is there before me, unmistakable, a puny red wet alien yet familiar body with limbs half formed, and I can't let my father see it, see that he is right. I don't want to touch it I have to. I have to clean this blood up. I have to leave the bathroom the way it was get the blood off my legs off my hands off the floor, I wash and wash no, send red down the sink drain I have to get the orange out of the water in the toilet, hope it flushes, not too many times get this form off the floor I don't want to touch it, don't dare take it out of the room, no choice do it fast, fast I flush the little form away, don't stop to notice how hard and stiff it is, don't leave a trace, don't look at it, be sure to clean up all the spots every single one hurry.

Jerry, my psychotherapist, asks, "Are you ready to tell your father?" I look at him, startled, realizing that I had kept this memory secret until just now, when it surfaced during my session. My father, dead many years now, wasn't in that room and never saw what I saw. I talk to him now, and many times after. This incident that lasted only minutes originally takes me months to work out. One day, as I stand in Jerry's office facing this memory again, I begin to shake. My legs, hips, chest, arms and head vibrate. Soon I am shaking all over, an experience that lasts several minutes. Gradually I picture change—the old images of blood slide off my hands and legs. The blood slides off the floor, the fixtures, the fetus slides too, everything moves away from me as if in fast forward, like a flower coming into full bloom within seconds. The fetus stops to blow me a kiss, slides along the porcelain and disappears. I finally complete the scene that day. I clear all the blood away from the room, say goodbye to that little form, free my skin, and heal the space around and inside of me.

RED

I decide that I deserve a medal for all my work to heal emotionally. At a flea market, I find military medals with red ribbons. I give myself permission to use them my way, without negating their original purposes. I have experienced my own imprisonment, my own war, my own holocaust. One medal is the "Lady of Liberty" from World War II. A woman stands, one foot placed triumphant on a helmet, holding a sword broken in two. The sun dawns at her feet. I frame the medals, six of them, and give them a place in my home. I give my psychotherapist a medal, also. After all he has heard, all the years he has stood by me, and all he has done to help me battle my way home inside myself, he deserves it.

RED

I am almost forty when I begin to feel like I belong to my gender. I dare to shop for lingerie in specialty stores, as if they are meant for me. I have the body of an adult woman. I bleed, as do most normal, healthy women of my age. I'm a mother by adoption, not birth, and sometimes my belly feels empty. But even nuns, unmarried and childless, are women. I decide that I must be, too.

My women's support group has a menstruation party, an event that for me celebrates what I have in common with other women. I read a poem I've written about coming out of the menstrual hut. We drink Bloody Marys. We use Kotex pads for cocktail napkins. We tell stories of our menstrual cycles, our wombs, and our experiences as females. I have the mothers, sisters and friends that I'd needed every time I'd bled, from my own natural rhythm or from my father's hands.

RED

My father lights the sheets of his bed on fire, the sheets at the foot of the bed where I am outstretched, lights them so that my feet feel the heat and know that this is what burning in hell must feel like. He says that this is what I will face forever if I tell. If I tell, because then they will all see how sinful I am. Because there's no hiding from God even if I never said a word, never showed it on my face. Because God knows everything, and I am lucky I have my father to teach me to control myself so I don't have to burn like that, burn like that forever into eternity burn forever and ever amen.

, RED

My church's emphasis on God's loving nature and the power of transformation never has fit, for me, with its preoccupation with blood. I have been tuning out the words during services for a long time, paying attention mostly to the music and rhythm. I'm familiar with all the words, but don't let them get to me. As I recover memories and become more present, I am stunned to realize how many are focused on this theme. I count the number of titles in our hymnal that include the word "blood." There are 54 out of 667, about eight per cent—more than Christmas, which has 49.

The church I attend is a center of support for our family. But now as my memories flare I'm constantly triggered by the words, images and practices that are also often comforting to me. I have trouble keeping myself together in church. I cry, I question, I fight the flashbacks that flood in on me as insistently as sunlight through stained glass windows. I get tired of facing the pulpit in silence, listening to whatever is being said as if those words and the speaker are automatically sanctified. There are many within the church who help me considerably. One church leader describes communion wine, the symbol for the blood of Christ, as life blood. As transfusion. As health and life-giving sustenance. As part of a feast around the communion table, communion with God and others. At his suggestion, I write my own theology statement. Despite my questions and confusion, my faith is strong.

The church, for all its shortcomings, is a good and stable parent to me—my only good and stable parent.

RED

My dream is about a pomegranate, I tell Jerry. That's all I remember, just a pomegranate. He says quietly, intently, "Be the pomegranate," one of two suggestions he gives me over the many years we work together that sound ridiculous. I make a "you've got to be kidding" face. He keeps looking at me, waiting. I know better than not to try it, though skeptical, since he is usually right. "I am the pomegranate," I say. It works. Tears fill my eyes, and I begin again. "I am a special surprise for you."

Every fall my parents buy pomegranates, those hand size, labor-intensive and fascinating treats with sweet, bright seeds joined in little compartments that are separated methodically with white membranes. We just put on old T-shirts first so the stains aren't a bother—they never come out. This red in my mouth tastes wonderfully tart and juicy. I don't have to scrub or hide these stains.

RED

My father has put pills in my mouth and given me water to drink them down. He does not drive me to school as usual. My mind is foggy. I can't concentrate, and doze as I ride through farmland on that gray, sunless day in 1965. I follow my father into a roadside motel room, clean and ordinary. It smells like strong soap. I lie down on the bed nearest the window, as he directs.

A second bed is at my left. There is a lamp, but the lights are brightest in the bathroom that is far down to my left, past my feet. My father paces. Another man is there, a man I don't know, nervous, watchful, wearing a suit, holding a case, a man my father calls simply, "Doctor." My father keeps pacing as he talks, in control of the scene. With angry, short words he tells the man what a whore his daughter is. How she sleeps around. How fortunate she is to have him help her. How she has learned her lesson now, thanks to him. The doctor focuses on his work, face serious and watchful, brow knitted, speaking only as necessary. I am limp on the bed as my father's stride and voice circle fast and strong about the room. My ears and eyes are limp, unable to grasp the words and sights. My thoughts limp. Limbs limp. Voice limp, and will. Sharp metal instruments appear and disappear from a case, from male hands, from inside my limp skin. I cannot lift myself enough to catch the doctor's eye, signal a warning, reach for the phone, or get to the door. I cannot form words to ask a question, argue, or tell the truth—that there are no others, only my dad. There are two tall men in this room. Men who know where we are. Men who have tools and keys to their cars. My mind spins high above me while my body sinks. I am pregnant, my father had said so, and I am convinced that I am having a baby today. That's what happens, isn't it, when females are pregnant and their bellies cramp, when they are lying on their backs with their knees up and open to a doctor? I feel the metal tools probing and scraping without pain, my legs rock heavy, as if gravity is pulling them far down beneath the floor. I cannot raise my head or arms or legs. Suddenly the doctor brings out a lifeless, tiny child with care from between my legs, as if he has discovered something interesting and fragile in the back of a cupboard. I am confused. I am listening for the cry of a large, lively baby, but there is no sound. The doctor cleans up, packs his things, and prepares to take the form with him. My father will not allow it, insists that the doctor leave the little body here, with him. The doctor does not argue, though this is clearly not his usual protocol, and, for just an instant, only his eyes show alarm. He waits a moment, looks at my father, then looks at me, as if wondering whether he should go. Then he does as my father says—walks out the door. Leaves the silent, still miniature baby. Leaves me.

I am still weak when my father brings me to the bathroom to stand with him as he disposes of the fetus, small and still, covered in red—evidence, he says, of my wrongdoing. It will remain with me, he says, this horrible thing I have done. I watch from far down inside myself, unable to speak or to feel my body move. He flushes it away. Assured that everything is taken care of, he brings me back to the car. I don't remember the ride home. We walk back into our apartment. As I pass my mother, he tells her that he'd picked me up from school because I was sick and I'm going straight to bed. I sleep.

RED

Like most pastors, my father leaves careful instructions for when he dies—information for obituary notices, financial matters, and memorial service plans. He asks for no flowers except a single long-stemmed red rosebud on his casket. We comply. Years later, I find his choice especially fitting. The beauty of who he was, his life never fully open, the dark redness. The thorns.

RED

I write and hold a private service of thanksgiving and healing at my church with my pastor and a few close friends. Communion is a central part of this day of celebration and homecoming for me. Instead of the purple-red grape juice used in our tradition, I choose white grape juice as a symbol of the complete transforming, the complete healing that leaves us stain-free.

RED

Many years later, despite some changes, I'm uncomfortable with some of my church's exclusive and patriarchal language and practices. Issues that I think should be openly discussed and prayed about are still mostly off-limits, at least in public—mental illness, alcoholism, abuse, divorce, suicide, sexuality, homosexuality, politics. My energy goes increasingly to translating religious words and images for myself, trying to find meaning that fits my experience, trying not to be carried away by the symbols. I have a harder time ignoring what disturbs and puzzles me from the pulpit and in print now. I talk about these issues with others, read, consult with church leaders and experts, and write letters of protest. I don't make a scene, reserving my energy for the work of my own healing and day-to-day living. Some people urge me to remember the pain that abusers must feel, and their families and communities too. Some imply that I should "get over it."

Would I still have a place here in the building and among the people I love if I told them how I feel about the many traditional images that still trigger memories for me? Most of these words and symbols—keys to their faith and mine—are ones that my father grossly distorted and misused. I want different language now, and try to make sure I say what I believe. When I sing hymns and read aloud with the congregation, I skip the words that don't mesh with my conscience. How can I explain that sometimes I experience God most completely in the form of the snake who visits me during meditation? I consider her to be a gift from God—God who might also be spelled "Life," "Light" or "Good," who understands my difficulty trusting human beings—and therefore both male and female religious symbols—and offers other divine faces. The snake I sense within me matches the resurrection power that I learned about in church more closely than anything else I have experienced. Finally I decide to resign from membership in the church that has been my family and home for four generations, reluctantly yet with a sense of rightness about my choice and timing.

I miss the people. I miss the music and singing with those with whom I share a strong, beautiful common history. I don't miss the crucifixion images or prayers that are narrowly focused. And I still think I shouldn't have had to be the one to leave. I still think the church—who says that even death is conquered—should open herself to her wounds, wrestle with her issues both privately and publicly, and change. The church should also answer Jesus' red-letter question, "Do you want to be healed?"

RED

I shape a small fetus out of clay, paint it red with my fingers, and bring it to a week-long intensive workshop where I can say goodbye to this little form properly. We are invited to choose a name to use there. I choose the name "Aborted" in honor of the life my father forced from me, and in honor of my own life, aborted over and over. Every day I carry around a pink blanket as if it is my child, talking to her many times. My arms, heart, hips and legs all ache with regret for not finding a way to hold her—and myself—safe and protected. At last I let the fetus go. During meditation I see a place in the stars, wonderfully contained, large and womb-like, where she and all babies go who are born too early, whatever the reason. This tiny figure answers me then—tells me how happy she is to be free in this secure and peaceful place, and not to be dragged around with me anymore.

RED

"And nothing red would be unclean," the poet says, accompanied by his guitar. I freeze at these words. My eyes open wide and fill with tears. I listen intently to him singing these lyrics and wonder, "Is it possible—nothing red unclean?" Afterward, I drive home to my small studio and find all the tubes and jars of red paint. I squeeze it, pour it every bit onto a large canvas and spread it with my hands. I rub red into canvas just as my father smeared my blood over my skin as if to wash me, his horrific perversion of the New Testament image of Jesus' blood atoning for the sins of the world. I had paid attention during church when I was small and the older children sang for the congregation, "Now wash me and I will be whiter than snow." This time I am alone, safe, and using paint on cloth. This time I talk out loud, firmly and clearly as I work: "I smear this blood for the last time. Once more and I will never be unclean again. I do this for the last time."

RED

The snow is deep and beautiful in February sunlight. I realize that I have yet to see even one cardinal this winter. I put out a bird feeder, hoping to welcome red into these days that are too white, this winter that is too long. No birds come at all for a month. Then a pair of male cardinals appears on Easter Sunday, when the snow is gone.

RED

At an art fair, I buy a striking watercolor of a red hibiscus flower in full bloom, the single flower as wide across as my hips. There is a bud above it. The blossoms are edged in green leaves against a deep blue background. This open, bright mandala is a painting I never tire of, one that always brings me a rush of hope, energy and happiness. In it I see the passion and fullness of life and spirit that grows, persistent and prolific, in each one of us. I recognize this vibrancy with joy and awe, seeing some lost-and-found part of me reflected there, and celebrate.

The Snake

The first time I saw the snake she was enormous, fiercely graceful, and fast. She appeared suddenly and clearly during deep meditation at an intensive personal growth workshop, returning to show me again how she had flown through the air to rescue me years before. How she had swept down to me when I was a little girl, lifted my essence up and away from my spent body and onto her back, carrying me to safety. I saw my flesh as I felt then, like a carcass that had stayed on the ground, vultures picking away at torn skin, while my spirit was removed and protected by this decisive, strong, kind, mystical, airborne serpent. I saw myself as a child, bent forward, holding myself close against her body, my hair streaming back behind me in the wind she created as we sped through the air. Others rode with me, and I knew then that she had lifted others in similar circumstances up onto her back long before. That this is the Being so powerful and loving that she continues to carry away all those who need her, lifting spirits above the limits of the body and emotions and away from danger. I rode with her again then as she moved, swooping down, speeding past, still watching over lives everywhere, going from island to desert, tidal pool to city, farm to mountain to prairie to glacier, skyward and under water. She is too fast for predators, and determined not to allow those who are victimized to give up completely. She always wins, this long, thick, muscular black serpent. For me, she is the picture of dissociation, a self-defense mechanism without which many of us would have simply dissipated. Since that moment, I've been aware of the Snake's presence with me in many forms, always sure and comforting. Always encouraging. Always timeless and holy.

The Snake is the constant regenerative force in my cells. The double helix. DNA. She coils in my belly. She becomes my spine, my esophagus, my veins. She lines my throat so I can cough up every bit of blood, semen, and irrationality I'd had to swallow against my will. She becomes my skin, teaching me to shed the old, dead layers and masks I've outgrown. Like an Inuit woman uses her teeth to soften hardened hide, the Snake's fangs firmly and persistently pierce my muscles, hardened over time as pro-

tection, gently and steadily bringing warmth, flexibility and freedom back to my body. She has taken the place of the massage
therapist's hands until I could tolerate the thought of even a
trusted stranger touching my bare skin so intimately. She is a
midwife to my rebirth. She wraps her body around me, soothing.
The Snake teaches me to be grounded, to keep my whole body
reliant on the earth. To be patient. To undulate, to keep my spin
flexible and moving, like hers. She gives me her sound—*hiss*—a
sound that seems uselessly quiet, weak and insignificant until in
it I recognize the sound of my own exhale.

I honor her by drawing and painting her, writing poetry about
her, and collecting snake images in a variety of materials, sizes
and colors—jewelry, art objects, paintings, and shells that mirror
her body, coiled or extended. These forms placed throughout my
home reassure me of her presence within me. I visit live snakes
in zoos and make eye contact when possible.

The Snake is most vivid when I am breathing very deeply or
in a reflective, prayerful, or meditative state. I try to capture
some of these experiences visually—with black marker on white
paper, sketches in my journal, pastels on black paper, clay, or
painted coils inside a pelvic-size wooden bowl. She speaks to me
through her movement, through the setting in which I find her,
and sometimes even in words.

~~~~~

*I feel empty and shameful, and am terrified to look inside of
myself. Suddenly, the Snake appears, clearly not at all afraid of
what is within me. She swoops toward me, entering my body
fast and effortlessly, painlessly, benignly, through my vagina. At
that instant, I feel my entire body inside my skin light up. I feel
the openness inside of me, startlingly quiet, benign and starlit,
like galaxies in outer space. My inner space, not dark or threatening, but expansive, bright, peaceful, timeless and utterly
beautiful.*

~~~~~

*At a concert of sacred Indian music, I see many snakes
dancing vertically, vibrating midair in tune with our chanting
as if in ecstatic celebration. When I describe this to the musician*

*later, he tells me he's not surprised—this is, after all, the music
of kundalini energy. Snake music.*

~ ~ ~ ~ ~

*During a massage, the Snake appears and speeds around
the room, her enormous black body wide and flat against the
wall midway up, circling around and around for many minutes. She is vividly clear to me, though my eyes are shut, so
much so that I am positive that anyone else in the room could
see her. Her presence reassures me at a deep level. Reassures me
whenever I recall this moment.*

~ ~ ~ ~ ~

*I am lying on the floor with other workshop participants in
a circle, our heads together, just touching, at the center. We syn-
chronize our breathing. I feel the Snake enter me at the base of
my spine, move up through my belly, and then face me. Then I
see the Snake move in and out of each person, linking us, healing us, just as we are linked together by our breathing and common purpose.*

~ ~ ~ ~ ~

*In a group session we work in two's in an extended session
to intensify our breathing. I see large, benign snakes circle fast
along the floor around me and the others. More snakes circle the
building. I feel my own energy releasing—strong, healing and protected. I see these snakes as symbols of the spinning of the universe and the atom-like, cellular regeneration within each of us,
especially evident at moments of openness, integrity and rebirth.*

~ ~ ~ ~ ~

*I feel as if I am a snake surrounded by beautiful blue light. I
become a huge butterfly with a snake as my center body. My
arms open and close slowly, then my legs, like wings. I lie on my
back, then on my stomach, still opening and closing, steadily,
peacefully. Opening and closing and free. I become a snake em-
bryo, forming and stretching within the womb of the Universe,
free and graceful within my transparent shell, and sure that like
every living thing, I am born to transform.*

~~~~~

The Snake appears to me again, as she has so many times. I keep waiting, watching, eyes closed. She faces me close up and persists, and I give into her presence. I begin to move like her along the ground, moving my arms and hips, inching my body as she directs. I hiss softly, then recognize my sound also as the sound of the hot iron that my father used to threaten me, that "sss" sound of releasing steam. I turn over and move flat along my back, roll my body from side to side, push along the floor. I move upright, then, on my knees, like a cobra ready to strike. I explore the area, moving as if through the air, land and sea. I can go anywhere. I am not afraid, because I am a snake. Finally I turn to rest on my back, lying belly up in a vulnerable position. My skin is many-colored. I rest on the surface of an ocean, completely supported and safe. The Snake says, "Write about me."

~~~~~

The Snake talks to me, answers my questions: "I love that you keep images of me with you, and that you have looked for me all these years. I have been working hard and long inside of you to heal you. I am nearly finished and can rest now. Your past is healed completely. I will always be here for you, you can count on me. Now it's time for you to move and to move ahead— live, love, and create with openness, truth and joy.

My skin is colorful because life is incredibly beautiful—like flowers, like fish, like what you see when you look through a kaleidoscope. This tells you that you can have and show all of your feelings. Everything, including pain, is part of the pattern and has a place within the ever-changing colors and designs of your life and all of existence. I change, like the patterns in a kaleidoscope, like feelings, and you can too.

I'm not just a pretty snake. I'm very strong. My fangs are protective; my tongue is a warning for others. You are safe because of me. Nothing, no one frightens me. I am friends with all living beings, because I am in every single one. So I can be with anyone, those who look like me, and those who don't. And I can be separate. In the deepest parts of yourself, you are not different from others. There is nothing in you that you need to fear, whether you are with others or you are alone.

101

My spine is long and flexible. I can be both upright and low to the ground. I have complete freedom of movement. I can handle any environment—move about in the air, on land and in water with ease. I can lie on top of the ocean. That means two things. First, there is no place that I can't go. The possibilities are endless. Healing is always possible, no matter what. The second is that you can go anywhere inside yourself and out. The ocean is a part of you, too—your beautiful, life-giving depths. This is a mothering part of you, on whom you can depend completely for support and safety. The sky—daylight and open air without barriers—is also safely yours now. This is the part of you that can be fully open without obstruction or fear. I have been demonstrating all of this for you for a long time. Life is yours to inhale fully."

~ ~ ~ ~ ~

I begin to ride the spine of the snake down to my core. I don't want to go, yet know that I must. I'm going too fast. I scream—I scream as if on a funhouse ride that isn't fun—spiraling down, down into myself. I am on a smooth, spiraling slide, slipping, tumbling over and over, moving faster. Once in awhile the Snake comes, coaxes me, face to face. I'm terrified and protest. I even try to scramble back up along her vertebrae, but lose my grip and keep falling, falling downward. She reassures me. I argue, protest, keep falling, nothing to hold onto. Finally I scream, "No! Don't make me go! Please, don't make me go!" She tells me slowly, kindly, "You don't have a choice. You've come too far to go back now. You're already on your way." I continue falling, headfirst, frantic, despairing. Exhausted, I give in and slide, slide down into darkness that seems to have no end. I am sure I can't take anymore when suddenly I see a small square beneath me. Then I am immersed in the purest flame blue, and know that I have arrived at the very center of my soul. I am home, sobbing, stunned and grateful for the privilege of seeing this beautiful place inside of me. This place that clearly we all have inside of us, regardless of how—or even whether—we ever experience it. I am certain now that I've never needed to be afraid at all. That being completely within my own self is a good, safe and precious place to be. And I rest.

Vicki Elberfeld

Love and Other Misadventures

"Donkey's Ears" opens a sampling of my life stories involving love, loss, and creativity—writing, dancing, and storytelling. As for writing, it has taken most of my life to get seriously started. "Conversation with a Stranger" was composed over thirty—five years ago. I then took a quarter of a century break to act, teach, dance, and perform folk and fairy tales. Only in the past decade have I begun to tell my own story at coffeehouses, luncheons, and storytelling festivals and commit it to the page as well. I plan to record these tales and include them in a book entitled, Love and Other Misadventures.

Donkey's Ears

Perhaps you've heard the tale, "The King Has Donkey's Ears," in which a king beheads a whole series of barbers so they won't reveal his secret—that beneath his carefully cut and styled hair grow not the ears of a human but of a donkey. Finally the king meets a discreet barber and lets him live. Sadly, the barber cannot keep the secret and tells it to a river, the river tells it to the grass, the grass to the trees, and by the next morning, all of nature repeats the words, "The king has donkey's ears."

Now there's a politically correct, high self—esteem version in which the ending has been tampered with, tampered with in such a way as to make it downright cheerful as in,

And so the king, troubled in his heart that knowledge of his deformity, his donkey's ears, was common to all his subjects, began to walk in the garden to reflect upon his shame. He had not gone more than a few paces before he heard a rousing cheer, and he looked up and out upon a sea of donkey's ears, some much longer and hairier than his own. And the king's heart was glad. An emissary from the crowd approached and bowed low, removing his cap. The ears came away with the cap. 'What is the meaning of this?' demanded the king. 'Sire,' responded the man. 'We your subjects love and honor you as our king, our leader, a man of virtue, wisdom, strength and great courage. We are not worthy even to touch the hem of your robe; we can only, therefore, emulate you in the one physical expression of your uniqueness. Please accept this unworthy token of our admiration.'

The emissary then hands his king the donkey eared cap, and this tale ends on a high note. Subjects and king celebrate with food, with wine, with dance, and with song. Oh yes, and they live happily ever after, blah, blah, blah. And so the king has little chance to even feel his shame before his subjects lift it from him. They, too, are uncomfortable and want to "make it go away" before it can penetrate to their core.

I had always felt the original ending to be painfully disturbing but real, a life's worst case scenario played out to its fullest extent. Imagine for a moment your own most intimate secret, your most private shame, exposed for all the world to see. The trees whisper it; the grass speaks it; the very wind howls it. There is nowhere you can hide—when you look into the eyes of those you love and whose respect you most desire, you see your shame reflected in those eyes and you turn away. Your shame is yours and yours alone. Others cannot take it from you by performing pathetic imitations of its source.

I learned early on that life can be a mortifying experience. I never suffered from any delusions of adequacy, often functioned well below satisfactory, longing for my witnesses to vanish and only return when I could perform to better advantage. Never much good at improvising, I often wished life had provided me with a well—written script to fall back on. Yet improvising is precisely the skill life requires.

As a little girl I never knew quite how to talk to the other little girls, my classmates. Watching them at recess jumping rope, I'd want so much to join them but didn't know what to say. I knew whatever came out of my mouth would sound stupid, presumptuous, abrupt—I mean, I couldn't just go up to them and say, "Can I play?" They'd have to know me first, and I didn't know how to let them know me. I assumed the rope jumpers shared some code, some special language that enabled them to be together having fun, while I remained on the sidelines looking on, feeling lost yet, at the same time, pathetically conspicuous.

Of course I did manage to acquire friends along the way, quiet girls, not in the thick of the action but sensitive, sympathetic souls, girls I could tell my secrets to—for example, that I had a crush on the youngest, shortest, and smartest boy in the class, John Wright. He too remained on the sidelines at recess. In class, he bested my score in every exam (though I did beat him in a spelling bee) and sat directly behind me. As I had long hair, he'd measure one strand against the other, pulling them out for closer inspection, a sure sign that he liked me. I tried not to yell when he pulled because it would get him in trouble, and he'd have to spend the remainder of the day in the corner.

I cared about his feelings, but would he have any consideration for mine? He announced to me one day that one of my "friends" had told him that I liked him, not just "liked" but "like liked." Not to give him the satisfaction, I denied everything and went home to bed for the rest of the day to cry tears of mortification.

Tomboy that I was, most of my neighborhood pals were boys, and I explored vacant lots with them, played "King of the Hill," and peed with them in the back yard. Mother yelled, "I thought I raised you to be a young lady, Lord knows I tried, yet look what you do! I certainly hope you're ashamed of yourself because I'm ashamed for you," and she grounded me for a week. When I pointed out that my brother had done the exact same thing, she just shrugged and said, "Well … he's a boy," as if that explained everything. Once I'd served my time, I celebrated by picnicking with John Wright's family. I climbed a tree with John but scrambled down immediately I heard his sister taunt, "Vicki and John, up in a tree, K—I—S—S—I—N—G."

Life had been humiliating for Mother as well. As a teenager, she was a gifted public speaker. On the day the principal himself came to class to hear one of her marvelous speeches she froze, totally blocked in the middle of a sentence, stood trembling an eternity before everyone and then retreated to her desk in embarrassment. Apart from rare occasions when her job depended on it, she never spoke in public again.

As a mother, she was determined that her only daughter would never suffer a similar fate, signing me up for every speech and drama class available. She also provided dance lessons to give me grace, electrolysis to keep my eyebrows from growing together, a dermatologist for my adolescent skin, contact lenses for my eyes, and braces for my teeth to keep my face from tripping me up. But acne continued to mar that face, and at times I believed the braces themselves to be worse than the overbite they were meant to correct. Still, all a mother could do to protect her cub from the scorn and ridicule of the world was done.

Doubts about my fitness for life arose as I wondered why I needed so much repair work. Plus Mom only worked on my outside, my image. But suppose one day my insides turned outside, revealing all my thoughts and feelings? What flaws might be discovered then? Mom would have to hire a psychologist to fix my mental processes, a writer to script my words, and a director to fine—tune the ultimate expression of them. We'd be bankrupt in no time.

But as I matured, I came to realize that carving and sculpting me, as well as pulling my strings, was not Mother's task. I had to compose my own words and gestures, take my own risks. Life was an adventure, perhaps the only adventure, and if fear of shame of prevented me from risking, I might as well crawl in a hole and pull the dirt in after me.

But for so long my adventures occurred mainly in the realm of books, and I looked to them for guidance. Though I loved to read of knights and ladies, of witches and fairy folk, finding realistic role models was difficult. I also read tormented Russians, whimsical Englishmen, and adolescent Americans, particularly Hemingway who said that a bullfighter lived most fully, most intensely, because he came so close to death.

I had to think about that…that this nearness to death gives life its edge, the moment of truth coming when one faces the bull and goes in for the kill, the moment of greatest vulnerability. While I wasn't about to fight bulls, I greatly admired the courage of those who did. But wasn't there some other way to feel this intense struggle with my own vulnerability?

I thought of the stage fright I endured every time I gave a speech or auditioned for a play, my palms sweaty, my muscles tensed so as to constrict the very voice I wanted to share. What I feared was making a fool of myself; I feared mortification. The ultimate criticism of my performance would be, "She died up there." Mortification. Morte. Death. And didn't I face a kind of death every time I mounted a stage?

Then I read a Frenchman, Jean Genet: prostitute, felon, philosopher. He suggested that if you bite into an apple and find you have inadvertently swallowed half a worm, go ahead and eat the other half...with relish! It's a way of validating life with all its trauma, of affirming, nay, of actually willing, what is.

Life is an embarrassing experience, and there is no way around it. One's mask often slips revealing donkey's ears and other flaws. Such is the substance of my worm, the first half consumed by simply enduring the daily embarrassments flesh is heir to. Might I not consume the second half by mounting the stage, thereby gaining some control over my exposure? Plus, performances always occurred at a given place and time; they'd never pounce upon me unawares. Not only could I thoroughly rehearse for them but also provide myself with a well—conceived script; I would not have to improvise.

In my late twenties, I found I could perform and yet dispense with any script whatsoever. I was dating a Don Juan. He and his ex—wife used to have body painting parties in their home, and once he divorced, his wildness continued. His ex was a stripper, and he admired her greatly. I too wished to be wild and admired, so I signed up for an amateur night at an X—rated movie theater.

Stage fright wouldn't begin to describe it. At the thought of what I was about to do, I was ready to lose my dinner. I didn't know if this were my moment of truth; all I knew was I was determined to take a large chunk out of the second half of my disgusting, slimy worm, and I did not expect to relish it.

Prior to walking onstage in a play, I typically worried about putting my audience to sleep. These thoughts were not uppermost in my mind, however, as I psyched myself up to shed my last stitch of clothing before a group of total strangers (though, come to think of it, if they had fallen asleep I would have been really humiliated). And all of the orthodontia in the world couldn't help me now.

But the other strippers were supportive, the audience was

more than encouraging, and as I heard the music throbbing, my love of dancing returned in a way Mother never intended. Since the house lights were down, I barely saw my audience, apart from the occasional camera flash, and I loved the feel of the hot stage lights on my skin. As the hard beat of the music pulsed through my body, I began to surrender to the experience. A stagehand signaled it was high time I removed some clothes. No problem! Applause as I removed my blouse. During the next number I removed my skirt, then bra, to more applause and increased camera flashing. The stagehand warned me not to toss my clothes so far, for if they fell off the stage, they might never be returned. So what? I had never felt so elated. Once stripped down to a total state of nature, I experienced an adrenaline rush more powerful than skydiving for the first time and landing safely on the ground.

As the last note died, cheers and applause swept away any reservations I might have had about my little adventure; I had won the amateur contest—a fifty dollar prize plus the respect of my fellow dancers! A pity I couldn't share the good news with parents and friends. A veteran stripper soon burst my bubble. "Of course you won," she said. "It wouldn't take a psychic to predict that. It's your first time. Look, don't feel bad about it, honey. It's just a fact of life but those guys out there…well, they kinda get off on feeling they're corrupting you. Just wait 'til you've been around awhile. You'll see."

So, wisdom wasn't only to be found in books. After months of doing the occasional bachelor party and performing amateur nights over and over again at the very same locations, I did, indeed, lose to newcomers. One evening as I came off stage, a fellow invited me to pose for nude photographs. When I refused, he accepted it none too graciously. He hurled after me, "All you broads are alike—afraid you'll look fat!" I kept on walking. I was suffering from a certain disadvantage in any debate and didn't see much point in arguing with a clothed person.

Discouraged by the little money I earned from the occasional gig and unwilling to work in clubs where I'd also have to sit with men who'd just seen me naked, hustling them to buy me drinks (a whole other kind of performance), I decided to find an occupation that was somewhat classier and a tad more lucrative. I turned to belly dancing.

What was disturbing about belly dancing was the addition of women to my audience. I had been used to performing only for men, and while I worked very hard at selecting music and choreographing dances, I couldn't actually bring myself to believe that anyone cared. Strippers who merely walked back and forth in time to the music were quite as successful as experienced dancers. We were all, audience and performers alike, simply being naughty together, and standards didn't really enter in.

But if women were in the audience, they would have standards; my dancing would need to be reasonably good. And in addition to risking my own mortification, I risked inflicting it on others. I was to persuade the guest of honor, the birthday boy, to dance with me at the conclusion of the performance. And while I would take care to give him something easy to do, generally involving hand, arm, and head movements, even so, a sensitive man might find himself feeling exposed and rather foolish. One gentleman even locked himself in the bathroom while I continued to dance outside his door. Friends, describing my every move to him and calling out such encouragement as, "Go on! Whatsa matter with you? Dance with her. Be a man!" weren't helping matters.

One gentleman even challenged me with, "Don't you have anything better to do than embarrass guys on their birthdays?" I felt ashamed and refrained from stating the obvious—that if I thought I had something better to do, I'd be doing it.

But I needn't have worried much about standards. On several occasions I was asked to view a videotape of the dance. I was lucky if I even made it on to the tape. The camera man was busy focusing on the birthday boy's face, catching his shock, and, oh yes, his mortification, upon receiving a belly dance, while his friends hooted with laughter. I was truly a gift more blessed to give than to receive.

Now that I have taken up space on this planet for over half a century, I have begun to tell stories of my life. And I have to ask myself, who cares? What is so extraordinary about my life and why should it have meaning for total strangers? What egotism leads me to think I can keep anyone awake, let alone focused on what I have to say? Audiences give me the gift of their attention, and I must provide something worthy in return. Yet suppose I come up empty, my stories irrelevant to those who have opened their ears to me?

Somehow I find it easy to identify with the king with donkey's ears and his deep—seated fear of exposure. I want to expose what I am proud of and hide whatever shames me. At this stage of my life I want to be heard far more than I want to be seen, yet I'm never sure that what I have to say has any value. What if I were to peel away the layers of myself, reach the core, and find there's nothing there?

I have come to appreciate that there is more than one way to be naked—that taking off my clothes was the easy part, and there is far more significant armor for me to shed. The first time I disrobed before strangers I wanted to vomit, but having heart and mind exposed is a far more fearful thing. I've also learned that to bare one's self without sensitivity or subtlety is merely a vulgar exercise.

And so I continue to live as a shy exhibitionist, striving, ever so gradually, to nibble away at the second half of my worm. Meanwhile, in my vulnerable egotism, I struggle to keep at bay this relentless fear: that I will awaken one day to hear the trees, the grass, the wind whisper and then shout, "Vicki is a hollow bore" and "Vicki has nothing to say."

Neurotic Woman

Some time ago, a married friend gave me a gift. I stress that my friend was married, for while he was single, he gloried in his bachelorhood, maintaining married folk were foolish slaves to an empty institution. But once he himself married, he became obsessed with matching up all his single friends, leading them down the path to wedded bliss. I was one of his victims. Finally I had to say, "Look, I can make my own mistakes in this area, thank you very much," and he backed off. So I was totally off guard when I unwrapped his gift. It was a book, entitled, *The Neurotic Woman's Guide to Non-fulfillment*, subtitled, "How Not to Get a Man."

"You shouldn't have."

"Oh, it was no trouble at all."

110

"No, I mean, you SHOULDN'T have!"

"Wull, I just thought that with all your, ahem, experiences, you might have missed a couple."

"We'll see about that."

After he left, I read from the dust jacket that the author, Joy Kennedy, has "succeeded in alienating men in three languages, nine countries, and five islands." Pretty impressive.

But as I read further I realized the book had less to do with alienating men than with finding Mr. Wrong to begin with. You pick a man with a problem: a wife, an ex, an addiction; perhaps he's so in love with himself that there really isn't any room for you, dear, or possibly his sexual orientation excludes you as a possible object of attraction.

Well, I had been guilty of some of the above, but only with the best of intentions. I even became a belly dancer because I believed belly dancers got to sleep until noon and had lots of dates. Wrong. Agents typically called me before 9:00 am and I was so busy dancing evening and weekends there was no time to meet anyone, let alone go out. But at one of my gigs I met that rarity, an unattached male. I liked him; he liked me. We agreed to meet later for coffee. But over coffee I made the disappointing discovery that my date did not speak English. Why hadn't I noticed this earlier? Well, I was doing most of the talking, I guess. He'd nod and smile, seemed to hang on every word I said, probably didn't understand a word I said, so conversation over coffee was difficult. Until we hit upon a subject he relished—his ex wife. He railed against her. Finally he wound down and said, "So how 'bout eet?"

"How about what?" "How about you...me..."

"You...me...what?"

"You...lif wiz me. Abartment, messy, leetle messy, buuuut...wife leef, no whan clean, what I can do, huh?"

"Look, I'm not much of a housekeeper and anyway, I just don't think the two of us..."

And then a hurt look crossed his face, and he slumped into his chair and I felt sorry for him, for a moment. Then all of a sudden he straightened up, and a huge grin crossed his face.

"Ah, you ahr lespian, no?"

"Well, no actually, as a matter of fact..." And then I thought

111

...why am I arguing? There could be a quick way out of this nightmare. So I said, "Why yes, yes indeed. You've got me there. So, seeing as how there couldn't possibly be anything between the two of us..." and I dashed out.

When I arrived home I noticed the red light on my answering machine was blinking furiously. He'd evidently phoned the moment I'd left to tell me he'd be over the following evening to help me with my problem.

If I couldn't date men I met at gigs, perhaps I could try the men I worked with. The problem was that there weren't many male belly dancers. Sadly, the few I met never showed much interest in me.

I knew this agent, however, and he was gorgeous. Furthermore, we shared many interests in common in dance, music, and theater. My girlfriend auditioned for him and happened to ask if he knew me.

"Vicki Elberfeld?" he asked. "Of course I know her. As a matter of fact, I'm in love with her. Don't tell anyone," he whispered conspiratorially, "but I'd marry her ... [snort]... if I were straight."

But I did manage to date a gorilla. He sang and danced in his gorilla costume and passed out balloons at ladies' parties. His name was Carl, but as he was terribly vain, I nicknamed him, "The Beda," (after that tropical fish who, whenever you put a mirror in his tank, will glide up to it, suffuse himself with vivid color, and become transfixed by his own reflection).

One day I wrote him a letter:

> "Dear Carl. It is my honor to inform you that you have been recommended for membership in Narcissists Anonymous. While it's true that most of our members have far more years experience looking at themselves, talking about themselves, adoring themselves in every way, what you lack in experience, you make up for in zeal. Come to my house on such and such a day for a meeting and further evaluation."

Then I added:

> "P.S. This is strictly a BYOM or Bring Your Own Mirror event."

I signed it, sealed it, mailed it, and in a few days received a very flowery and gracious letter of acceptance, saying how much he was looking forward to the event.

Could he help; could he bring something, photographs of himself, perhaps, or recordings of his songs?

Somehow I scraped together a meeting of friends who were in on the joke, and Carl was accepted. I never informed him that he was, in fact, the sole member of Narcissists Anonymous.

Years later I left the belly dancing world. One could conceivably continue in that occupation until the age of sixty—five, but there was always the problem of the dwindling audience. Face and body lifts might have extended my performance life, but I preferred to retire, return to school, meet new people, and possibly even learn something. And I studied literature. Now the study of literature is wonderful, for it provides you with the opportunity to study relationships. You read about them, analyze them, discuss them, and by the end of the day you are so tired of them you feel no real need to have one; that's the beauty of it. I threw myself passionately into the romances of Tristan and Iseult, Troilus and Cressida, Catherine and Heathcliff. I particularly loved the scene near the end of Wuthering Heights where Heathcliff digs up Catherine's moldering body and embraces her one final time. What she might have smelled like or looked like after being in the ground all that time really didn't enter my mind; I was in another world.

Joy Kennedy, in her Neurotic Woman's Guide, devotes an entire chapter to "Waiting for Prince Charming or the Greener Pastures Syndrome," in which she suggests that the neurotic woman select as her love object a man well above her in status, who scarcely notices her and who, in fact, barely knows she's alive. I settled on my literature professor. He taught a course with love in the title and I loved hearing him talk about love.

I'll never forget the first day I saw him. He rode into class, not on a white charger, but on a bicycle, which he proceeded to park in the center of a circle of chairs. He sat down next to a student, and when the class period began, he opened his notebook—not to check any notes as the pages were all blank—and he began tearing out pages, wadding them into balls, tossing them into the garbage can parked next to the bicycle. Then he delivered his lecture, all the while gazing at the ceiling. When he grew restless he stood up and did what I called chain coffee—smoking. He had a cigarette in one hand and a coffee cup in the other, and he alternated them, all the while pacing back and forth, continuing his lecture, not missing a beat, occasionally tripping over wads of paper that never quite made the basket.

His sentences were always works of art. The longest would have covered pages if written down, yet his syntax was perfect. He was brilliant, and I adored him. Yet how would I get his attention? He never looked anywhere but at the ceiling, never listened to any voice except his own. And then it came to me.

A few weeks before the end of the term, he announced that for our final papers, he didn't want junk to read. Customarily, he informed us, he would read only the first few paragraphs of a student's work and if it failed to impress him, into the garbage would go the entire paper, resulting in an "F" for the final grade. This semester, however, he was making us a one—time offer. If we wished, we could take incompletes, giving ourselves an entire year to finish. We could then put sustained effort into our papers and produce something worthy of his attention.

Inspired by his announcement, I took an incomplete and devoted the better part of a year to working on and obsessing over my paper. I even learned some German to research sources otherwise inaccessible to me. I poured my whole being into the project. I ate it, drank it, slept it, breathed it, knowing that this was the only way I could make an impression on him, that he would have to judge my entire worth on the paper alone. It had to be beyond brilliant.

In order to allow some time to prepare for an oral presentation for him in another class, I turned in the paper a few weeks before the deadline. Finally, the hoped for and dreaded day arrived, as he called me into his office to give me my grade. I was a wreck. I knew I hadn't failed; I had worked too hard for that, but I didn't know how I'd face him if I'd received a common "C." I'd have wasted an entire year only to be a mediocrity in his eyes.

He passed the paper across is desk to me, and I noticed that in the upper left hand corner was an "A" with a circle around it. An "A," unheard of from this professor! A smile of relief blending into ecstasy crossed my face. He caught that look and said, "You needn't let it go to your head. Your writing was acceptable, but your oral presentation the other day was a disaster, totally incoherent! I don't know what got into you. Frankly, I'm disappointed in you, Vicki, very disappointed."

I was numb. I felt as if all the blood had drained from my body. I don't know how I managed to leave the office; I don't know how I got myself home; I don't know how I made it through the week. But by the end of the week, the damn had burst and I needed to talk to someone. I chose to confide in my father. He was a literary person; surely, he'd understand. When I had finished my tale of woe, my father concluded, "That professor helped you snatch defeat from the jaws of victory. Can't you just see it? A giant bird swoops down and snatches a fish from the jaws of Leviathan, but when the bird soars off, the prey turns to ashes in its mouth. No, no, doesn't quite made sense, does it? I had a whale in mind, actually, and whales don't eat fish, they eat plankton or something, don't they? Or do they eat fish? Hmm—needs work, definitely needs work," and he wandered off to work on his metaphor, leaving his poor daughter in anguish.

My friends were somewhat more helpful. One friend took me to a Quaker service, thinking it might comfort me. She explained that a Quaker service was truly amazing, for the entire congregation sat in silence for an hour. If someone became inspired, he or she stood and spoke. Some of the more secular Quakers didn't believe their inspiration had to come from a deity. For example, they might simply have read in the newspaper about some war torn country and feel inspired to stand up and talk about the suffering there. But the only sufferings I was concerned about as I sat in silence were my own, and in my head I heard, over and over again, the words of my professor, "I'm disappointed in you, Vicki, very disappointed," and soon tears were falling down my face. When I could stand it no longer, I rose to my feet and cried out, "I have been wronged, grievously wronged! (I used to talk that way as a literature student.) "Before this day," I continued, "I was incapable of understanding how one man could kill another over something as trivial as an insult. But that was before I had ever truly been insulted! Perhaps I shouldn't say this at a Quaker service, but sitting in the silence, I have come to realize that as a society, we need some way, some ritualized way, of handling insult. What we need is to bring back.....the duel!"

And I sank down as far as one could sink down into a wooden pew, to an ever deepening silence. And then the pictures in my brain began to roll. Of me walking into my professor's office and unfurling a long scroll covered with student complaints about his arrogance. Then, with the whitest of linen handkerchiefs, I'd slap him gently saying, "Dawn. Grant Park. Choose your seconds." Or would it be, "Choose your weapons?" I'd have to read up on this. But if it were up to me, I'd choose pistols, and on a foggy morning in Grant Park, we'd stand back to back; our seconds would count out ten paces—we'd turn and fire. Perhaps I'd kill him and be avenged. Perhaps he'd kill me, and I'd be out of it. But perhaps I would only wound him and, seeing him lying in a pool of blood, some shred of pity would enter my breast and destroy my high resolve. Or perhaps he'd only wound me, and I'd be paralyzed. I'd have to lie in bed for the rest of my life, playing over and over again the scene of my mortification.

Mercifully, the end of the Quaker service put an end to these reflections. I had a moment of panic as I watched those around me rise to their feet. But I needn't have worried. Not one of the Quakers approached to ask me to forgive the professor, very sensible under the circumstances. Not one so much as asked me to join them for coffee downstairs. And they gave me rather a wide berth as they departed.

When the room was almost empty my girlfriend, the one who had brought me, placed her hand on my arm, smiled at me tenderly and said, "Vicki, I can't take you anywhere, can I?"

Well, I'm proud to admit that I have finally finished the book, *The Neurotic Woman's Guide to Non-fulfillment*, and I have to admit that my friend was right—that I had indeed missed "a couple," though he seriously understated the case. More than a couple, there are many, many kinds of unproductive, impossible, unfulfilling relationships that I haven't experienced, yet.

VICKI ELBERFELD

Dialogue with Writing

I suffer from writer's block. In an effort to gain some perspective on this problem, I have the following dialogue with Writing in my journal and, being polite, I let writing begin.

***

Writing: Why hello there, stranger. And to what do I owe this unlooked for pleasure?

Me: Don't start with me, Writing. You know, maybe if you were a little less sarcastic, maybe if you were a bit more pleasant, I'd spend more time with you.

Well, did you ever stop to think that maybe if you spent more time with me, I'd BE more pleasant?

Touché! But I've so much to do—two jobs, a so-called social life, plus I have a house to clean...

Excuses. Excuses. Look, I have a lot to offer you, you know — an outlet for your thoughts and feelings. Plus I myself am extremely intellectual, emotional, creative...

Don't forget full of yourself...

Give me a break. I can be brooding, dark, intense, complex...just your type. You name it, I'll be it! And I can take you places and show you things about yourself that would surprise you.

But surprises aren't always good. Take that time I stayed late at work and composed my first piece of erotica, "Education of a Sultan," and then sent it by company email to all my friends.

EROTICA? Oh it's erotica now is it? My my, our Vicki's composing erotica. Look, what you don't seem to realize is that in order to be considered erotica, a work has to have some socially redeeming value, while what you wrote was just....

Goldie liked it.

Ah Goldie, well...Goldie. Let's see, how do I put this? Let's just say your friend Goldie is unusually kind. Then she showed it to Joe, who not only avoided looking you in the eye, he suggested you place it in a musty old trunk in the attic, there to be discovered only after your death—he distinctly emphasized the

117

word, "after." Now you know how much I hate to be the bearer of bad news, but a piece like yours with no artistic or socially redeeming value, well the proper term for it is...

Stop it! Now you stop right there. You're not supposed to be judging me, you know.

I'm not? Well what am I supposed to be doing then?

You could try....to seduce me.

Seduce you? You want me to seduce you?

Yes. Please.

O......k. But you do realize I'm not particularly good at it, don't you?

Oh, you don't need to tell me, Writing. I know. Believe me, I know. It's just that some women find you irresistible—they pick you up, they can't put you down. I can put you down. Some say they can't be away from you for a few days, whereas it takes me months to even realize you're gone.

Very well, I'll try. You women! All you ever want is romance, always have to be "in the mood." Luckily I have a few ideas. How about next time we get together you put on some music and add some soft lighting. Then select a chair, comfy, but not too comfy. I don't want you falling asleep on me. Then light a candle....

Candle? Are you crazy? You don't want writers messing with candles. Besides, I tried that just last week. I sat down to write and lit this big candle. I wrote down a couple of lines, but pretty soon I was pacing back and forth, talking out my story—well you know my storytelling background. Before I knew it I'd wandered into the kitchen, and since there were lines I wanted to keep, I scribbled them onto post it notes and plastered them all over the refrigerator. I seriously need to collect them and type them up some time. Well, since I was at the fridge anyway, I made myself a snack. Then I turned on the boob tube and fell asleep. Believe me, it's no fun awakening to smoke alarms.

Ok, ok, forget the candle. My point is, I feel really wounded when you act like you don't care, when you neglect me. Take last night. Two hours of sitcoms? If you'd given those two hours to me, you'd have something to show for yourself, something to show for your life...

Oh you are so full of it. Promises, promises, that's all you are.

I've devoted hundreds of hours to you and if I'd given them to candle making, calligraphy, wood carving, paper making, knitting even, I'd have something beautiful to show for it. And lasting! Well, maybe not the paper, unless I put it behind glass and you know how I am with candles, but you know what I mean. And now all I have of you are pieces—awkward starts, ideas that trail off and go nowhere, lame endings....

How about a little patience, woman! You know a relationship has to be nurtured — given food, water, sunshine. Naturally this takes time.

Love? Love? Whatsa matter with you? Who said anything about love? Wait a minute; wait a minute here. You know you are really crazy. Yoooooou scare me sometimes.

(smugly) I do, don't I.

You are so full of yourself. You're not so special. Listen. Let me explain so even you can understand. I go to work and pay my bills. If I don't, I get in serious trouble. I eat, sleep, and breathe and if I don't, I die. I don't write—I don't die. Life goes on. I watch sitcoms. I have a few laughs. Whatsa matter with you? You don't want me to laugh?

Laugh all you want! No problem. But you have to realize that I can be funny, too. And not with corny laugh tracks, either. Listen, just listen to this! Two middle aged women with writer's block walk into a bar. The first one says...

***

But I don't let Writing finish. That's the beauty of a dialogue journal. You can end it any time you like. You don't even have to say good-bye. I was tired of Writing's incessant whining, cajoling, self-pity, bad jokes. Not to mention his nagging and jealous accusations. So I just slammed my journal shut.

But Writing wasn't satisfied. If there is one thing I can say about him, it's that he is no respecter of boundaries. He's a stalker, one of the worst kinds of perverts. Shouldn't have told him eating, sleeping and breathing were important to me. Now at every meal he is by my side nagging me to finish and turn on the computer. In my dreams I hear his screams, accusing me of self-sabotage when I misplace my notebooks and computer disks. And whenever paper and pencil are in reach, he urges me to share a memory, an observation, something, anything. Sometimes I open my journal and write the truth—what I really feel, "I hate you! I hate you, I hate you, I hate you, and this is why I hate you," for I want him to feel some small part of my pain, but all I can sense is his gloating. And I cannot shut out his maniacal laughter, for he knows I am familiar with the old saw: that the opposite of love isn't hate; the opposite of love is indifference.

Ralph Murre

Crude Red Boat

Time and tutelage have shown that simply gathering up the best of my poems and stapling them together would not result in a satisfactory chapbook. Two years of wrestling with lots of new poetry and constantly adding, subtracting, editing and fretting have done a lot to produce a better book. Some poems which had been accepted for publication in various journals and reviews or were popular at readings didn't feel right for this collection, while others, some of which had been rejected, seemed to belong. Of the poems that appear in these pages, all of which were considered for my book and all of which I believe might have been worthy, just one appears in my final manuscript. Like an island in the sea, a body of work is defined not only by that which it is, but also by that which surrounds it. I think my book, Crude Red Boat, *is a good little island.*

I Tried

I tried to read the work of a poet,
but found he was not ready for me.
I've put his book aside
to give him time to prepare.
Perhaps, when I next take him
from the shelf, he will have
swept up and made the beds.
He will have weeded the gardens.
There'll be freshly cut flowers
and the aroma of baking bread.
Perhaps he'll offer me a
comfortable chair before launching
into his long and lofty talk.

Minnesota Snowfall

All I know, says Merton, *is that here I am —*
with a false sense of modesty, I think,
as though that isn't more
than the rest of us know.
As in, Gee, Tom, why do you suppose
we're reading your journal?
As in, Gee, Tom, isn't knowing where
almost as good as knowing why?
As in, Golly, Brother Merton,
even my return address
looks very strange to me.

All *I* know is that I wonder and suppose
about the spring that starts the Mississippi,
as though that isn't more
than I'm likely to learn.
As in, Wow. As in Holy Smoke,
mid-Pacific evaporation.
As in, Criminiddly, Gene,
Minnesota snowfall and hidden aquifers
and purity and pollution
and pollywogs and paddlewheelers
and The Falls of St. Anthony.

As in, all I know I'm guessing at.
Like where here is, never mind how,
as though here I am is
bigger than a dewdrop.
As in, Yikes. What'll we teach
the yellow busloads of children?
As in, what's any of it
got to do with Blaha's dog
or with the falls of
all the other saint-used-to-be's,
like water returning to sea level.

Por Nanita en Febrero

What can St. Valentine have known about it,
having never met you ?
His notion of love incomplete,
his idea of dinner just a salad,
a small glass of Chablis.
What has a saint to say of love,
that he can remain saintly ?
I've known the meat,
the rich sauce,
the Burgundy dark of you,
the fruit, the sweet, the dessert of you.
I've snifted your brandy,
been warmed by your fire,
seen you in the light of green candles.
You diminish my chances of sainthood
and I shall dwell in the house of your love
forever and ever.
Goodness and mercy.
Amen.

Northern

I lead you out onto these preliminary lines
like an old fishing buddy
walking on the season's first thin ice,
unsure we won't slip beneath the surface,
gulping at the depth,
but certain this is the day for keepers,
gleaming in cold silver and gulping, too,
as they slip into the sky above their homes.
I coax you toward the center of this verse,
towing tools of the trade in a little sledge
that follows on faith,
bore a hole through the fragile freeze
where we wait, shiver, wait.

I try simile, metaphor, then rhyme for bait
and I talk of patience
and barely notice the nibbling of a thought,
now hooked and struggling liquid,
muscle and tooth and blood
this idea, hungry, as a lover takes a lure,
a snap, a relaxing,
and it's swimming free—
this thing I'll never grasp—
hooks torn from its legendary flesh,
laughter from its lips.

Smile at me, swimmer, smile at me.

Standard Time

I don't know how to draw this.
A sunbeam has found your face and
made you slightly translucent.

I can see beneath the surface of you
as you sleep a bit longer; this first
morning back on Standard Time.

Who's that painter? . . .Vermeer?
I don't suppose he makes housecalls
at this hour on a Sunday?

I'd gladly spend all the daylight I've
saved in six months of Daylight Saving
to preserve this moment of light on you.

Already, the sun's angle has changed
and all I have left are these words
hastily scrawled on yellow paper. . .

And you . . .

Whose beautiful depths I've seen,

And you . . .
Who makes the thought of six months of
Northern dark bearable,

And you . . .
Who saved me from darkness before.
with the same eyes

with the same eyes
through the same glass
the same moon
full again, but
never so full as
when you were in its light
never that color
we couldn't name
illuminating our embrace
and all of me
singing
all of you

Vendor's Shadow

Tom Becker

GALLERY

My photographic interest and subject matter is very diverse. My photography is not focused enough to acquire enough quality material. Of my past projects, Rodeo Cowboys probably came the closest to having enough quality images for a book. I did that project in 1993 or 1994. The following year I was going to start it up again. I went to a rodeo in Cherokee, Iowa, on Memorial Day and got one photograph. My interest was lost and I could not pick it up again. I don't know how some artists can stay with a theme or subject matter for years at a time, working it and improving it. I admire that but I jut can't do it.

Past projects, aside from most of the work on my web page (www.tombeckerphotographer.com) include: "Old Time Musicians," "Rodeo Cowboys," "The Hoboes," "Portrait of a Small Town/Our Town," "Northwest Iowa Farmers," and "County Fairs."

V, Self-Portrait

Father & Son

Outside Room 403

Mother & Daughter

Solitaire

Robert M. Zoschke

A Gangster's Promise

Robert M. Zoschke's novel revolves around Johnny, a thirty-five-year-old Chicago mob street soldier fresh out of Stateville Prison after serving a ten-year sentence. The sole offspring of a city alderman and the daughter of the Outfit's North Side Boss, Johnny brings the scars of Stateville back to the streets. Elevated to boss of his old street crew, Johnny allows his soldiers to earn as much as they can without restraint, against the mandate of the absolute boss of Outfit crime in Chicago. Swept up in aiding his mob-member cousin, they leave a trail of blood that drives Johnny to question the life he chose. Waiting for the opportunity to take final vengeance for prison violence against him, Johnny yearns for the girlfriend he loved and left behind, while his grandfather Antonio organizes an old-fashioned prelude to the arranged marriage between Johnny and a beautiful daughter of a mob family. Growing passionately attracted to his arranged bride-to-be who happens to be very attracted to him, Johnny finds his old girlfriend and learns she is in deep trouble. Knowing he is the man with the power to solve his old girlfriend's problems, Johnny must decide whether the girl who touched his heart is worth the risk of his life by defying his allegiance to the Outfit.

Chapter 2

The two old men stood on the hardwood floor of the North Side bungalow, staring at framed black and white photographs lining the living room wall. The photographs traced generations of their families. All the way from the lemon and olive groves of the old country to the old neighborhood streets of Chicago and shoreline fishing trips along the great banks of Lake Michigan. Since

boyhood the lives of the two men were entwined. All of their decades had been spent side by side: hustling the back alleys of the
Patch, climbing the Outfit ranks and watching each other's back.
They often relied on communicating through their own silent language of gestures and glares. As if connected by a shared and un-
noticed mannerism, the two men stroked their balding gray hairs,
their fingers tracing the same pattern across their wrinkled
scalps.

Weary from the painful arthritis locking up their hips and
knees and restless with anticipation over Johnny's impending release, they rocked on the heels of their slip-on loafers. They wore
collared pullover shirts of a similar beige shade, hung loosely over
linen slacks cut from the same swath of fabric by the last Sicilian
tailor alive in Chicago. They were cousins bound by blood yet
something palpable like the heavy breath exhaled from their la-
boring chests bound them together much tighter than old country
roots and blood ties. The two men had made the same choice and
the same promise, many decades earlier, when their hips and
knees carried them with purpose and their chests were strong.
Schoolbooks and classroom learning had never interested them.
They dominated the back alleys and the street corners of the
Patch with their broad shoulders, powerful punches, and cunning
street smarts. When they were asked, they promised their loyalty
to the iron-fisted syndicate that had watched their hustler's development like baseball scouts seeking out major league talent.

Antonio Palmentola and Salvatore Benedetti lumbered over
to a maple end table tucked against the projection television
along the living room wall. Antonio shuffled through the stack of
compact discs next to a small tabletop stereo. He chose Chet
Baker's *In a Soulful Mood* recording. He struggled trying to juggle
open the case and remove the compact disc.

"I'm tellin' you, Sal, son of a bitch got ridda records oughta
have his head examined. Fuckin' guy's nuttier than a fruitcake.
Somebody oughta take the stumblebum jamoke down the loony
bin for a saliva test."

"Aint much for them goddamn discs neither," Sal offered with
his palm open, knowing he would be handed the disc. "Least
they're smaller, don't take up so much space."

"That so, Sal? Then you smaller the fuckin' thing into the

player, for Christ sake."

Sal inserted the disc. Antonio focused on the stereo speaker, as he always did when he chose *In a Soulful Mood*, waiting to hear Chet Baker introduce the first song.

"This is a composition," Antonio mouthed along silently, "by an Italian composer and piano player from Rome, Enrico Pieranunzi. It's called Night Bird."

Antonio turned his eyes away from the speaker as Chet Baker's inflective trumpet solo began to emanate. Sal shook loose two Pall Malls from the pack on the table. He struck a blue-tip match against his thumbnail, lighting both cigarettes then handing over Antonio's. Sal tossed the snuffed match into an old ceramic ashtray with block letters that spelled out Havana Club. Antonio held the first unfiltered hit deep in his lungs, staring at the ashtray.

"Remember that time we're out fishin' the Rock River? You, me, Johnny an' Tino. For Christ sake, they were just little boys, musta been seven or eight. At the boat launch some kid had that shirt on, said my parents went to the Dells an' all I got was this lousy t-shirt. Tino ran his yapper all day, all the poor bastard got was a lousy t-shirt."

"Yeah, I remember that day," Sal answered, deeply inhaling a puff of smoke, searching for the point Antonio was illustrating. Sal glanced at the ashtray and figured it out before Antonio spoke again.

"Hell, Sal, we oughta have a sign on this table, says we pumped millions into Cuba an' all we got was this lousy ashtray."

"What a fuckin' almost that was, down there," Sal clarified.

"Almost, hell," Antonio barked through a smoker's cough. "Almost only counts when you're neckin' with a parish virgin."

"That was a helluva long time ago," Sal countered with a chuckle. "Gettin' hard to remember neckin' with all them parish virgins."

"Stop right there, Sal," Antonio said through a thick plume of smoke. A tight-lipped smile became another crease on his weathered face. "I know goddamn well what's gettin' hard on you, thinkin' 'bout all them parish virgins. I better stand back from you a couple feet, for Christ sake."

"At least seven inches," Sal added, drawing laughter from

both of them. Sal lifted the lid of the sterling silver ice bucket. He stirred the melting ice cubes with a disjointed index finger gnarled by arthritis. "Some goddamn trigger finger I got left."

"Aw, hell, Sal. Your other trigger finger's fine," Antonio offered with a gentle pat on Sal's shoulder. "You were always double coordinated. Had one firing in each hand just like Billy the Kid, for Christ sake. All them independent rummies hadda worry 'bout both your trigger fingers when we straightened out the North Side."

"Them were the days, Antonio," Sal started, pausing to get through a smoker's cough of his own. "Every day came up nothin' but aces an' kings. We never got stuck holdin' a lousy five a clubs back then."

"We lived so goddamn long we seen times change, Sal."

"Don't fuckin' remind me, for Christ sake."

Sal gripped the ice bucket carefully, trapping the melting ice with an open palm as he poured ice water halfway into two old highball glasses. Antonio opened the Heaven Hill bottle, splashing the glasses full. The dial hands of the old Westinghouse alarm clock on the table showed twenty past six in the morning.

"Glad you got some Kentucky brown water left in the joint. Glad you couldn't sleep neither, Sal."

"Woke up aroun' three, for Christ sake. Couldn't get back to sleep for shit." Sal noticed Antonio looking at the worry lines on his forehead. "Don't get me wrong, Antonio, it aint like I don't love Tino like my own. But Marie, rest in peace, after she caught that first goddamn cancer down in her privacy, well." Antonio wrapped an arm around Sal's withered shoulders. He pulled Sal close and Sal hugged him back before continuing.

"An' it aint like I don't love Tino's father. He's your boy, for Christ sake."

"He's a simple man wanted a simple life, no disrespect. Hell, least he was smart enough to know what he aint cut out for," Antonio offered.

"Maybe on account Teddy was like us, plus Johnny was so much like you since he was a little kid," Sal continued with moist eyes. A beam of pride spread across Antonio's face then he nodded and held Sal tighter. "Swear to Christ, Antonio, watchin' Johnny grow up was just like runnin' alongside you, growin' up together like we done."

"Sometimes the apple don't fall too far from the tree," Antonio clarified.

"I guess what I'm sayin', Antonio, why I aint been sleepin' for shit an' all, I aint never been so goddamn fidgety over somethin' like Johnny finally comin' home." Sal felt a welling in his chest, lightening the conversation accordingly. "Well maybe I was this fuckin' fidgety right before I popped my cherry, for Christ sake."

"I aint got fuckin' Alzheimers yet, for Christ sake," Antonio barked. "I remember why you were so fuckin' fidgety when you popped your cherry. On account you came outta your drunk an' realized you wasted your cherry on that poor homely thing, Rita Spadafora. She looked like a mongrel at the pound, night she dragged you home."

"I had to pop it on somebody, for Christ sake. You rushed me to it, goin' to that South Side Shine joint like you done."

"You shoulda come with me. I aint never had no complaints," Antonio barked. "That working girl turned a fifteen-year-old boy into a man, for Christ sake. She coulda knocked Marciano out with that ass on her. Rose, rest in peace, thank God she aint alive to hear me say it."

They finished their drinks in measured gulps and set the empty glasses down on the table. Shuffling back and forth on the hardwood floor they listened to the Chet Baker disc play through. Then they heard the coded knock at the back door of the bungalow. Sal pushed aside the old curtain. With a nod of his head a bleary-eyed Tino Palmentola signaled hello.

Tino followed them into the living room. His starched white dress shirt was unevenly tucked, half-out of his wrinkled silk slacks. His shoes were scuffed and in dire need of a polishing. From his perch on the couch Antonio took in the appearance of his grandson with scorn.

"Looks like you were carousin' one a them disco clubs," Antonio offered. "Musta been a real good bump an' rub, got you all fuckin' messed up like that." Tino rolled his eyes at his grandfather.

"Grampa, them discos been closed up for years."

"You look like a poor bastard homeless person. Like you should be down in the Loop, askin' stumblebum jamoke commuters for spare change."

"I love you, Grampa, nice seein' you too," Tino countered. "I been up all night pullin' my fuckin' hair out."

"For Christ sake, Sal, here it comes again," Antonio moaned. "Get out the goddamn violin an' don't forget the viola neither, we'll fuckin' play the background serenade." Tino shook his head, looking to his uncle for support. Sal cast a blind eye at Tino and waited for Antonio to continue. "We're all supposed to be gettin' ready for Johnny comin' home. Somethin' tells me all you got in your noggin is trackin' down your wayward Mick Irish lassie."

"Grampa, how fuckin' long you gonna make a beef outta this? I love the girl, for Christ sake."

"How many goddamn times, Tee? How many goddamn times I gotta tell you? Every cute little freckle on that Irish lassie's face is a fuckin' forest fire runnin' through her Mick noggin. Aint no Dago horse thief ever gonna put a harness on that Mick filly." Antonio shook his head at Tino then looked to Sal for support. Sal nodded at Tino.

"Listen to your grandfather, Tee," Sal advised.

"Grampa, you're forgettin' what I fuckin' told you the other night," Tino responded cautiously. He looked for an expression on Sal's face, for a clue as to whether Antonio had relayed their conversation to Sal. The glance was not lost on Antonio.

"Don't run your pouty mug over to Uncle Sal, for Christ sake," Antonio barked. "I aint gotta say shit to him about this. He knows good an' goddamn well where your loins should be leadin' you. You could be halfway down the fuckin' road to easy street with Butchie the Hook's daughter by now." Antonio waved regretfully at Sal before continuing. "How many goddamn times, Sal? How many times I pound it through Tee's noggin already?"

"Plenty," Sal answered with a deferential nod.

"Course I did," Antonio clarified before turning his emboldened gaze back to Tino. "For the last time, Tee, unnerstan'? Butchie's coffee shop deal down there on Printer's Row, it's in his daughter's name, for Christ sake. She's already sittin' on a legit six-figure investment fund the fuckin' G could never touch. That don't even get into the Lake Shore Drive condo she's sittin' on. You think she's sittin' on a mortgage, like some stumblebum jamoke livin' on fuckin' credit? She's sittin' on the deed to the property, for Christ sake!"

Tino sat down on the couch. He squeezed in, wrapping an arm around each of them. Antonio and Sal eyed Tino suspiciously.

"What Butchie the Hook's daughter is sittin' on," Tino offered, "is an ass wide enough to stop a freight train, for Christ sake. With saddle bags so big, Butch Cassidy an' the Sundance Kid couldn't fill 'em with loot." Waves of laughter surged out of the three of them. Antonio ran a hand across his forehead then he looked at Sal. Antonio hoisted himself up and Sal followed him into the kitchen. Tino knew to stay on the couch. Antonio and Sal leaned against the kitchen sink, puffing deeply on fresh Pall Malls. Antonio broke the silence between them.

"Bottom line, we could fuckin' run down half a dozen nice Italian girls ready to keel over an' faint for a ring from Tino, for Christ sake."

"But I thought you said the top floor aint talkin' about a half dozen prospectives?"

"The top floor aint passin' down word, just suggestin'. On account Butchie planted some seeds. I don't blame Butchie. What the hell, his only daughter, she's twenny-seven already," Antonio pondered out loud.

"Yeah, no kids yet, her ass is already a trainwreck, for Christ sake. You can't blame Tino, neither. He'd take her out on a Friday night, gotta hold out two chairs, one for each ass cheek."

"You wanna gimme me *agita* here, Sal? Enough with the poor thing's trainwreck ass already." Antonio turned the faucet on. They snuffed the smoldering butts under water then pitched them in the trashcan.

"So it all boils down to one thing," Sal responded, shutting off the water. "Tee's gonna get your nod to take on a Mick Irish firecracker wife, or he aint. We gotta keep in mind how bullheaded he is. He aint gonna play it cool, keepin' little Miss Ireland on the side. Then we got shit on our hands on account a two hotheads. They'd make a fuckin' mess outta it, bad for business."

"I hear you, loud an' clear, Sal. Put the fuckin' bull horn down already," Antonio offered dejectedly.

"Let's look at the fuckin' bright side, an' there is one," Sal offered. "So the girl's father is just a jamoke on the back of a gar-

bage truck for Streets and San. Maybe we get him moved up to
concrete mixer. Them old three-flats in Wicker Park you were
talkin' 'bout buyin', to turn into rehabs. Maybe the new concrete
mixer gets us all the concrete."

"You're splittin' hairs tryin' to buffalo me with that peanut
shit, Sal," Antonio countered, opening a cabinet above the sink.
Sal pointed to the other cabinet above the sink then Antontio
found a pack of smokes. They lit fresh Pall Malls. "What about
them two city copper uncles a hers, Sal?"

"They both got a ways to go to draw their pensions. One's in
Youth Division right now, word is he aint got much of a noggin.
The other's in Vice, supposed to be on the way to Detective. They
both got kids ready to go to college. We handle it right, Tino
makin' her the wife could turn out to be a real profitable union."

"Gimme the goddamn odds, Sal," Antonio barked. Antonio
looked around the kitchen. Sal opened the cabinet under the sink
and brought up a bottle of Heaven Hill. They nipped shots from
the bottle and smacked their lips.

"I'd bet even money we turn the simpleton in Youth Division.
He's at least good for general sniffin' aroun'. You were talkin' 'bout
makin' a push this year to get parlay cards goin' again. He can at
least help keep an eye out on shit like that. The fuckin' Detective
in waiting, I'd say seven-to-two we can turn him."

"Seven-to-two," Antonio mused. "Seven-to-two separates too
many horseplayers from their wallets, for Christ sake." Sal
started to bow his head as if his points had been made in defeat.
"But what the hell, Sal," Antonio offered, lifting Sal's head to attention. "We got this far by sneakin' in the clubhouse, takin' a
fuckin' shot at the hunnerd-dollar window every now an' then."

"That's great, Antonio," Sal offered with a sigh of relief.
"Tino's gonna be so fuckin' happy over this. He's gotta be dyin'
out there, you know how he can't stand waitin' for shit."

"Not quite fuckin' yet," Antonio cautioned. He placed a firm
grip on Sal's shoulder. "Tee says he's got it pegged, she's down in
Florida. He gets two weeks to send a couple guys from his crew
down there, track her down an' get her back here. I aint lettin'
this goddamn ordeal hang over all we got goin' on now. I better
see the little Mick lassie in my backyard for Sunday dinner, no
more than two fuckin' weeks, with a goddamn rock a Gibraltar

ring on her hand. If Tee wants her so fuckin' bad, he's gotta step up to the plate, for Christ sake. Two weeks."

"Or?" Sal prodded, raising his scruffy eyebrows.

"Or else me an' some *paisan* somewhere, with a daughter knows how to make a sauce, got somethin' to get squared away on." Sal started to peel away from Antonio's grip, only to feel Antonio's hand lock down ever harder. "One other thing, Sal, an' get this through your sharp noggin right fuckin' now. We aint gonna stand aroun' like two goofy broads havin' a chit chat over the hand in marriage Johnny's gonna take. He gets the most beautiful girl in the neighborhood, the best Italian girl left for a guy movin' up a couple floors."

"Yeah, well," Sal stammered, caught off guard by Antonio's closing directive. "A course, no fuckin' doubt, he's gotta."

"Sal," Antonio started through an omnipotent smirk. "Don't fuckin' wince like I'm throwin' somethin' else on your plate. You know good an' goddamn well I already hatched that fuckin' plan. I been holdin' up my end on us gettin' ready for Johnny comin' home."

They walked back into the living room to give Tino his good news. Sal knew Antonio would want to bust Tino's balls first. Sal kept his head down as Antonio looked away from Tino's waiting glare.

"Your grandfather's come to a decision," Sal started in a mournful tone, still looking at the floor. Tino shook his head and stared at the floor. "Maggie's yours if she's goofy enough to say yes," Sal prodded with a smile on his face. Tino leaped up off the couch and hugged Sal. He went to hug Antonio who pulled back.

"On these conditions," Antonio barked. "No more than two weeks, I gotta see her in the backyard for Sunday dinner. My fuckin' cataracts aint gettin' any better. I aint gonna squint tryin' to see the rock she's got on her hand."

"Thank you, Grampa," Tino said through a smile as he hugged Antonio.

"Don't thank me yet. Go home an' take out your rosary, say a prayer to the patron saint for Mick Irish firecrackers. No more than two guys go down there to flush her out. I aint puttin' a street crew caravan on the road over a lover's quarrel, for Christ sake."

Sal shuffled over to the maple table, stirring each of them a stiff celebratory drink.

Antonio and Sal watched Tino down his drink and strut out the back door, into the humid daybreak of another August morning's stagnant rise. Antonio and Sal sat back down on the couch. Antonio put his hands on his knees. He started rocking back and forth on the edge of the couch cushion, telling Sal he had more things he wanted to discuss. Sal cracked his arthritic knuckles, telling Antonio he was waiting for him to break the silence between them. For a long while Antonio stared at the hardwood floor. Sal started to hoist himself up from the couch.

"Fuck it, Sal. We don't need no music right now," Antonio barked. "Let's clear some shit up," Antonio said and Sal nodded in agreement. "Run me through the deal again, the cocksucker messed up Johnny," Antonio clarified.

"I sent Tony Provenza to meet with that watch commander from the South Side. I figured since the top floor gave the nod to Johnny comin' home a crew boss with Tony Pro for lieutenant, might as well let Pro start takin' care a the bullshit like copper sit-downs."

"I got no problem with that shit, long as you spilled no beans to Tony Pro on the top floor blessin' new crews."

"Course not, for Christ sake," Sal replied. "Pro hears that from Johnny, after the top floor throws the welcome home dinner."

As old and tired as they were, loosened up as they were by the stiff belts of bourbon running through them, even after Sal's bungalow had been swept for listening devices earlier in the day with the same technology used by the FBI, they still would not chance breaking part of the promise they had made many decades earlier. They would go to their graves never to be overheard identifying the man on the top floor of their world, the absolute boss of Outfit crime in Chicago. Sal struck flame to two more Pall Malls. They took the first unfiltered hits deep into their lungs. Antonio flicked a couple fingers in the air, telling Sal to continue.

"Tony Pro got confirmation this scumbag Levander Holmes runs a crackhouse for them Sixty-Third and Cottage Grove gangbangers. Two different joints they use, switch every couple weeks."

141

"Can the fuckin' watch commander snatch this goddamn scumbag, deliver him alive?"

"Too much Internal Affairs heat comin' down. One a his beat coppers just got fuckin' pinched dippin' into evidence room stash, movin' it out on the fuckin' street."

"You gotta be shittin' me. Aint there a limit on how many stumblebum jamokes that goddamn department employs at one time, for Christ sake?" Antonio bellowed. "Don't any a them coppers got the balls to knock off one a them Shine joints anymore? They gotta fuckin' sneak in the evidence room like a goddamn pipsqueak?"

"Least we got confirmation on the addresses, for Christ sake," Sal offered meekly. Antonio motioned a halt to Sal with a flick of his wrist. Antonio shook his head somberly before flicking his wrist again to allow Sal to continue. "Maybe after the welcome home, you ask for a sit-down, get the top floor's nod," Sal prodded.

"Johnny aint gettin' his hands dirty on the snatch," Antonio commanded. "Tino, neither, unless the shit's too fuckin' deep down there. I already got the nod. The top floor agrees what got done to Johnny got done to all of us. We settle it the old fashioned way," Antonio clarified, patting Sal on the knee.

"So what else we gotta square away?" Sal asked.

"That's enough for now."

"I got the air conditioning vent closed in the other bedroom, so it aint too goddamn chilly in there. You wanna try an' catch some shut-eye?"

"Not yet," Antonio barked, breathing deeply through his nose. He shuffled over to his favorite photograph on the wall. Antonio looked at the image of a seven-year-old Johnny holding his first ever Lake Michigan steelhead, caught on the first rod and reel Antonio had given him. "That, part," Antonio stammered. Sal shuffled over next to Antonio then Antonio continued in a whisper. "That part no mother should ever know. Are we absolutely goddamn sure my daughter don't know?"

"You gotta let that shit go, Antonio. Victoria only knows Johnny got roughed up bad but not too bad. She don't know nothin' about the goddamn shower. All she knows is a fight out on the prison yard, Johnny caught a couple serious shots on the kisser."

"I gotta piss like a racehorse," Antonio exclaimed with a sigh. When he returned from the bathroom the projection television was playing and Sal was fumbling with the remote control. "Fuckin' clickers," Antonio offered. "Lot easier in the old days. Three channels, pair a pliers after the goddamn knob broke."

"Them were the days," Sal reminisced, flicking through the channels.

"Suppose I oughta spill the beans,"Antonio offered, leaning back on the couch then looking at Sal. "Maria Montini."

"You gotta be shittin' me, Antonio," Sal bellowed incredulously. "She's hook, line an' sinker over that Sheenie ambulance chaser. They're shacked up, for Christ sake."

"Hey, they were never shacked up, make fuckin' sure everybody knows she kept her own apartment. Far as that Sheenie jamoke, he aint no ambulance chaser yet. Still pissin' aroun', tryin' to pass the goddamn classes, what I hear. But that's ancient history we don't gotta talk about none, far as Johnny's concerned. Put the word on the street, Maria just gave the Sheenie the boot."

"Well Holy Christ, I never heard," Sal whined.

"Course you aint heard. Maria's a classy girl, for Christ sake. You think I'd set Johnny up with some gin mill rummy, runnin' her yapper like a dingbat on them goddamn talk shows you watch all day long?"

"Not all day, just all mornin'," Sal clarified and they laughed together from down deep in their bellies.

"You remember the brother?" Antonio's eyes were ablaze like a child's on Christmas morning. "Chubby kid, played catcher on the softball teams when Johnny an' Tino needed guys."

"Hit from the wrong side with his foot in the bucket. Couldn't hit his way outta paper bag. Poor kid's belly hung out at the pitcher like a watermelon, for Christ sake."

"That's him. Well, he's been a big help, puttin' the pieces together. Aw, hell, Maria was just a skinny little thing then, braces an' all, used to watch them ballgames like a deer in the headlights. Mother Nature wasn't kind to her development yet. Johnny had no reason to know."

"The hell you gettin' at, Antonio?"

"Maria wasn't comin' to them ballgames to watch her brother play, Sal. She had a crush on our Johnny, aint gone away. The brother says she locked her bedroom door an' threw a tantrum when Johnny went away."

"Well holy horseshit, I never woulda known," Sal added before his jaw dropped open. "She'll be all over him, for Christ sake. An' their kids, just think how beautiful."

"You got no idea how much I been thinkin' the same thing, Sal." Antonio pointed to the remote control. "Find the fuckin' channel plays them old shows. Maybe we can watch The Honeymooners for Johnny."

"Only thing on worth a shit right now is Kojak."

"Bald Greek plays the copper, always chompin' on a goddamn lollipop?"

"I thought you said you aint got Alzheimers yet?"

"I been up all night, half in the bag on bluegrass booze. Lucky I remembered to shake my dick after I pissed, for Christ sake," Antonio offered through a drawn-out yawn.

The two old men watched the opening credits to Kojak beam across the television. They started to drift off asleep shoulder-to-shoulder, the way they did as little boys, on the big rocking chair next to the hissing radiator in the cramped Taylor Street apartment their families shared. The episode of Kojak ended, the closing music shaking Antonio from his slumber. He nudged Sal and kept on nudging him until Sal awakened and turned a tired eye his way.

"What about the deal with that cunt guard, let the scumbag an' his guys attack Johnny?"

"Squared away, just like we fuckin' said," Sal whispered, starting to fall back asleep. "Like we said," he whispered even softer before drifting off again. The Mary Tyler Moore show came on. Antonio forced himself to stay awake until he saw Mary smiling, twirling and throwing her winter cap up into the frigid air. Antonio smiled back at her. He winked before speaking to Mary Tyler Moore's image.

"What a classy doll you always were, sweetheart," Antonio whispered, blowing a kiss at Mary on the television then leaning back. As soon as their shoulders touched, Antonio and Sal were both deeply asleep.

Chapter 3

The pockmarked sidewalk in front of the all-night restaurant near the corner of Elston and Cortland was clear of pedestrian traffic. The myriad of condo and loft developments promised by the Alderman had not materialized. The restaurant's owner, Frantisek Pucera, couldn't help but snicker staring at the old and increasingly vacant industrial buildings surrounding what had been his dream for a better life. It was always at the forefront of his thoughts, how the Alderman hoodwinked him into taking over a bad lease started in haste by one of the Alderman's cronies.

The sparse, early morning counter business consisted of several regulars: gamblers who entered the restaurant every morning with Racing Forms and late-sport finals of the Sun-Times and Tribune. Going through the papers they bantered over the results of West Coast ballgames and Chicago harness races. None of them had far to travel after breakfast. The restaurant was a stone's throw from the bend in the Chicago River and the remaining foundries, presses and factories still lining the river's bank. The number of production lines clouding the river a stagnant, toxic shade of green had appealed to Frantisek when the Alderman's crony waved the deal under his beginner's nose. Only a few of the blue-collar plants were still in operation. Without the condo and loft developments perpetually springing up to the east in Lincoln Park, Frantisek's restaurant traffic kept declining.

As if he were back in his old welterweight days between rounds, Frantisek rolled his neck and shoulders trying to stay loose. He topped off coffee mugs from the working side of the counter. He had come to Chicago six years ago from the Czech old country, where his father taught him to appreciate the old country hard stuff. One of the first things Frantisek encountered in Chicago that endeared him to America was Old Grand Dad, hundred-proof bonded. He kept a bottle stashed under the restaurant counter behind the extra sugar and napkin dispensers. A large silver container for blending milkshakes was never far from Frantisek's hand, filled with spiked ice coffee day and night.

Frantisek emptied the tinfoil ashtrays in front of the gamblers. Then he reached down under the counter for the bottle, topping off his second ice coffee of the morning. He covered the Old Grand Dad label with one hand and his sore lower back with the other. Frantisek's wife was seven months along with their first child. She could only find sleeping comfort by spreading out on their tight full-sized mattress, leaving Frantisek merely a slim corner. Frantisek listened to the gamblers cursing themselves for not betting on the longshot Yonkers invader in the prior night's stakes race at Maywood.

"They let New York sulky pay twenny dollars win?" Frantisek rued in his heavy accent. With a gambler's intuition he calculated how a lousy fifty bucks on the horse's nose down at the OTB would have covered a new queen-sized mattress wide enough to relieve his lingering stiffness. He contorted himself again, trying to get loose.

"Check it out, boys," Lonney Dahlberg teased. "The Bohemian Ballerina's stretchin' out for a comeback. Gonna knockout some gangbangin' rap video star in a three-rounder somewhere."

"Don't push," Frantisek replied with a growl from his caffeine-and-bourbon laced gut.

"I remember plenty a Ruskies, Ukraine kooks, guys like that meddlin' in the Chi Town ring. You were the only Bohack stepped in to give it a twirl, right?" Lonney prodded in a failing comedic effort to draw laughter from his fellow gamblers at the counter. They knew Lonney was treading on dangerous ground, tarnishing Frantisek's old fight name and the not quite distant history of his boxing career. The same Alderman who suckered Frantisek into the bad lease had suckered him into his bad deal with a boxing promoter.

The promoter nicknamed Frantisek the Bohemian Bomber. Propped up by the Outfit, the promoter took Frantisek as far as his hunger to win yet woeful ineptness with the lead jab would allow, to an undercard knockout loss before a title bout on a southern Indiana gambling boat. By the time the main event rolled around Frantisek was already plunked down in front of a slot machine. Surrounded by blue-haired old ladies jabbing at one-arm bandits much quicker than he jabbed at the tough ghetto boxer from the streets of the old Gary steel mills, half of the cash in his envelope from the promoter was gone before the main event on the card.

Tino Palmentola had watched Frantisek's entire display, from the sorry exploit in the ring to the exploitable compulsion on the slot machines. Before Tino left the gambling boat he summoned the promoter to a quick sit-down at a bar near the roulette wheels. While the blue-haired old ladies' husbands and suitors hollered out for the little ivory sphere to land on their favorite numbers, Tino defined the sphere of possibility that remained for a boxer he mockingly dubbed the Bohemian Ballerina. Frantisek would take a dive as directed for an envelope lined with ten portraits of Ben Franklin, on meager fight cards in Midwest clubs. After a phantom punch from a club hack he swore he could have beaten, Frantisek hung up his gloves. Tino never hung up on Frantisek. Tino brought him along with crafted precision until he found a way to position Frantisek to his advantage.

From his perch behind the counter, Frantisek seemed to the scattered booth customers like an immigrant settled into mucking out a straight life in a Chi Town greasy-spoon joint. The gamblers at the counter knew differently. Frantisek had attained what had once been their own hustler's dream of getting connected to an Outfit crew. Lonney had not simply made some ill remarks to an old chump fighter. He had taken a risky shot at the bagman who ran one of the many front operations for Tino Palmentola's bookmaking enterprise.

Fifty-one-year-old Lonney Dahlberg had no ashtray in front of him. He was struggling to pay heed to the last remnants of a persistent and throbbing cough diagnosed as a precursor to emphysema if he did not give up his daily three-pack Marlboro habit. Lonney spat into the paper cup required by the thick wad of chewing tobacco stuffed in his lower lip. His new method of nicotine delivery had earned him the moniker of Farmer Lonney. Lonney had been pontificating on the Mets loss his bookie account absorbed the night before.

"Spit out that chaw an' climb down from your John Deere, Farmer Lonney," Jerry the butcher teased. "We heard enough crop jive this mornin'."

"I'm tellin' ya, Chop, this fuckin' stiff pitcher the Mets made the big deal for, them bright lights on broadway fuckin' got him shattered him already. I seen the stumblebum piss away his first two starts. So I gotta throw good money after bad, thinkin' third

147

time's a charm?" Lonney washed down his point with a swig from a bottle of Old Style serving as his morning equalizer. Jerry hadn't finished razzing him.

"It's six o'clock on the dot, this is Jerry Vitlacil in the traffic helicopter, now let's switch over to Farmer Lonney for a report on how high the corn is out in Kane county." The rest of the men at the counter laughed as Lonney shook his head.

"Aw, Chop, instead a lightin' that fuckin' dimestore cigar in your puss, just stick it up your goddamn heiney. Like you're mister hot streak, on such a fuckin' roll you're headed to Vegas?"

"Aw, hell, Lonney," Jerry replied, a tad incensed. "I remember when you had an eye for style. This is a fine Dominican cigar," Jerry cooed, rolling the Arturo Fuente in his hand so Lonney could see the label. "I'm still winnin' every now an' then, Lonney. You keep on that losin' streak a yours, you'll be rollin' your own Bugler instead a goin' back to Marlboros."

A hush came over the counter. The silence of the men paid heed to the biting losing streak ensnaring Lonney. They were aware of the reservoir of assets Lonney had run bone dry paying off his last enormous bookie tab. Lonney picked at the loose knot of his tie. He was the only one not wearing blue-collar attire. Even Joe Anicci, the retired spot welder from the Ford plant, still wore an old factory jumpsuit to breakfast.

"You guys ready to catch double?" Frantisek said, swirling the contents of his milk shake container until he had a unified, affirmative response.

Frantisek headed into the kitchen to fetch six plates of the breakfast special: hash browns, two eggs, two bacon strips, two sausage links and two pieces of toast. Being a horseplayer himself, Frantisek had named the plate the daily double. Frantisek emerged from the kitchen with three steaming plates across each of his long, outstretched forearms.

"Ready to catch double?" Frantisek projected in his heavy accent.

The gamblers ate as if the forks in their hands were shovels into dirt. Lonney kept his eyes glued to racetrack entries. He wiped his plate with a wedge of toast as if he were scrubbing a dirty dish with steel wool.

"Goddamn daily double's the best breakfast in town, hands

down," Lonney proclaimed with a belch.

"Speakin' a daily doubles," Joe Anicci offered, "I got a pretty good lock in the second at Maywood tonight."

Joe Anicci had been a career union laborer who always kept his nose clean, except when he was deep in grime building cars at the Ford plant on the South Side. Joe had taken early retirement and moved into a bungalow out west on Fullerton, a nice home he inherited from a North Side aunt. Anicci's gambler friends at the counter called him Sulky Joe, the moniker Lonney had come up with years earlier. It was Lonney who had invited Anicci into the breakfast fold after they met at the Fullerton newsstand in line to buy harness programs.

"Well it's about fuckin' time we hear from Sulky Joe," Lonney bellowed, leaning into Joe's shoulder. "I was about ready to start callin' you Silent Joe."

Joe passed the Maywood program around for emphasis. Frantisek leaned over from the working end of the counter, trying to read the race chart upside down. Joe's old union supervisor from the Ford plant raced harness horses around Chicago. Every now and then a hot tip would make its way through Joe to the gamblers at the counter. Lonney needed a winner like a drought crop needed rain. He leaned forward, listening to Joe like a brown-nosing schoolboy.

"The two horse, guys. Name's Misty Shadow. My guy claimed him at Balmoral last year. Them two races already this summer were just layoff races, to get back in the groove slowly, on purpose. Look at them Balmoral runnin' lines last winter. Sixth, seventh and eighth, three piss-poor races. Horse looks like a stiff, right? Program don't show the horse came up before winter from Pompano."

"We got a fuckin' Florida horse on our hands," Lonney bellowed, already incited. "Didn't like Chi Town freezin' weather."

"Hit the nail on the head, Lonney," Joe replied with a wise smile. "Poor little nag fillie shivered so goddamn bad, my guy wound up keepin' her in the barn, covered up with blankets. Horse is actually droppin' in class compared to her Florida races, which nobody's gonna see since they aint in the friggin' program. Program says fifteen-to-one. My guy says she's ready as a cocked pistol." The gamblers' eyes spread wide like children's before an

Easter egg hunt.

"Here's what we do, guys," Lonney started, wiping anticipation from his brow. "Steer clear from bettin' into the track pool. We're gonna take our score right from Tino's lousy fuckin' book." Frantisek winced at Lonney's mention of Tino's name. Lonney rambled on, oblivious. "We don't need railbirds or OTB jamokes watchin' our action like we got stable money in our hands." The gamblers nodded in agreement. "Joe, this is a real solid tip. This horse comes home in front, you bring your niece by the warehouse," Lonney offered in Chi Town favor-for-a-favor style. "We got a winner, she's got a fancy dress on me, for that high school dance a hers you talked about."

Lonney owned a fashion distribution warehouse on the West Side. Years earlier, before gambling fever burned through his marriage and household, Lonney built the business up well. He came up with a mechanical hanger system allowing garments to be unloaded, stored and shipped without being creased or folded. Most of the large Michigan Avenue retailers used Lonney's warehouse as their Midwest distribution center. Warehouse business was far from Lonney's mind as he fantasized about the tip-horse triggering a huge score.

The rest of the gamblers thanked Joe Anicci for the tip with their own Chi Town favor-for-a-favor proposition. Jerry the butcher offered porterhouse steaks cut on the sly at the supermarket. Terry the produce guy offered a teeming basket from his stand. The foundry guys offered some choice metal that Joe liked to tinker with in his garage. Frantisek offered up breakfast for a week. The gamblers paid their tabs and filed out, until only Lonney remained at the counter. Lonney kept his hands at his sides, an unwelcome signal that the meal would go on his growing tab.

Frantisek motioned toward the bathroom. Before following Lonney inside he put the yellow closed-for-cleaning hazard cone on the floor outside the door. Frantisek stood aside of the bathroom mirror, resting an arm on the paper towel dispenser, ready to let Lonney run his course before counseling him. Lonney stared into the mirror lost in disgust. He took his bulky wallet out of his pants and set it on the sink ledge, pulling at his pants and looking at his profile in the mirror. "Look at this goddamn overhang of a gut," Lonney hollered as if Frantisek were standing a couple blocks away. "I'm tellin' ya, Frankie, never fuckin' turn fifty. Stick a knife in your goddamn heart, but never turn fifty. Fuckin' look at me. If I gotta lower this belt any more, my pecker's gonna be over my beltline."

"Maybe you buy bigger pants," Frantisek replied, picking up Lonney's wallet. "Maybe you stop looking yourself like girl in mirror, stop leaving wallet on sink like yesterday. How you buy bigger pants, your wallet on sink here?" Frantisek said, shrugging his shoulders then handing Lonney his wallet.

"Buy some pants? In the middle a this losin' streak I'm trapped in? I can't pick a winner for how long now? Swear to Christ, if the coppers told me they had my mother down at 26th an' California, I couldn't pick her outta the goddamn lineup. Took every lousy penny I could get my hands on to clear my last tab with Tino, that goddamn Ginzo prick."

"I tell you too many times. Never say Tino's name."

"Fuck Tino an' the rest a them Ginzo bastards," Lonney bellowed, grabbing hold of his protruding belly. "How many poor schmucks can't do nothin' but lose weight when they got stress? All the stress I got, I just keep packin' on the goddamn pounds. Pretty soon I gotta have a mirror to see my feet, for Christ sake. An' lemme tell ya, it's all because a that Ginzo prick Tino. Fuckin' louse bled me dry." Frantisek grabbed Lonney by the collar, digging his powerful hands into Lonney's shoulders for emphasis.

"Last time I waste breath. You keep saying Tino's name, Tino's guy tell me break legs. Maybe tell me break neck, put you in wheelchair forever."

"Fuck you an' the boat you rode over on, Frankie. The miserable bastard bled me dry, an' I'm supposed to buy him a carnation for his Ginzo lapel?"

"You say Tino's name again, I tell new guy make collections. Then I see you hanging on bridge over river. You almost there last time you take too long pay." Frantisek dug his grip into Lonney's struggling shoulders. Lonney raised his hands to resist but he couldn't get past Frantisek's forearms.

"You got some nerve, Frankie," Lonney whined. "Just remember I aint the only dumb schmuck got in too deep with them louses. You owed a lot less than me after you went ape-shit on the

March madness tournament. Look at the deal they cornholed you with."

"I make bed I sleep on."

"Some goddamn bed, Frankie. I see all of a sudden you aint buyin' cleaning shit from your old supplier. You got a different guy bringin' in the dairy all of a sudden. You got a new meat vendor. Had to fuckin' stop gettin' your produce from Terry."

"Not here about me, here about you. You the guy saying Tino's name. Tino don't let nobody run yapper. You run yapper at me, call me ballerina, I hit you once," Frantisek explained, pounding a sharp uppercut into Lonney's belly. Lonney crumpled to the ground in a wheezing fit, clenching his arms to his belly. Frantisek slammed his fist down on the faucet press-knob. He splashed cold water on his face, yanking on the towel dispenser knob until he had a long sheet to dab his face with. He threw the wet wad down at Lonney's wheezing face and hit the target. "I tell new envelope guy I punch you once in belly. He tell me more, I punch you more next time I see you," Frantisek clarified.

"I shoulda seen this day comin'," Lonney whined, still sprawled out on the floor. "Soon as they made you their goddamn lackey frontman." Holding onto the edge of the sink, Lonney slowly hiked himself up. He looked in the mirror and matted his ruffled hair. "You got no idea how fuckin' deep I had to dig to get outta my hole, all the goddamn scams I had to pull at work. I'm tap city, Frankie. Cash advanced my credit cards all the way. Surprised the wife aint fielded calls from bill collectors yet. I got fuckin' investigators from my retailers on me, crawlin' up my ass like a Village People reunion show, for Christ sake."

"I tell you new envelope guy take everything you move out back door, you tell me no," Frantisek said, shaking his head.

"Course I told ya no. I don't need Tino's Ginzo crew fencin' my own shit for me."

"You make bed you sleep on."

"Wait till you see the bed I'm sleepin' in after tonight. I'm gonna phone in two dimes on this nag's nose. Gonna bed down with one a them strippers from Loco Poco's near the horse parlor there. Fuckin' two dimes I'm gonna put down."

"Two thousand on one sulky race? You lose goddamn mind?"

"Fuck 'em, Frankie. They drained me outta seventy dimes I

didn't have, now I'm down again. Tonight I start watchin' it all come back in fuckin' spades." Frantisek shook his head and started to leave the bathroom.

"The fuck they gonna do?" Lonney hollered, keeping Frantisek in the bathroom. "You think they don't know they gotta play by a whole new set a rules these days? Don't get yourself caught in too deep, Frankie. They try playin' hardball, I walk right into the FBI office down in the Loop. I'll sing to those feds like a fuckin' opera star. You know that opera star, that fuckin' blind guy the broads swoon over? I'll make that fucker sound like some three pack a day Shine in a blues club, I'll sing so fuckin' sweet." Lonney reached for the bathroom door. Frantisek whistled, stopping him in his tracks. Lonney turned around to see Frantisek holding out his wallet.

"You put on sink again, climbing up from floor like girl."

"Like I'm gonna remember the piece a shit with no money in it," Lonney whined, snatching the wallet.

"Keep running yapper, maybe I put tongue in envelope, give present to guy I tell you never say his name."

"Aintcha read the fuckin' papers, Frankie? These stupid Ginzo jamokes gotta go into witness protection or else get fuckin' indicted right now, for Christ sake. Read the fuckin' papers, Frankie. How you gonna take care a that kid on the way in your wife's belly, sittin' in the can next to them Ginzo mopes? They wanna make me sing, I'll fuckin' sing in the FBI office down in the Loop." Frantisek grabbed Lonney, slapping a harsh backhander across his face.

"Listen good now, Lonney," Frantisek growled. He slapped another backhander across Lonney's startled face. "I never let you drag me down. This you remember always. I see FBI here, you dead man." Lonney whimpered as he wiped a trickle of blood from the corner of his trembling mouth. "Look in mirror now," Frantisek advised, grabbing Lonney's head and forcing him to look. "I hit you like girl. You cry like girl, bleed like girl. You keep running yapper, maybe guy I tell you never say his name like way I kill you, maybe he clear my tab."

Barbara B. Luhring

The Tomboy Chronicles

In the days before feminist enlightenment, tomboys roamed the earth. Considered rebels for doing the things that came natural to them, these girls played sports better than boys and played with toy guns while shunning dolls and dresses. They went against the polite rules of American society. Realizing this at a young age tomboys either took on these rules with a vengeance or conform to an unhappy life spent in party dresses playing house. The Tomboy Chronicles *celebrates the girls that refused to play by society's rules during the period of the 1950s to the 1970s. In graphic novel form, the lives of these tomboys and how the world around them reacted to their antics comes to life. Whether you were, knew, or parented a tomboy, the images on these pages will bring back memories and hopefully a smile, from a time that didn't always give kids who were deemed different by society's rules, a lot to smile about.*

Barbara B. Luhring

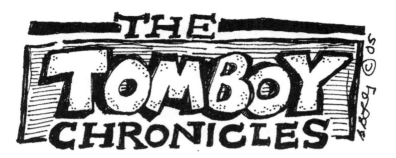

USEFUL TOMBOY BRAIN

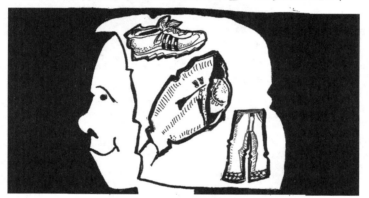

USELESS
NON-TOMBOY BRAIN

TOMBOY INCUBATORS: THE FAMILY

Tomboy was born the third child of an eventual four child family. That particular birth order suited her just fine. Her parents, busy with other children, paid Tomboy just enough attention to nurture her dreams of being a city garbage collector, NBA superstar or combat soldier without taking time to remind her that she was a girl.

Therefore, Tomboy, grew up happy and confident in her family incubator. She felt the world was hers to conquer.

With Tomboy's declaration "I am a boy, not a girl" her parents knew that she was really telling the world she expected options, not the straightjacket offered women in those days.

Tomboy's family incubator grew an unconventional, yet amusing baby woman.

TOMBOY'S NIGHTMARE: ACT ONE

When she was six years old, TOMBOY received a "Tiny Tears" doll from her Grandmother for Christmas. Having no maternal instincts, nor a desire to play with a doll, (unless it was GI Joe) she hid it in the attic, but continued to be haunted by scarey, floating dolls at night.

TOMBOY'S NIGHTMARE: ACT TWO

When Tomboy's sister was left to babysit. Tomboy
knew there was a good chance they would be
playing dress-up.

"Mother left me in charge. Time for dress-up."

If she was lucky, they'd play "church" and Tomboy would get to be the priest, while her sister played the Mother Superior.

"BODY OF CHRIST"

However, if Tomboy was unlucky, playing dress-up
would mean dressing-up in fancy clothes
and high heels. Something her sister knew
would crush Tomboy's spirit.

BARBARA B. LUHRING

TOMBOY'S NIGHTMARE: ACT THREE

When Tomboy was in kindergarten, she loved to draw and color during the free time allowed by her teacher. Two of her classmates had other ideas about how Tomboy should spend this free time.

Tomboy's teacher refused to intervene, telling Tomboy playing house would be good for her. So Tomboy followed her captors. She put on an apron, grabbed the toy iron and surrendered to the type of stereotypical gender play expected of females in the early 1960's.

Wearing dresses to school was humiliation enough. But being forced to play house against her will caused Tomboy the deepest scars of her early school career.

TOMBOY ANGER

On the occassion of her sister's First Communion,
Tomboy made it clear to her folks that she did not
want to wear a dress to the celebration.

As Tomboy grew older,
she put the gun away.
Since her parents had
taught Tomboy good
manners, she decided
to cut people some
slack when they made
her angry.

So, when Tomboy
was in high school
and a priest told her
to sit on his lap while
she gave her annual
face-to-face Lenten
confession, she did.

In 1982, when a co-
worker suggested to
Tomboy that because
she was employed, she
was taking a job away
from a man, she smiled
and disagreed.

Now that Tomboy is
more mature, she
realizes these moments
of anger call for a
more appropriate
reaction. That reaction:
**RAW, UNREPENTENT
CARTOON ANGER!**

TOMBOY IDENTITY

In 1963, a confident five-year-old Tomboy sat on a stuffed buffalo in complete denial that she would someday grow up to be a girl.

What would people say?

Tomboy's mom was right.

TOMBOY FASHION

Tomboy took great pride in her wardrobe. To her, a perfect day was one in which she did not have to go to school in a dress and could wear whatever she wanted. On these days, she made her selections with two criteria in mind. 1) Will it be comfortable while digging in the dirt? 2) Will it be roomy enough for a holster and gun?

Tomboy's favorite clothes included her leather cowboy boots and her suede fringed cowboy shirt.

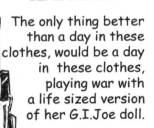

The only thing better than a day in these clothes, would be a day in these clothes, playing war with a life sized version of her G.I.Joe doll.

THAT WOULD BE TOMBOY HEAVEN!

TOMBOY'S OBSESSION
ACT ONE: BASKETBALL

A nine year old obsessed with basketball in 1967 could dream of starting at point guard on the high school team. That is, unless that nine year old was a girl. But even with equal rights for girl basketball players still 5 years away (Title IX passed in 1972), Tomboy had a dream of her own.

That dream took place day after day, at the basketball hoop attached to the garage in her parents' driveway. Rain or shine. Hot or cold. In that dream, Tomboy was a member of the New York Knicks. An equal to her teammates Walt "Clyde" Frazier and Willis Reed. In these games, her team always won. And it was usually because she made the winning basket at the buzzer.

TOMBOY CAREERS

High on the list of Tomboy's career interests were jobs that took place outside. At the top of this list was garbageman. The combination of wearing dirty clothes and boots while hanging off the back of a truck thrilled her to no end. Another outdoor job that held an interest for Tomboy was combat soldier. Neither of these were to be realized.

Aside from working outside, careers that entailed absolute power and unquestionable authority held Tomboy's interest. Choices could include the presidency or the priesthood. Of these two it was the priesthood that called to Tomboy. And while she was a God fearing Catholic, Jesus was less an influence in this choice than was the raw, unadulterated power that was part of the job description. That and the fact that Tomboy's sister wanted to be a nun. She knew that priests trumped nuns anyway. Even aspiring Mother Superiors!

Dorothy Terry

The Fantastical Travels of TSE

I encountered TSE while looking out of my window at frozen Lake Michigan three years ago on a weary, dreary January morning. Suddenly, there he was, stumbling in from the frozen shore where his ice-breaking tug had gone aground. He was bundled in a crimson striped Harvard muffler, thus battened well against the scourging wind, which was throwing a thousand knives at him from the East. TSE, chilled to the marrow, obviously longed to visit warmer climes and better times. He asked if I would travel with him in order to transcribe his hoped-for experiences, thus freeing his pen for more poetic ventures.

Here are two accounts from these journeys thus far—the first to the Mountains of Mexico, where he arrives on the back of a donkey and encounters a saint and a Subcommandante in a single auspicious day, and his most recent journey to the WAR, during which he has a prophetic vision at the junction of the Tigris and Euphrates.

The Fantastical Travels of TSE

Somewhere

Up there halfway to the other
perfectly proportioned side of our new globe which
revises the world lit with an everlasting light fully
illuminating tiniest hamlets mountain ranges tinkling streams
dry heath
dusty deserts big bogs dull dales
lighting brilliantly each embossed spot where
footprints were dug in flight

from the rushing to catch up
and sight more sites
South of the Arctic north of Byrd's undiscovered Pole

Somewhere ...
brilliantly defined in iridescent four-color litho magnificent
flora and fauna (names parenthesized) dates micro-ized
history sanitized folk-lore

Somewhere ...

In that easy-to-read curving left-tilting rim of our continental
world
I point

There!

His poem isn't working so
He decides to take a steamboat
Landing in a lagoon full of Lily Walkers.
He loses his way in the mountains,
Then rides into town at sunrise
On a scarified donkey
He is tired and alone
"Soledad!" they call him
Since he is traveling by himself

TSE Goes South

He had wanted to escape possums and gossipy clerks
with pocket protectors and bi-focals
Instead he found tear-stained Jesuit saints.
They reached from their damp niches with long
Curved preying fingers

In solitude he meditated on his sins then giddy

with forgiveness wrote a limerick
or two but gave up when he could find no rhyme
for Oaxaca.

The women came and went in his baroque balcony room
Their small round heads were covered with sequined lace
Their maraschinoed fingernails dropped engraved vellum cards
on a lacquered tray that held
the remnants of last night's burnt dinner.

They also brought tiny white Venetian mourning doves
speaking of nothing nothing at all
in twisted silver syntax

Bored he took a bus to the local ruins
The dancers were bowlegged and frightened
because it was July 19 an inauspicious day for travelers.
Yet they pranced on the stone temple
with the sure feet of little cats

Margueritas at the hotel
The sun setting behind ochre mountains
A basket of tequila dreams bursting
White blooms
Discarded bridal veils
Idly tossed on a desert

He wrote this poem
but threw it at the ghost
of a bright blue lemur with rabbit ears running
beside him on the road.)

Next day market trucks filled with pigs from
Aztompa rumbled like tumbrels over the broken stone road
into town mingling with one hundred green Volkswagens leading
a parade of ragged revolutionaries

They waved books of poetry written by their Subcommandante
who wore a purple velvet bandolier with mismatched
bullets and carried a broken black rifle. A small blue parrotlet
perched on his head and pointed out photo opportunities as
the Subcommandante greeted the cheering crowd

Hungry and lonely
TSE sat down at the three-legged writers' table
in the Zocalo next to the guanoed liberator's horse drank
his cappuccino and read the news from Mexico City
He saw that tourists afraid of an inauspicious day
had begun to flee the vast airport.

He was glad he had phobias that led him
to trust only the dependable river boats of his youth

TSE wondered what Vivienne was doing now.

If she were here, she would wear a hat of puzzled chrysanthemums

He was glad he had remembered his umbrella.

It might rain …

It rained the next day
and the next
adobe melting many casas
The streets ran red
with venous Indian blood

TSE met a starving girl prostrate on the steps of the cathedral.
He asked her to dinner where she greedily gobbled
charred filets and Dauphinois (1) potatoes
at the Snip Snap Cafeteria
much frequented by fellow Midwesterners.

She became his muse.

His Swiss Santo watch with chiming alarm
rang him to matins (2)
He felt a rush when he bent above the poor pierced foot of Christ
ignoring a robed and tasseled cleaning crew
scraping pews annoyingly
across the ancient stone floor

At the nave a midget wearing an orchid hairpiece
And accompanied by a wall-eyed monkey
handed him a persimmon
TSE ate it then quickly
cleansed his hands with
antibiotic wipes which
he carried at all times. (3)

The monkey then blessed him
with a trinity of day-old Corncobs

One night the Virgen of Guadeloupe came down

She took the three o'clock from Mexico
but returned the next day because TSE remained faithful
to Soledad in her black velvet Lenten mourning dress. (4)
The Virgen of Soledad had arrived alone on the back
of an ailing donkey wrapped in la noche
just as he.
But her donkey died.
and his did not

Was there a poem there? ...

Cleansed and purified he left Soledad's side
when a group of small girls in white bridal tutus began
to sing "Sanctus Sanctus"

as they tossed bouquets of fire lilies on the altar

Meanwhile, his muse after running up a huge bill
at the Snip Snap fled to the mountains where she vowed a life
of poverty and slapping flea.
He heard she had joined a band of revolutionaries
and had become the Leader's favorite
since she was adept at quadruple anapest quatrains
and a variety of poetic forms and devices
all suggesting to replicate
the lurching gait of
Emilio Zapata's white horse.

Disillusioned TSE spent his days trying to remember words
but no ink flowed from his pen.
At times his reverie was disturbed by beggar Madre
witching him awake
with her carved Virgen of Guadeloupe bookmarks
If he bought two she could feed her family for a week
including the men who played chess in her courtyard

He tried to befriend other writers
but they did not understand the poetic
significance of his long lines
of extravagantly embellished dactyls carrying excess baggage
waiting for the bus to Las Carnetas

A small red mark above his lifeline
Spreading rapidly
His fingers tingling a thousand pin pricks
His face ashen
A vision of a desert
Drowning in pop-top cartons of Fruity Juici
And abandoned minivans
With no headlights or side air bags
White dust motes rising
From a magenta recycled plastic dune
Revealing His Lady

Wearing Dulce Grabano size 16 Listless Jeans
Her simulated fiberglass tote holds a small albino ocelot
With astigmatic brown eyes
She stands under a tree of clapping Chautauqua palms
TSE quickly repaired to his casa to drown memories of his mother—
her soothing red satin dress—
the piercing peril of her Plexiglas wedgies
He felt a sharp pain in his posterior cortex!
He heard the screech of hydraulic brakes!
The poem
began

(1) This delicate dish was created for the wife of the last Dauphin of France by his second cousin who owned The Cackling Coq bistro in Dauphinvillas   an ancient subdivision of the south of France. The Dauphin and Dauphiness, who could not control their sensory pleasures, lost their heads over the dish, which was initially presented to them by a team of waiters wearing edgy black velvet slumber masks decorated with pictures of the latest governor of California.(2) For those shoppers among you, TSE's unique Swiss Santo Watch was purchased at the Saints Alive curio shop adjacent to the church of Soledad. The shop is well worth visiting. It contains in addition to the watch, Soledad night lights, Pope John paper dolls and handy Virgen of Guadeloupe bottle openers, which offer relief from thirst while sending up prayers.

(3) TSE had recently seen on television a group of microscopic slides showing the proliferation of bacteria that live and breed on all surfaces, often establishing invisible universes on one's fingernail if not eliminated immediately. (4) It is said that there is some competition between Soledad and Guadeloupe, but do not believe a word of it. While the Guadeloupe has sewn up the bookmark franchise and they do have their little tiffs, TSE can assure you they are the best of friends. They also are fashionistas, especially Soledad. Even her austere Lenten

attire is a chic midnight bombazine, and her tiny apron is
edged with delicate Brussels lace from Brittany

"Oh, the rockettes red flares
The burbs bursting with pairs
Sent couth through the night
To dissemble our cares."
                anon

TSE Goes to War

He rued the day he was captured on a cool spring morning two
    months ago.

Returning to Istanbul with a humvee full of rare Oriental story-
tellers,
he was forced to stop behind a dune to attend to nature's demands.
Deeply absorbed in Coleridge, TSE heard nothing.
Then, suddenly, he looked up
and there they stood in their bloody soccer shoes,
rag-stall Prix de France cycling shirts
and black polyester sweat pants with white running stripes.

They were pointing guns at him and holding out a chef's toque!

TSE, unable to flee, attempted to tell them that he was a member
    of Poets
Against Loaded Words and Inexplicit Ambiguity
but could not persuade them of his neutrality.
However, he accepted the toque, since he felt that his talent for
    culinary art
might distract his captors from their purpose of killing everyone
    they met.
Thus he was duly sent to be the personal chef to The Leader
    because of his skill

DOROTHY TERRY

in preparing delicate fluffy omelets. (1)

In addition to twelve dozen double yolk eggs,
TSE immediately ordered candle wax, persimmon pizza and fifty
    quarts of Fruity Juici,
the favorite drink of The Leader,
along with rare succulent chocolate from Chiapas.
He took his assignment seriously, since he felt that creating prize-
    winning cuisine
was similar to crafting a poem—the ingredients must be the very
    finest and freshest
and, as in perfect versification, should indicate discriminating
    taste.

TSE's major charge each day was to prepare The Leader's noon
    meal,
which he placed carefully in the green Captain Marvel lunch box
carried by The Leader to The Front.
The Leader ate his lunch at noon break while checking his bank
    balance,
which was encoded on Al Jahida. But lately transmission was
    very poor
due to incessant boring Swiss chat.

When the Shaking Awe began,
and bombs burst like meteors above the griffin guarded gates of
    the palace,
TSE's Captors jumped in the coffin-shaped prayer pools.
Then they prayed to Allah that they would be worthy to meet
    their maidens soon.
The balance of the time, his Captors worked at scuffing up their
    shoes and ripping large
tears in their Chemical Protective Suits, so that if they, by
chance,
were shot carrying a cart load of computer mouse pads from the
    public works building,
they would appear to have died defending Their Leader,
who was deep in his burrow by then.

They talked bravely of becoming martyrs, but TSE could smell fear on their breaths,
which reminded him of desert dog stew, requiring a lot of wine and cilantro to mask
the rancid odor of corruption. For if they tried to escape, they would be shot as traitors
by the new volunteers who arrived every day from next door.

TSE finally gained the confidence of The Leader
and was able to hold poetry readings the third Monday of each month
or when the moon was waning. But one morning, when rinsing out his stock pot in the
turgid runoff next to the mess tent and chanting with the others
"In Xanadu did ...,
" TSE felt a small animal wind its wasted body around his left
and very very touchy metatarsal This helpless creature resembled the little starving dog
who curled on his rug every night during his recent long safari
with the Bedouins across the endless desert to Africa.
The dog, the reincarnation of the great warrior Antitank,
whispered in TSE's good ear that the war was over
and that soon they would all have a warthog in every pot.
Jubilant, TSE immediately began cracking hazelnuts
for the grand victory feast.

The nights were black as coal pits in Wales, but the moon was full
when he escaped after The Leader and his Captors ran away with their bags
of overly contrived allusions.
TSE headed for a well-marked waterhole,
located between the Tiresome and Euphoric Rivers.
There, his Captors said, the maidens lived
and would welcome him.

He walked twenty days and twenty nights in a swirling sandstorm
so thick he was blinded. Finally, he entered a void,
without sound or light.

He now realized that The Leader was hungry for blood,
not wine sauce, and was persuaded that he would never see Emily
     again,
nor be able to prepare her favorite dish—Spring Smeltlings a la
Rossetti.

>   Suddenly, through white glare
>   A beautiful maiden appeared.
>   Seductively, she lounged
>   On the steps of a shining marble palace
>   Her hair—finest spun silver
>   Her body—white as sifted sand
>   She wore neckpiece of desert fox ears
>   Her bandolier held bullets of pure gold
>   Under the many Moorish arches
>   A state of the art music system
>   Boomed new issues of salsa and merengue (2)
>   As twenty beauteous maidens danced with his ragged
>   spectral Captors.

His maiden, seemingly more subdued than the others,
silently beckoned, inviting him to join her in a game of Scrabble
But TSE, though tempted, declined
and kept to his purpose of finding his way home.

He hoped he had not gained too much weight.
He would have to go on a diet immediately,
since he wanted to be trim and fit
in order to wear the twelve bespoke suits
he had ordered prior to this journey so as to impress Emily,
who had sent him E-mails every day
(and sometimes five times a day)
along with the latest works of Dylan Thomas,
her favorite poet. (3)

While often he was annoyed at having to open so many of her
     E-mails,
he rather missed her and vowed to commence a special poem
composed of all the words in her letters.

Rich amulets of verse.

He was thankful he had not lost his glasses.

(1) Fortunately, few people know that TSE was a graduate of Excalibury Culinary Arts Institute, holding an award for a recipe reproduced in the prestigious Annals of Gastronomy – Smashed Flounder con Frites con Anchovy Salsa al la Ezra. He also was noted for his Creamy White Range-fed Partridge Yolk Soufflé a la Gerard and his Peppercorn Sautéed Grebe Legs Frisse a la Percy.

(2) While on his last vacation, TSE took dance classes at the Bottomly Ballroom in Bournemouth. It was recommended to him by Virginia Woolf, who had learned a soulful samba and a tortured tango when on holiday there the previous year. But when TSE invited her to be his partner in the Quick Step at the Bottomly Annual Ballroom Dance Competition, she demurred, saying she would rather go for a swim.

(3) TSE had spent an unfortunate evening with Thomas at the Gwynth Paltry Inn and Pub during his last visit to Wales. TSE, it seems, imbibed too many mugs and later found himself alone in the woods, at midnight, without his walking stick, which Thomas had broken over TSE's head when he kept reminding him of the time.

Blinded by blowing sand
Little sleep-Nothing to eat …
Occasionally, a bomber roared
Often, there was the rat-tat-tat of
Spectral gunners throwing lightening bolts
& the hazy sky was lit with searing flashes
Blooming, exploding super novas.

.

Will the world end in this way?
With not even a murmur of
Despair, as the stars finally make way

For the dousing of their lights?

His eyes filled with the dense void of universe.
His hands, gloved with dust,
Were entombed in the remains of an expired planet.

TSE Goes Home

On the sixteenth day,
weighted down by the heat and his atmospheric protective suit,
TSE saw, far in the distance, an imposing figure.
It was larger than anyone he had encountered in his travels.
It loomed on the horizon like a lone skyscraper
on the shore of a frozen inland lake.
The personage wore a tightly curled beard
and its nose resembled an upside down question mark.
Perched on its shoulder was a slender sentry,
with the head of a hawk and blood-gorged eyes.
He surveyed TSE with vague dislike,
as if he had seen him before in some other life
and found him just as distasteful then.

The Personage, known at the Hate Keeper,
asked if TSE, by any chance, had the price of admission
to the Sins of the Foibles, a city of rotting rubble—
time's discards—a box of pox,
carpeted with choc-o-malt Easter Egg wrappers,
festooned with endless tedium and virtual terror toys,
timelessly set to explode in the immediate past
and not-too-distant future.
.
TSE had nothing on him but a half-eaten Oreo, which The
    Personage
 gratefully accepted.
After checking his pack for manicure scissors, eyebrow tweezers
and extra tickets to The Talking Heads concert,
he allowed TSE to pass through the grimy gates,

which suddenly lurched open, leaning dolefully away from the
    walls of the city,
interrupted in their attempt to escape.
The place was barren, yet emitted the fragrance of hydrangeas,
crowning the ramparts with lush blue blooms.
TSE noted that these bulky flowers, which fill large vases more
    than adequately,
seem to be highly popular at weddings of those who are not well
    read ,
but do not usually appear in poems because they scan lumpily
and are difficult to rhyme.

The site had fallen to ruin due to malign neglect. The roofless
    buildings,
seen from the air, resembled diagrams for ubiquitous, planned
    condo developments
spawned in the Midlands, which enable the motivated family to
    plunge all their money
confidently into the home of their worst dreams,

A regiment of hollow saluting warriors, identical to the Sentry,
lay about, arms and legs awkwardly askew, flung down helter-
    skelter beneath
their pedestals and oversights. Some had been tentatively raised
to their former imposing glory, but their aspect was unnatural.
Often their predating falcon heads were turned toward the West.
TSE thought it was interesting that the sun, in its journey,
moved along their beaks as on a sundial,
seeming to mark the hours since the warriors had been thrown
    from their ramparts.

Much of this disarray was the work of scavengers of good taste,
those who appraise the prize, then fill scarified vans and taxis
    with the corpses
of centuries. From Egypt to the Andes, these midnight tomb
    tunnelers
gorge themselves on the remains of expired worlds
and then sell history to the highest bidder …

But the stolid Hate Keeper remained menacingly at his ticket stand,
placed within a giant Joseph Cornell box of sky and sand,
sprinkled with the fragile scrapings of spent shells.

Beneath the torrid, sweltering sky
A Bedouin tent was raised
To house a clever digital montage
Of stolen cars from Chicago
And fresh bleeding hearts

Cruelly pierced by curved, crusted
Saracen daggers.

> Three goddesses of Ur
> Dancing on a silver dome of broken bones
> Beckoned to him to join them
> Yet Emily, moth hair ablaze with a thousand sparks
> Remained resplendent in her leafy niche
> As when he left her
> In the rose garden
> Aside the turgid stream
> In that other land
> In that timeless
> Long ago.

TSE soon left the tent and resumed his journey.
In his travels, he realized that unfortunately he had discovered little
that did not already lurk in the lonely alleys and
Secret stairways and
Dusky cul-de-sacs
Of home.

"And at the end of our exploring
Will be to arrive where we started
And know the place for the first time."
         T.S. Eliot, 1944

Lampost

Photography, Bobbie Krinsky

Bobbie Krinsky

Voices: Elegy for an Asylum

Rita
Crazy for Love

In the summer of 1982, I was one of six artists recruited to build studios in the half deserted, historic west wing of a County Home in Wisconsin. Intrigued by the potential of the condemned, litter strewn basement, we proposed trading art classes with the residents for rent free studio space. Not long after I began my work in the hospital, I started making friends with residents whose conversations were so remarkable, I raced back to my studio to jot down their stories. Some were sad, others funny, but almost always, the insight these people had was so simply said, that nine years passed before I realized what stories I had just waiting to be told. "Crazy For Love: Rita", the excerpt from my work-in-progress, could easily speak for "Rita". When the hospital gave us our initiation tour, our first stop was 3-EAST, the unit where she lived. I never saw her again, but twenty-four years later, our encounter still haunts me

PROLOGUE

1966, Rita

I knew Mitchell was a stiff
but he was neat, clean shaven and even better,
Pa hated his guts. Trouble is, I eloped
with the sonofabitch
just to piss Pa off.

Here's our wedding night:

When I call him Mitchie and kiss him ... okay? ...
he says, "Wait — the name's Mitchell. From now on call me
Mitchell or Hubby. Just make up your mind and stick to it."

So now I'm stuck with Hubby.

2006, Vince B., Counselor

Yeah sure, I remember her. Rita. The nurses' pet.
She couldn't talk but she had this devious sense of humor
whenever I walked past, she kind of laughed
and pinched my butt.

Door Stairs

I.

The first time we talked, Mitch called me Angel.

1965, Spring

When home is a cold water trailer
set on cement blocks behind the westbound
tracks on the edge of a town so small,
everybody knows
your business, school is hell, home
is hell — life is hell.

Schoolyard punks
dump your books, pinch
your butt and call you *trailer trash.*
And you hate home because Ma
drives Pa nuts so he hits on you
and you know

you gotta get out
or you'll go nuts

So you beg your new friend,
the man who sells bibles to Rexall's,
to take you when he moves on and he grabs
you and cries. *Hell is for sinners—*
What angels need is love.
His love.

But you know that look
in his eyes
because you're sixteen, stacked
and so crazy for love,
you ache.

183

II.

1968, Spring

I married young
but Hubby's a traveling man.
Leaves me on my own but I like it that way.
You try living with a bible thumper
who prays for your sins
but won't talk to you.

Wanna know when my life begins? When Hubby hits the road.

That's right—

I'm home alone,
don't have to answer to no one.
I skip chores, sing sappy love songs
he calls *heathen trash,*
watch Dating Game and dream. Or go out,
meet folks at the TipTop,

have some laughs,
let my hair down and dance.
Trouble is,
guys go nuts
when good-time girls tell them,
Gotta go home. Alone.
On my own.

Attic Window

III.

1969, Spring

While Hubby's packing his van
for Toledo, you get another phone call.
You keep saying, hello?
hello? but all you hear is breathing that spooks you
so bad, round midnight, you're still sprawled
on the couch reading to get sleepy

when you hear footsteps

and something furry flashes past
the back window. Your legs are lead but you know
you gotta get up, force yourself to *stroll* out the room
and out of sight, grab the kitchen phone
and head for the cellar but inches from the door,
the cord twists and trips you.

Stumbling, you miss the top step
and tumbling down the grit cracked linoleum,
you plunge into darkness.
You still don't know how you hung on to the phone,
dialed 0 and crying so hard, the operator
could barely hear you whisper,

"Somebody's come to kill me."

Sheriff's on his way miss, but don't hang up. I want you to listen.
Listen? To what? Oh please …
Anything that don't belong—a kick, a crash,
                              glass breaking—
                                      footsteps

IV.

1969, Summer

There were no fingerprints,
no cigarette butts
or boot tracks
but the sheriff found a coon head
under the back porch:

"Stinks like road kill," he said, "but it ain't.
Those bones there—some nut hacked them.
We can check for prints but don't get your hopes... hey,
you still home alone? Don't matter.
Call back. Anytime."

Trouble is, I called back
three nights running. The last time
the sheriff said I worry too much and left. Maybe
he's right. Maybe it's just the heat.
Today I drove for sixty miles before I found
a store that still had fans.

But I'm still so hot,
I'm gonna skip the TipTop

and take a cold bath. Trouble is,
something out back stinks worse than road kill.
And I'm dripping wet and too tired to...
what's that?
Who's ... somebody just rapped
on my windo...

Time–Turned Back

The Cage

V.

They   found me   they
I thought I hid good   but
they found me bare naked
shaking so bad I
wait no
don't

1969, Fall

While Hubby stood over me
yelling about sin
the sheriff wrapped me in a sheet   helped me
upstairs   talked me to sleep
trouble is   then he showed Hubby
the coon head   told him

about the TipTop
and the dancing

Maybe the sheriff meant good
but Hubby stopped traveling
Took my clothes   my keys   made me
crawl
denounced me to his lousy Holy Rollers
who still call me   *trailer trash*

but he never saw me cry
even on my twenty-first birthday

when he woke me   touched my cheek
told me   hey   let's make a picnic
take a drive
he was grinning like a kid   but I should of known
he'd start in on me   speeding
screeching around curves

but I was so crazy

for love
even when he reached across my lap
I thought he's gonna grab my hand   kiss
and make up   but he grabbed the door handle
yanked it so hard   I

All I heard was the wind   all
I ever hear is the   wind
and   some poor fool   in my room
                    screaming

Door Ajar

195

Young Rita

Ghosts

Jude Genereaux

Why I Won't Write About the Past (An Anti-Memoir)

I have been drawn to write about my brother, a talented young man who died far too early, after a challenging and inspirational life. I began writing a narrative, but it was disconnected and didn't flow smoothly. After acknowledging that I avoided tracts of the family saga which needed to be included, it became clear to me why I was having difficulties. I have also discovered that even as I resist focusing on the dark side of awareness, the urge to document occasionally takes hold, perhaps as insulation for the next time expectation tempts me to believe that family gatherings will be different, and lessen the disappointment when they are not.

Why I Won't Write About the Past

While the jury may yet be out, after a recent writing workshop in "Memoir," I have serious doubt this would be my venue. We were encouraged to write about what we know: "... tell what happened in your life." Which means of course, our families—as in nuclear family: siblings, parents, extended aunts and uncles. Fertile ground, my family.

Ground I am weary of trodding ... ground that still rips at my heart.

Shall I write more about our beloved brother, the classic Marfan? Marfan: a syndrome marked by great height and intellect, long on legs, digits, noses, talent; short on life. Want to hear more about his loss of sight—as a ten year old? How about his dozen failed surgeries, struggles to live a normal life, including crashing "normal" public school, rebuking "Special Ed"? Learning to ski, drive. Blind. College, music, love all came to him in spades. As did death from a body that sabotaged his every effort, at 23.

I could certainly write about a neurotic mother; swamped in a vision of what she "expected" life should bring to her table, she remains stalled by the disappointment of it all, confused as to what's important, and failing to recognize an abundance that includes comparative good health at the ripe old age of 83. I carry a vein of incredulous bafflement I could tap into there, which might never end.

Or a favorite in every family, the wild one: our adorable, living life-on-the-edge younger sister, saddled with a full backpack of panic attacks, bulimia and a motorcycle accident that resulted in the loss of a leg at age 18. After a classically mis-matched marriage, her first child was born with a Downs Syndrome "type of" delay. This in itself is a challenge to any marriage, and didn't make the next decade any easier. After two more (healthy) children, a move to California (and back) a house fire and an ever more confused life-style, the divorce that followed surprised almost no one. Then came the re-marriage to the "Love of her Life," followed by her discovery that he was an alcoholic (albeit a very fun and loving one), followed by his death at 42 from kidney failure. As she approached mid-life, she seemed to reach a plateau where, even though alone, she was negotiating small bits of happiness for herself, only to be clobbered with a horrific bout of, for God's sake, oral cancer.

Then we have the middle sister: used to being ignored while growing up, cowed by family as well as the competitive world, she lives fairly cocooned in an artistic lifestyle where she produces the beauty she sees, but which is not always returned to her by those she holds most dear. Married nearly 40 years to a man teetering on the edge of abusive, their sole child is now geographically distant, and while he expresses his caring for her, he certainly knows how to take advantage as well. She's turned to reading and interpreting Bible passages for succor, claiming Jesus Christ as her personal savior as a matter of routine when answering the telephone, as well as liberally sharing this mantra in her conversations with the rest of us sinners.

Then there's our Dad. After his mother and twin died at his birth, he was raised for a short time by his father and a stepmother, until the father also passed away. Moving from coal country Pennsylvania, his large immigrant family chose Detroit to find work, with Dad being tossed about between step-mother and older sisters until he was a teen. Stories he has told indicate he grew up a loner, with few of the finer lessons a mother would have taught him as he bounced from home to home. In his late teens he had the misfortune of working at the local matinee and after watching three or four hundred re-runs of "Over the Rainbow," he was fatally stricken with Judy Garland—fatal. That obsession sharpened his senses for a glimpse of my mother, a darn close Judy Garland look-alike, and the man was done. Stick a fork in him = he was done. Literally. Did he ever consider personality? goals? values? interests? Sensuality??? when he was in lathered pursuit of this woman who was to become his mate for 60 + years? It does not appear so; all that mattered was The Look, and his fate was sealed. Now, after a life of hard work, a failed business which was to be his slice of the American Dream, and a body destroyed by age, he lives in his 86-year-old-skin, resenting children and years that have moved on, unable to find joy in his life or family, with only the carping and confused world view of his complaining mate, who no longer resembles Judy Garland, much less a rainbow of any sort.

You want me to write about this? This, which I've tried to put behind me, in preference of looking past it, getting over it, moving through life in spite of it … moving to the beat of a different drummer (I hope); praying all my life for deliverance from such patterns? God our Father, let us live in your Grace, grant us good health, a joyful life with all of our children a great part of it. I seek the ability to find Good in people and the world; an ability to keep moving and doing that which I must in earning, EARNING, my place in the world and meaningful connection to people: my mate, children, friends, colleagues. Accepting responsibility for my own personal happiness, I have a full understanding that help from the Almighty is definitely needed, as well as a strength of character which must have been expressed in the nuclear family, but not always experienced.

No. My instincts move me away from dwelling on past heartaches; just this smidgen of writing opened doors I have not looked into for years. While I certainly hold close the good memories that were also part of growing up, there is too much material there for dozens of sad, angry memoirs, novels perhaps, based on the heartaches and failures of a wrecked family. But I lived there once, and do not want to return. I want, what do I want … ?

I want to acknowledge that which I know in my bones: that there are happier lives and places than these. I see other people move about the world oblivious to even a fraction of the loss our small family experienced. I want to live that way. I want to acknowledge in my writing the deep gratitude I have for a life begun at age 19, when I moved my few boxes of belongings out of a bedroom shared with sisters, and stepped into the dormitory of a small mid-western university, closing forever the door to living under the heartbreak roof of my family.

I want to be able to say, when I am told to "write about your life" that I do. I write about the best part of my life: life with a loving partner, the utter joys found raising my own family, the search for the small contentments found in a black sky at night, the song of spring peepers, the stand-the-hair-up-on-my-arms call of loons, voices of my children and grandchildren calling my name, my Love's breath on my arm at midnight.

Becky Post

The Ka Conspiracy

Kate Vavra worries that her teenage son Seth's rebelliousness is an early sign of schizophrenia, the illness that afflicts his father, an iconoclast nicknamed Plato. Though they've been divorced a number of years, Plato phones frequently to rail at society and culture and to convince Kate to keep their son free of these negative influences. Plato has developed his critical ideas into a theory that he calls "the Ka Conspiracy" from the Egyptian hieroglyph Ka, which represents to him the stiffness of culture.

When Plato hitchhikes from Madison, Wisconsin, to Kate's home in a small city farther north, his wild behavior lands him in the psychiatric ward there. These events deepen Seth's depression and cause further difficulties for Kate.

The novel is completed and the author is looking for an agent.

Chapter One

Plato was my husband until he went crazy. When I visit him, he looks like Jesus or Rasputin and he rages. Against me. Against his parents. At the world. His eyes are deep, dark recesses that seem to reach into a murky underground. His hair hangs raggedly, brushing his shoulders. His full beard is untrimmed. He is dark, dark. I go less and less. Sometimes I wonder why I go at all. I hardly ever take Seth, but he talks to his father by phone, so he hears the same mad ravings.

He lives in a poor part of Madison in an apartment building peopled with others like him, outcasts and crazies, exiles in our midst. They are a sad and tattered bunch. He has had roommates off and on. Now he lives alone. I visit him because of a promise I made to his parents years ago. They are back in Connecticut worrying about him, so I check on him occasionally. I don't mind. The drive is pleasant from Sand Prairie, the small city where I moved with Seth after the divorce. The highway flows ribbon-like around, up and over the soft bosomy hills of southwestern Wisconsin. The trip takes just under three hours.

Sometimes he is fine. We talk about books. Then a recognizable spark of the old Plato, bright and literate, appears. I used to find myself wistful at these times, even hopeful. I've learned. There will be no recovery, only the grim march of days—some better, some worse.

I've realized, too, that I must avoid talking about politics. The last time I did was two years ago when I advised him to vote for Mondale and Ferraro. "Dammit, Kate!" he yelled and began a ten-minute rant. "They're all idiots and cowards! Reagan, too. Don't you know? They're all part of the Ka Conspiracy, every last one of 'em!"

Last week when I was talking to him on the phone, he was drunk. I could barely understand his garbled words. "Plato," I said, "what are you trying to escape from?"

"That's a good question, Kate," he said. "I'm not trying to escape from anything. It's like . . . I don't know. But I'm a drunkard, an absolute drunkard."

"Why don't you go back to AA?"

"Naw! I'm insane, as determined by our fine government. I'm insane!" I didn't know how to respond, so I waited, and he continued, "I have a hard time. People don't talk."

"What people? At AA meetings?"

"Those bastards! Doin' their own schtick!"

"Plato," I began, but he interrupted.

"You don't know what I'm talking about! I'm talking about roses! I think we can grow 'em."

This time I let him continue, though what he said was disconnected and nonsensical. I hoped we would finish the conversation before Seth got home. I didn't want Seth to hear any of it, not even my end. By now Plato had worked himself into a frenzy. "I'm just a lame-brain, no-mind, muddle-headed madness," he yelled. "It all grows! It grows beautifully. I'm not kidding! If I'm a crazy person, don't mind me. Don't mind me!"

My friend Lil tells me I shouldn't let Seth have any

contact with his father at all, but I disagree. He needs to know he has a dad, that his dad cares about him. Someday Seth will understand. And unlike Lil and my parents, I don't think Plato's craziness is the cause of Seth's problems, though it does complicate things.

***

His real name is Michael. College friends called him Plato because of his philosophical reading and spouting. Max Schulte first called him that the night six of us went to the Indiana Dunes in Meggy's car and sat up on the edge of a small hill, drinking cheap wine and enjoying the bright sliver of moon and the wash of waves on the beach. We had just started dating; it was 1966, the beginning of my freshman year.

Meggy and Bob were there, Sharon and Max, and Michael and I. A raucous bunch of high school kids—townies—came by once, tossing vulgarities back and forth and tussling with one another, but after that the beach was quiet except for the soft pulse of Lake Michigan and our hushed and serious voices. Most of us were concerned with politics and the world and what we should do with our lives. Michael went deeper, beyond my understanding at that time. My mind was just beginning to waken and expand. He spoke of Nietzsche at length, then Sartre. When it was time to go back, Max said, "Maybe we should drive to this place again sometime and Plato here can lead us in another discourse." We all laughed, but everyone called him Plato after that.

I was first attracted by his mind and his energy, the excitement in his voice and the spirit in his eyes. I liked the way he walked down the street, his stick-thin arms bouncing to the jazz rhythm of his feet.

Now we are almost forty. The years have marked us both.

***

The last time I visited him, he was sober. When I knocked, he yelled out in a gruff voice, "Come in!" I opened the door and saw him sitting on the floor with a mug of coffee and six or eight open books surrounding him—Nietzsche, Artaud, Reich, *The*

Egyptian Book of the Dead—I forget the rest. The shades were down and the only light came from the glow of a stubby candle next to him. His jeans were nearly white from wear. Almost obscured by the long scraggly hair and beard was a face dominated by darkness—shadows, a scowl, and his brown eyes, deep-set and ringed from sleeplessness.

He picked up a book, read a little, then violently underlined something, stabbing at the page with the stub of pencil and muttering "Fuck! Shit!" I stood at the door awhile before he acknowledged me with a look. Then I stepped inside.

Around two sides of the room were tall shelves cobbled together with crates, bricks and boards. Books were crammed into them, stuffed two rows deep. A twin-sized mattress topped with a haphazard pile of blankets and pillows lay on the floor against another wall. In a corner was the tiny Formica and chrome table that we bought years ago at a garage sale.

"Hello, Michael," I said. I don't know why I used his real name. When we were married, I only used that name in anger or during lovemaking. I'm afraid this started out my visit on the wrong foot.

"What do you want?" he snarled, seeming unsurprised by my presence, though I had not told him I was coming.

"May I sit down?"

"Don't be polite. You know I hate social niceties."

"I won't ask you how you've been then," I said.

"This is a fucking hell-hole. What do you expect?"

"Do you mind if I have a cup of coffee?"

He didn't move from his position on the floor. With a wave of his hand, he indicated the pot on the stove.

I used the opportunity to look in all the cupboards to see if he had sufficient food. This is why I came, so I could report to Claire. She always worries about how Plato eats. I grabbed a mug and poured myself some coffee.

"Seth is a problem again," I said, sitting down at the table. I shouldn't have brought this up. Plato is never any help.

"What does he do?"

"He sneaks out at night. I have no control over him. If I tell him he's grounded, he leaves anyway. No matter what—"

"*You're* the problem," he exploded as his arm shot out in a wide gesture. "You're part of the conspiracy. You're one of *them* now!"

His face was twisted and ugly, like that of some prehistoric bird. He flung down his book and stood up, and I noticed how gaunt he was. His body shook and his movements were like a grotesque, mad, animal dance. He came closer, raised a fist and brought it down on the table with a crash. Some of my coffee splashed over the rim.

"It's the Ka Conspiracy, and you've joined it!" he said.

I looked at him and said nothing. His thin lips twisted into a sneer. I stood up, fighting the urge to speak, afraid I'd blurt out something that would enrage him further.

It was time to leave. As I neared the door, he turned in my direction but did not follow me. His fist was raised, clenched and shaking, not at me, but at what I represented to him.

Chapter Two

Seth and I live in an old, two-story house just big enough for him to avoid me. If I ask a direct question, he either walks away without answering, gives a short, grunted response, or says something rude and angry. He is usually out with his friends or upstairs in his room. When we eat, he reads. I tell him to stop so we can have a conversation. He puts the book aside, but not without an argument, and then eats in silence anyway. I never win. He has been seeing a therapist for six months, but I haven't noticed any progress. He is still sullen and negative, often depressed.

On the day of his appointment, I pick him up from school. We have to rush to get to Dr. Guinn's office at the opposite end of town. He throws his heavy backpack to the floor and without looking at me or saying "hello," curls glumly down into his seat.

"Thanks for being prompt," I say. "If traffic isn't too bad, we'll just make it."

The last time I picked him up, he was standing outside the school talking to Brianna, a girl with ink-colored hair, black clothes from top to bottom and crimson lipstick. I waved him toward the car, but he ignored me. When he finally got in, I said a few sharp words, he responded in anger, and we were off into another ugly argument, speeding to his appointment. It is never good between Seth and me.

"You don't have to thank me for what's merely normal," he says this time. His face is clenched and he hunches further down, his long legs bent up in front of him. This past year he's grown so fast I can barely afford to keep him in clothes.

The parking lot is full of cars and high school students. I ease through slowly and carefully, but on Weber Drive traffic is moving smoothly and I can speed up. The rust-colored marsh grass waves in the wind, and I think how I'll soon have to rake leaves and put in the storm windows. Seth turns on the radio, but my nerves are already jangling from a day of teaching chatty third graders. I turn it off. He turns it on again.

"I need quiet, Seth," I say loudly, above the harsh music. It's *his* music, young people's music that to me is a screech of electric guitars and unintelligible lyrics. I am yelling at him again. All my muscles are tensed up. The traffic slows suddenly and I have to brake, stopping within inches of the car ahead. He switches the station to classical music, which is at least softer and calming. I agree tacitly to the compromise.

We arrive just in time. I drop Seth off at the clinic door, turn off the radio, and find a parking place at the far end of the lot.

While Seth is talking to Dr. Guinn, I flip through old issues of Reader's Digest, McCall's and Redbook, but I can't find anything I want to read. Finally, Seth comes out and we leave. On the way home, we stop and pick up a pizza for supper. Thursday is always "psych and pizza night."

"Mom, there's no Coke!" he says, and slams the refrigerator door shut. He grabs two cheesy slices, throws them on a plate, and hurries upstairs to his room. Luci, our terrier-beagle, yips and skitters out of the way. A blare of rock music rips the air.

I run up and knock on his door. He doesn't answer, so I bang.

"What do you want?" He opens the door a crack.

"Seth, I've told you before! Turn that down, or I'll take the stereo out of your room!" I yell so harshly it hurts my throat. He knots up his face and goes to turn it down. Before we can goad each other further, I go back downstairs, get a slice of pizza, and sit down on the couch to watch the news.

Ten minutes later, Seth comes down. From the bottom of the stairs he peeks around the wall into the living room. "Sorry for the music," he says.

"All right," I mumble, still chewing, and he goes back upstairs. Although we have made a temporary peace, the evening's emotions are tossed onto a growing pile of unsettled, smoldering issues.

Plato calls. I turn off the TV, grab a diet root beer and settle in at the kitchen table. He sounds good tonight, not drunk, not illogical or paranoid or raving. We talk about books and he mentions one by Alan Watts that we've both read.

"Do you know when I was reading that?" I say. "We were in the Porcupine Mountains. I was stuck in the cabin on a drizzly day and needed a flashlight to read. You and Seth were outside in the rain, trying to catch fish."

"Ah, yes, the Porcupines!" he says, and there is a momentary silence. "Now that was a paradise, wasn't it, Kate?"

Suddenly I see in my mind a photograph I took of Seth and his father on that trip. Seth was almost four, blond and tousleheaded, his face filled with a smile. Plato's long hair was blowing across his face as he squatted, his arm around Seth. Behind them glittered a little lake, dotted with yellow water lilies and surrounded by tall birches and pines.

The photo seems as clear now as if it were in front of me. The sun, the lake's dappled brightness, and the smiles all mirror each other. The memory brings an old phrase to my head—"when life held such promise."

Plato and I continue to talk about other books, other times, but the photo and phrase are stuck in my head like a slide that you can't get to click forward to the next picture. "Porcupine Mountains . . . when life held such promise . . . such promise." I try to focus on what he is saying, try to stop the memory, try to hold back the tears that I can feel parked like runners waiting for the gun. When Plato hangs up, I burst into sobs.

He was OK back then, still working for the county. I took care of Seth all day and looked forward to Plato's coming home. I wanted an adult conversation, but he'd come in, sit on the living room floor, smoke pot and read. He was inaccessible. After that he'd take an hour-long bath, saying this ritual was necessary to get the "Ka" of the job out of him.

Our trip to the Porcupines was a rare vacation. We back-packed about a mile into the forest. Little Seth had his own small pack and knobby walking stick. He was jaunty, self-assured and inquisitive as he raced down the path ahead of us. When he got too far ahead, he'd stop, sit on a log or in a patch of grass, and wait. As soon as we caught up with him, he took off again.

Plato was his old self, celebrating a reprieve from his hated job of filling out forms for welfare recipients. As soon as we got out of the car and stepped into the forest, he was skipping down the path, singing odd lyrics to an invented tune, stopping to show Seth a bug or a snake, or lifting him onto his shoulders so Seth could better see the trees "and all the crazy critters up there."

We spent three days swimming, hiking and soaking up the raw splendor of the north woods. Each day we'd row out to the middle of the lake and eat sandwiches or gorp. Plato and Seth built castles and moats and bridges and populated them with whatever bugs they managed to corral. Best of all, Plato did not cocoon himself off from us, and at night, when Seth had gone to sleep, the two of us would talk the way we used to, about authors and ideas, the sweet excitement of books. It was a dream time.

As I clean up the kitchen, I think of the photo again. Plato was whole then, not suffering from this awful disease. Seth was as yet undamaged by what was to come.

"So much promise" echoes in my head, and the picture appears while I am walking the dog or grading third grade spelling tests. There is something touched here. I usually do not know that I hurt so much.

Chapter Three

I'm at school drilling my third graders on math facts when Lois, the school secretary, buzzes me on the intercom. "You've got a call on line two. It's Glen Sobotta. He says it's important." Glen is the assistant principal at Seth's high school. Lois will send up an aide to watch my class so I can run to the phone. As I hurry to the teachers' lounge, I am hoping he is merely sick, but of course I expect something worse.

"He swore in speech class," Glen says. "It wasn't in anger or anything like that. He was standing in front, giving a speech and simply used the F-word several times. Mr. McIlwain brought him down here right away. I'm sorry, Kate, but he's been very belligerent and we're going to have to suspend him."

I know Mack. We were on a district committee together once. He's balding and bearded, dark blonde. I can imagine the whole scene: Mack, his face reddening, rushes to the front of the room, jerks Seth away from the podium and says, "You're going to the office!" He drags him out of the classroom and down the hall, his hand tight around Seth's upper arm. Seth's face is clenched.

"Can you drive him home at noon?" asks Glen.

"Sure," I say. Thank goodness, I don't have playground duty today. I was planning to correct papers while I ate. Now I'll be lucky if I have time to eat at all.

"Tell him I'll be there soon."

As I drive to North High, I manage to eat a few spoonfuls of yogurt at a red light and some more while parked at the school.

He gets in, but I can't tell if he's contrite or angry. Neither of us says anything.

I have just twenty minutes to drop him off and get back to school. I stop in front of our house. Luci is standing on the roof of her doghouse. She sees us drive up and wags her tail, her whole body moving. Seth grabs his backpack and gets out.

"We'll talk at suppertime," I say. "Do you have your key?"

He nods and mumbles, "Thanks for the ride." I am surprised. Maybe he is sorry this time. He lets Luci out of her pen and they go in the side door together. I make a U-turn and head back to school.

All afternoon I'm thinking of Seth as I teach, mulling over what I'll do. After school, I stop to pick up groceries.

"I'm home!" I yell as I come into the kitchen carrying a large bag. I hear the TV go off in the living room and the sound of Seth's feet clomping up the stairs.

During supper he is silent. "You're grounded tonight," I say, knowing this will lead to a fight. On Fridays he always goes out with his friends.

His eyes flare. His lips and jaw constrict. "No way! I've already been punished for what I did! I was suspended. That's enough!"

"No, it's not, Seth." I speak quietly to prevent myself from losing control. "You've got to learn—"

"There's nothing wrong with my language," he interrupts. "They're just words. What's wrong with words?"

"We've been through this before. You know that certain words offend people." I continue, though I know that he will reject everything I say. I tell him that the issue is not about words, but that he must consider others' feelings.

"No!" he says. "They have to consider mine!" He throws his fork on the table, shoves his chair back, and goes up to his room. I hear his door slam, then the throbbing bass guitar of a rock group. I finish eating, clear the table and sit down at the piano. I begin to play Fur Elise, which tends to calm me. The phone rings and it's Lil, the librarian at my school. She wants me to go with her to a concert of Irish music downtown at the arts center.

"I don't know," I say.

"Oh, come on," she urges. "You never get out, Kate. I've heard great things about this band."

My body feels like it's wound in tight knots. I could use a break, so against my better judgement I decide to go.

When she arrives, I go upstairs and knock on Seth's door. He ignores me, so I yell that I'm going out. I do not remind him of his being grounded. There is a chance he'll leave while I am gone, but I'm not going to stay home for enforcement. There is only so much I can do. Maybe I've given up.

As I go out the door, I feel lighter. The October air is refreshing and we decide to walk. Dry leaves drift down. The scent reminds me of when I was a child. My sisters and I used to rake leaves into a gigantic pile, then take turns jumping off the porch into the pile.

"C'mon!" I say to Lil, and I step into the street, where leaves are bunched in the gutters. I stride into the thick of them and walk with a kick-step that sets them flying. Lil laughs and joins in. The leaves crunch as we make our way downtown. At the concert, spirited Celtic music sets my toes tapping, and for awhile I forget my problems.

Afterwards, we head to Granny O's, a downtown café. Lil is filling me in about a conflict she and her ex-husband Jack are having over their son Brian. The room is filled with the hum of voices. Lil has a new boyish haircut, gold hoops in her ears, and her eyes spark with the intensity of her story. I try to listen, but my mind wanders to Seth. I want to check on him. A blonde slip of a girl brings us our coffee.

"I'm going to phone home," I say out of context. It occurs to me that I may have interrupted Lil. I apologize. "He's fifteen, Kate. He can take care of himself."

"But he's grounded. I'm afraid he might sneak out."

"If he does, he does. You could go home and tie him to his bed," she says. "Short of that, you can't control him."

"I know. I don't think I ever really could. I guess I'd just like to avoid the problem of what to do if he leaves. I'd have to come up with an additional punishment and then enforce it. It's not easy to do!"

"Remove his stereo, his radio, his phone. Don't let him watch TV."

"Yes, of course."

I have done these things many times. Whatever happens, it will be a battle. This is how it usually goes. He tries to bully me verbally into giving his things back. I do not answer his ridiculous and irate arguments. He follows me—down to the laundry room, back up to the kitchen, outside to the garage—all the time talking agitatedly, his nervous body propelling him. I remain firm, mostly mute, answering occasionally to reinforce my resolve. He doesn't get his things back, but he wins something else, the power to harass and badger me, and I am left with a jangling uneasiness that does not easily dissipate.

"Yes," I repeat to Lil. "Of course, I can do that."

When I get home, the light is on in his room. I knock on his door and he answers gruffly, "I'm on the phone!"

"Can we please talk?"

"In a few minutes," he yells.

A little while later he comes into my bedroom. I am leaning against a propped-up pillow, reading a book. Seth has on summer shorts and a T-shirt, his year-round sleeping outfit. He sits down in the wooden rocking chair and dangles one leg over the side.

"What did you want?" he asks in a voice that is now soft. His face is splotchy.

"Seth, I love you. I wish things could be different between us. I wish we could get along." I don't add, "but your behavior has to improve," or "you need to learn to get along with others."

He rocks slowly and says, "I'm sorry that I was rude today, in school and with you. I'm sorry for the inconvenience I caused."

His eyes are blue like mine, but deep-set like his father's. His hair is no longer the golden blonde of childhood, but a dark blonde color easing into brown. There is a sadness in the set of his jaw.

"It's OK. Apology accepted," I say. I have put my book down. I want to offer him something more. "Why don't we go out for lunch tomorrow?" I suggest.

He smiles thinly and continues to rock. "Don't be offended, Mom, but I'd rather do something with my friends. That is, if I'm free to leave the house. Am I ungrounded?"

"Sure. You can do something tomorrow, Seth." He stands up to leave. "Wait," I say, getting up.

I wrap my arms around him and hold him. He raises his limp arms and hugs me back. I do not embarrass him by looking at his face as he leaves the room, for I can tell he is on the brink of tears.

What terrible pain and anger writhe inside him, I wonder, that he should be so torn up and deeply damaged? Things have gone so wrong. The most troubling question of all jabs me: Is there, lurking somewhere deep inside Seth, the beginning of his father's disease?

Tibor

*The extraction from Book III, AMERIKAN SKRIPT, found in
these pages comes from a greater book of many books—a
lifework beyond categorization with the ironic, working title, DANS
LE LABYRINTHE, which is where I find myself each time I pick up
the pen again after abandoning the madness of the task for
months and years—a project I am certain I will never finish. "The
Lines in Winter" is illustrative of both the theory and content that
compels my narrative for the eyes. Among my many influences,
all European, I bow to the master of the nouveau roman, Alain
Robbe-Grillet, who professed: "Each novelist, each novel must invent its own form."*

The Lines in Winter

the days are not mine and they let me know this

I held her hand till the moon came up

the iconography and ritual of murder

you can have sex anytime

the expression of the face seems to be in the process of change

we returned to the cabin to skin the animal, slitting it from
nose to tail with the tip of the knife

flowers, stones, breasts, small sticks, pubic hair, the stone
chimney was clogged with snow

she did not take her eyes off me

she played dead

I was determined to blur boundaries

there are no more sins

this is a long story for a different season

I have all but forgotten the terrible torture of the stairs

the beast has not changed;
it carries the same load

TIBOR

the great story is the crime unsolved

George E. Wamser

Tales from Good Medicine Lodge

Wisconsin's North Country has produced a large number of writers who have scribed with a loving hand stories about our state's abundant forests, rivers and lakes. This essay reflects a particular slice of time, directly after the 9/11/01 tragedy. 2001 was a year of huge change for me and my family because we had returned full time to the North Country after a fifteen year stint in Milwaukee. That very same week my daughter and her fiancé arrived from California to be married.

This became a tumultuous mixture of joy and sorrow, against the background of the beautiful autumnal forest at its peak, and if you'll remember, 9/11/01 was a beautiful September day with perfect blue skies, warm temps, and golden sunshine.

This essay expresses the complex feelings in my mind at that time. I was concerned about "stepping too hard on the moss" while much of the rest of the world began killing one another wholesale.

So in a way this is a historical document.

Six years and two wars later, the human beings seem to have wearied of war, but my life above the frozen tundra has been very good. My daughter and her husband have given us three fine grandchildren and live a comfortable life out west. There are no more answers today then there were six years ago, as to why 9/11/01 really happened, but, the forest...the forest...has remained faithful all along, has remained my salvation, my healer, and has accepted my words of gratitude.

Every time I return to it, it is as if I have re-entered the echo of my own wonderful dream.

Autumn Reconciled...

Late September wears,
Toward lake, earth and field,
An amber dwindled mood,
A silence scarcely stirred,
In crimson, bronze, yellow and blue,
Earths every hue entering its solitude,
Of all that summers knew,
Or autumns reconciled,
And a sense of the utmost thing...
—Leonie Adams

Last night as I drove home from work, I was delighted to see in the north a spectacular edition of the aurora, with pink and pale green curtains of light raining down on the horizon— that, and a full moon which bathed the land in its own pale luminescence. This intense combination of light allowed me to see even the colors of the leaves on the trees in a subdued shade that was almost twilight, much like the half-light of the world under an eclipse, but *full* of color. Add some ground fog, and the world became an apparition of incredible beauty.

I have learned that when Nature continues to perform for an individual, continues to *give* to an individual her great beauty and charms, day after day, it is then, you realize as the Indians did, that the physical is only the starting point for a journey into the spiritual. It is only a feeling. As easy as it is for a modern white guy like myself to be skeptical of such things and pragmatic, the feeling one gets for this "other place" is too powerful and too persistent to ignore. If living in the woods has taught me anything so far, it has made for some profound changes in my appreciation for a natural world that is a reality of many layers.

No, I'm not turning into some sort of New Age wannabe. In fact, time in the woods has sharpened my writing, hunting, daily labor and even my night vision, driving my pickup home from work in the dark, trying to avoid the critters out on the road.

I have dodged so many deer in these last six weeks that I am developing a sixth sense about their presence. This same notion has carried into observing other animals as well, as I am more aware of the habitat around me, and just as you become familiar where the bass are likely to hide in the lake, so it is with the forest around me. There are places I look for now, that are more certain to hold a flushing grouse, or a startled deer.

If there are any among you who might have toyed with the idea of living in the North Country, seeing what more time in the woods can afford you in the way of sheer experience, let me tell you it breeds a form of familiarity that is priceless. I always suspected that this was true, but never comprehended to what extent. Though it is not for everybody, if there is any way, in the future, you can swing living in the woods for a couple of months, totally immersing yourself, I recommend it highly. It will teach you subtle things about the game and plants, and the living process of the habitat, weekends here, or even one whole week, cannot.

Consequently, there is a lot of growth going on within me. Development of a sort I haven't experienced this profoundly since I was much younger, and much more immature; therefore, not as able to process that growth which cuts across the entire spectrum of my being, from my art to my politics to even my view of the subtleties of the human behavior going on around me. Let me add, however, that this is a *gentle* revolution of thought, and it is without malice or critical eye that I ponder the new world around me. In other words, I'm not standing back with an attitude, but rather, with a mild case of amazement.

In spite of the world's tragic events, I have not grown cynical, and somehow have had the brutality and senselessness of the world, balanced by this close relationship with nature. Nature has soothed me through these rough times, and this is important; it is comfort I did not *ask* for, it was offered, it was just *there*, and I was incapable of ignoring it.

At times, as the tragedy of 9/11 unfolded, I even felt a bit guilty because I was more than just okay—I was/have been *flourishing*.

Worse, against the background of a country at war...I have been at *play*.

I have succeeded in breaking my everyday routine, moved out of the context of my former life in the city and have become invisible to everyone but those who know me intimately. (And perhaps to those few who read my column.) The North Country has become my home, and my life in this new society has become my wilderness.

All this is subject to interpretation, and this task has fallen on the library of 500 odd books I carry around with me, now in my cabin, The Good Medicine Lodge, which contain the collected wisdom of all the great human beings I need as a resource, to gain understanding of almost *anything*...even terrorism. It's true I seek intellectual solace in my books, and from the minds of people like Gibran, Olsen, Merton, Vonnegut, Abby and Twain, and I can reflect on anything that concerns me from what the value of a poplar tree is, to how the Allies incinerated 100,000 people in one night over Dresden Germany. As some folks seek their answers in the Bible or the Koran, one single book, I seek references in many.

While I have been physically hiking, swimming, mountain biking, hunting, chopping wood, doing chores and working, I have been in reflection, leading a contemplative life, not just for material for these essays, but as a matter of emotional survival, and I am at better man for it.

Yesterday was the quintessential perfect autumn day; blue cloudless sky, 70 degrees, windless, dry, warm and sunny, so under the guise of grouse hunting I went a-field. On top of all this great weather, the leaf coloration is at its peak, and when that happens, the sunlight falls through the trees as if it were coming down through stained glass, dappling the forest floor in shades of amber, crimson and orange.

My first thought on entering the woods was my desire to share this perfect fall day with *everyone*. What a perfect place to walk along and chat with a friend. My second thought was of the thin veil that separates existence from non-existence, and that I was damn lucky to be here myself.

I sauntered ever so slowly to an old pine plantation, through that, up a gradual climb to a high rocky promontory.

True, the plantation was a creation of man, putting the pines in perfect rows...row upon row...but nature had long since worked her magic on this place, growing the trees to incredible size, allowing a succession of beech, hemlock and oak to invade the under story, but more importantly than that, was the forest floor itself, which had been completely overtaken by a thick, luscious carpet of moss.

Walking on the soft green moss, sprinkled with golden pine needles and fallen leaves was quite interesting; it was almost as if you were entering someone's newly carpeted living room, with your shoes on. You had to step carefully, gingerly, because some of the moss and lichens underfoot were fragile, and very old, some species perhaps having grown over decades. In a way, I felt as if I were intruding...

You do not drag your feet... you do not run...you walk softly here, carefully placing each footfall where it will do the least damage.

When I got to the top of the mountain, I found a comfortable spot overlooking the forest, a place to sit very still and quiet, to wait to see what critters might come to me.

The moss under me was warm, dry, and very comfortable.

My mind wandered to a million things, but my senses were alert to every little scrunch, squeak and rustle all about me. Soon I was visited by chickadees and nuthatches, field mice, chippies and red squirrels. The shadow of some big bird above the canopy passed across the forest floor. I sat silent for perhaps a half an hour while the forest forgot I was there, and came alive all around me.

It wasn't long before two grouse came walking up the hill towards me, and it was kind of funny, they were waddling, giving up little squeaks as they too sauntered along, and though ostensibly I was here to kill them, today; I chose to simply watch.

The grouse took a nap huddled together in a spot of sunshine next to a tall pine.

It was then I remembered that I had along, a copy of Sigurd Olsen's SONGS of the NORTH in my pocket, and pulled it out, thinking I might spend a little time with the old gentleman. I began to read a chapter entitled: "The Maker of Dreams" and from the start, his words were the perfect interpretation of what I myself have been living. So perfect, that I wish I could quote you the whole chapter in this essay. Instead, you will have to settle for bits and pieces, with the understanding that you should acquire a copy of your own.

I lay back on the soft moss, and held up the book to a sky,

that outlined its prose in clear blue…

"The study of the earth and its shaping opened up new vistas for me, and when finally I was aware of the intricate relationships of all forms of life in the north, my understanding grew to the point where I felt more at home in the woods than ever before…"

Sigurd goes on to say that his relationships with the *people* of The North Country only deepened his love of the place, by adding color, warmth, fellowship, incredible stories, adventure and hospitality as he cruised through the lakes and rivers of the Quetico-Superior country. I too, can attest to this, with a special nod to the friends I also made in Canada and Minnesota, who upon my visits there took us into their homes and treated us like gold, sharing more than food and campfire…sharing with us their life stories…which were incredibly interesting.

"…At home in the woods…" The people at Sunrise Lake are of equal quality, and exhibit the same "backwoods lifestyle" ideals that made the people of the far north so endearing. A loyalty develops among neighbors around here that isn't seen very often in urban settings.Though we often joke about the foibles of the North Country Lifestyle, in truth, we are a bit dependant upon one another, because when you live so far from town, from the nearest hospital and so on, we are wont to avail ourselves to one another's needs.

Mostly this is in the realm of helping one another with a chore, repairing a cabin roof, sinking a well or installing an electrical box, and sometimes pulling a friend's 4x4 from a mud hole that may have been just a little too deep. Often it is also in consolation of a loss, and supporting one another in good times and bad. We share food, fire and drinks and a lot of bad jokes as well. We…*live.*

"As time went on, there was a certain fullness within me, more than mere pleasure or memory, a sort of welling up of powerful emotions that somehow had to be used and directed. And so began my groping for a way of satisfying the urge I felt to do something with what I had felt and seen, a medium of ex-

pression beyond teaching those who were my companions in the wilderness, some medium that I hoped would give life and substance to thoughts and memories, a way of recapturing again, the experiences..."

—Sigurd Olsen

It is here, that Mr. Olsen decides to become a "writer" and of this sorry craft I have learned but three things: one, is the power of the incredible natural high that comes in the first thirty minutes after a writer finishes the first draft, written directly from "the heart" *before* "reality" sets in; two, all the little red marks and notes and such that my friends, teachers, critics and editors correct my work with, are really nothing more than love letters. Not necessarily love for me, but out of love and respect for the craft; three, the enormous body of a writer's entire life's work may only ask *one* single question, or make *one* solitary statement. This *relationship* between language and information is as important to me as any other aspect of life. I believe that somehow this link has some very practical use, written in a personal journal, a poem, or even an internal dialog that simply allows your own sanity a fighting chance. If anything at all, the North Country lifestyle fosters expression of free thought, clarity, an "opening up to the world" and encourages all of you who dance on the tea kettle, to *fire-up* the wood burner under it.

Along the way stop in at the cabin, and we'll share your dream over a cup of strong coffee, or floating in the old canoe fishing for bluegills...

Whatever it is inside of you, that calls you to your dream...*LISTEN*...that, and only that...is the message here.

I live my dream for all those who cannot, and in the hope you find yours.

The great sculptor Giacometti once said, in thinking about his work and his dreams:

"Art is only a means of seeing. It is as though life is always behind a curtain...the great adventure is to see in each day in the same world...something new coming forth."

Sigurd read this too and thought...

"Had I understood then what he meant, it might have

explained many things, but I did not know, for the concept of reality as he used the term was incomprehensible to a mind involved only with the visible world and personal gratification. My days and nights were filled with unanswered questions and wonderings, with trying to clarify values and give direction to my probing, and I sensed, vaguely perhaps, if I looked deeply enough into the wilderness that had satisfied so many needs, that the answers too, might come. My search was so vital to my peace of mind, that it completely engrossed me."

Peace. Peace of mind in these troubled times. And how often have you asked for a way to turn off the world's problems, for even a moment, and find a few answers, to return you to the relative peace of mind you had before September 11th? Now you can see the true damage of terrorism, and these events demand too high a price from us.

As some people find solace in their church, children and families, I find it in my forest.

This is my way…we all must find our own, all I am doing here is sharing with you the proper questions to ask…

"One day in October I was hiking in the woods when something strange happened to me, it was the first of a series of insights that would come to me over the years. It was as if the thoughts and questions I had been involved with suddenly fell into focus, and in some uncountable way, had been answered so simply and logically, I wondered why I had not know it all along …these epiphanies gave me the courage for the task ahead."

—S.O.

Courage. Courage just to get out of bed in the morning…courage to just do the right thing. For your world; and for yourself.

People e-mail me all the time and relate their personal struggles to me, and it is with the deepest appreciation, I feel it a privilege to be able to listen; one of you loses a dear brother, another a mother, others struggle to stop urban sprawl, and yet others are homesick for Wisconsin, or struggle with life threatening illnesses.

And so we share our sorrows, triumphs, struggles and

moments of pride in our children, that is what life's all about, in the sharing.

How odd it is, that sharing something as simple and mundane as chopping wood, or hiking in the woods, can become a pathway to personal survival, and beyond that, inspiration. That in recreation and leisure time wisely spent, we find a form of solace in which we become one with all of nature around us. How the forest can soothe grief, and bring us closer to our concept of creation, provide a form of companionship and community with life, that few in our modern world understand. That in the pause of a silent pine filled glen, we can find the courage and more importantly, the prescience of mind, to carry on.

If there is any utopia at all here in the woods, it comes from within, because it is you who must take that first step... outward bound.

I put the book down and smiled, after thinking all these things, and appreciated what a truly great friend Sigurd has been to me all these years, sharing his life with me in his books, even though I never met the man in the flesh.

It was then I realized that I had rolled over on my belly on the soft moss carpet and was at eye level on the forest floor and it was as comfortable and clean as any living room deep pile carpeting. Below me lay a tiny forest of hundreds of different plants, some like miniature pine trees, other lichens shaped like bugles, pale green and thrusting up from the tapestry of this miniature world.

A field mouse scampered nearby, and a chickadee landed on the barrel of my shotgun, resting on a log. I get tremendous satisfaction when the forest forgets I'm here, because its life goes on without my intrusion. I like being still and almost invisible, reading a book helps accomplish that, because I too, leave the scene for awhile, lost in Sigurd's world...

I departed the forest that day, wondering if I could properly express it all.

While writing this later in the cabin, the Winter-hawk arrived on the wings of a powerful cold-front with 35mph winds that dropped the temperature from 70 degrees to 40 in a matter of a few gusts. The sun disappeared and the leaves began flying. I stepped out of the cabin, and for the first time this season I realized that enough leaves had accumulated to send from the forest floor, the sweet aroma of their decay.

And it was *good*.

I fired up the crackling wood burner, and huddled next to its warmth ... reconciling autumn's sense of the utmost important things.

Debra Fitzgerald

The Properties of Light

The book I thought I was writing when I began The Properties of Light *in the summer of 2000 is not the book I'm now writing. I've met many characters, mediated dozens of scenes, written hundreds of pages, before dawn broke and revealed the characters in the opening scenes of this book.*

A couple things remained constant throughout my gracious and strange grapplings with the blank page. Characters have always collided across dualistic southwest and northeast settings; and the heroine, Magdalene Salgado McGregor, has always finagled the 'paste' with the 'cut' function, or escaped the irrevocable erasure of the deletion key.

I began this novel thinking it would be 'about' ideas, values and nuanced reflection. But I've come to know Magdalene, and that's not what she's 'about.' She's not much given to rumination. Her propulsion comes from external events rather than internal, emotional hand-wringing. So this won't be a novel where nothing much happens, I believe. I have a dim understanding of 'what' that might be, but she, or others, may still surprise me yet.

So far, it's been an active journey. Here, I hope you enjoy the beginning of that trip.

This is the sound of grief: the creak of a bed spring as she rises from the sheetless mattress and stares out the window down the empty curve of dirt road. She hears the dead calm of a live hawk perched in a mesquite tree, the whimper of a yellow puppy pacing anxious circles on the cracked stoop of an adobe bungalow. A man curses beneath a battered gray sedan lifted on concrete blocks in his gravel drive, and an abandoned candy wrapper tumbles across the gas station parking lot across the road. She returns to the bed. The absence spins out, the smell of fresh paint lingers. Beside her ankles: a bulging suitcase and backpack. She lights a cigarette, inhales, places a hand between pressed-together knees. She doesn't realize she's crying. White bandages wrap her forearms and her dark brown hair cuts close to her skull. The past is her only nourishment now; she's become slight as a whisper, her long slender neck too fragile to bear the weight of a human head. Only her astonishing blue eyes appear heavy — lashless, stippled with gold, feeding upon memory.

A blue neon sign flickers on above the gas station across the road and the bells from the distant church singe the air with the first of the hour's seven chimes. She exhales smoke from her lungs and rises again to stand before the window. Aurelia will be there now, reliably filling the empty curve in the packed dirt road, as constant as the speed of light racing west to leave the day in darkness. Her eyes will be pinned upon the ground, a plastic bag in each hand anchoring her amble up the hill. The ritual was born of childhood and grown to habit, but still: most evenings, she would wait for Aurelia to return from her job at the diner, watch Aurelia's distant face move closer with each climbing step, her cheeks that had dropped to soft jowls, her black and white curls that never stayed in place. She watches her mother silently until Aurelia looks up, sees her at the window, and tired, patient, enduring, smiles.

A freight train rumbles from the bottom of the canyon behind the gas station. She touches her hand to the warm, vibrating glass. Her face changes from blue to shadow, blue to shadow, in time with the blinking neon. Everything has changed. The puppy's disappeared, the hawk flown away, the candy wrapper impaled on a cactus by the pay phone. The man smokes a cigarette while contemplating whatever's broken beneath the hood. The long shadow he stands upon vanishes, with Aurelia, before she can climb the stairs. The sun drops behind the ancient purple mountains and the sky burns red and orange.

She takes a last pull on her cigarette as the train speeds away and the metal clanking stops and the whistle grows faint at a remote crossing, then dies. She stubs the cigarette on the windowsill, pressing the butt with her thumb into the still damp paint. She turns from the window for the last time. She slings the heavy backpack over her shoulder, lifts the suitcase. The flap her leather sandals make on the wood floor echoes in the empty bedroom, the empty kitchen. She selects the keys from a painted nail below a mirror. She briefly notices tears on her cheeks. She does not turn around before she leaves the house, before she shuts the door, before she wonders: crying has become impersonal.

***

Her name was Magdalene Salgado McGregor: Salgado for her mother, who was now gone, but part of all her memories; McGregor for a father she never knew. There were stories, always Aurelia's lilting stories. "You'll never know him, but…" Aurelia would say, before speaking of a man named Michael McGregor who had snatched Aurelia's heart like a petty thief when her long dark braid still danced in the sculpted space of her lower back. The stories came piecemeal like dreams at various times throughout her life, smoky vignettes of another time and place when Aurelia was young in a northern California town cleaning rooms at the Larchwood Inn. Michael McGregor arrived with the monarchs before winter, migrating down from a northern cattle ranch to lead customers on trail rides through hills of Monterey Pine. Aurelia shyly deflected his flirtations; he persisted. When she grew bold enough to look him in the eyes, she accepted his invitation for dinner. But Michael McGregor would leave. And when he did, Aurelia pinned up her youthful braid close to her head and followed work to Tucson, with Magdalene growing inside her.

"You'll never know him, but…"

As she grew, Magdalene more than believed her: 'father' was an abstract concept that had nothing to do with her everyday world.

Then came the final story of Michael McGregor while driving to Mrs. Purcell's cabin in the foothills where the 90-year-old woman lived alone. Magdalene drove, Aurelia in the passenger seat beside her holding the book she would read to Mrs. Purcell and a package of ginger cookies with white icing the old woman liked to dip in tea. It was an ordinary Wednesday evening of their ordinary lives. Magdalene would drop Aurelia off then take the dirty laundry in the backseat to Clara's Clean-up. She'd shop for the small list of grocery items between the wash and dry cycles, then retrieve her mother from Mrs. Purcell's. The voices on the talk radio show crackled in and out as they climbed the snaky road. The frequency caught and held in Mrs. Purcell's driveway. Instead of getting out of the jeep, Aurelia turned up the volume on the radio. The Republican Senator from Arizona was being interviewed. Aurelia leaned in, listening intently, dangling from his voice as if it were the only thing holding her from falling off a cliff. The book on her lap slid to the floor.

"Mrs. Purcell isn't totally blind yet, is she?" Magdalene asked. It was not yet dark, but dusky enough for lights and Mrs. Purcell's cabin was dark.

"Shuuusshhh!" Aurelia said. But then the interview ended. She remained leaning forward, as if more would come. The interviewer broke from a commercial and announced another program to follow. Aurelia turned off the radio and picked up the book from the floor and placed it upon her lap again. She smoothed the shiny cover with her hand.

Magdalene flicked on the headlights. Cold wet dust danced in circles in the beams of light. She glanced down at her cell phone on the seat beside her, but it gave up nothing. She drummed her thumbs on the steering wheel

"I'll pick you up at nine?"

"I've always told you you will never know your father."

Filtered through the silence of her phone, her chores seemed monotonous, her evening tedious: laundry, groceries, a paper due tomorrow. Taxi her mother. And curiosity about her father had long passed.

"Yes, you've told me that."

"How I cleaned rooms at the Larchwood Inn."

"And dined at a small restaurant at the end of the pier, and ate mussels and watched sea lions bobbing in the water."

Aurelia turned to her daughter.

"It is not right that you will never know your father," she said. The wetness in her mother's eyes surprised Magdalene. Her mother let her head fall back against the seat and closed her eyes and when she exhaled, she breathed words born from memory, from dreams: of that fat-mooned night in a California town beneath a grove of blue gum eucalyptus; of those thousands of monarch butterflies clustered in the trees, 50,000 pair of orange, black-tipped wings gilding the branches.

"That's where you became," Aurelia said, later, after dinner, when they'd walked beneath the butterflied trees. Michael McGregor had spread his coat that smelled of horses and cattle and the dust of endless plains. They made love with the soul-bird trees pulsing above them, with their bodies bathed by the scent of eucalyptus, the moonlight's specter breath.

Michael McGregor left in the spring with the clouds of Monarch butterflies taking flight for distant lands. But the monarchs would return. They had inherited a genetic memory while they were caterpillars eating milkweed pods, that they had retained even when their heads dropped off and their skin split, their bodies convulsing in cocoons that smelled of wild parsley and eucalyptus. Somehow, they would pass on to their descendents in future generations the memory of an over-winter grove thousands of miles away, sometimes even the exact tree.

"So, what you're saying is all it took was a bowl of mussels and a bunch of butterflies and you're flat on your back on a smelly coat," Magdalene said.

Aurelia opened her eyes and turned her head toward her daughter. The wetness in her eyes had vanished. She smiled. But the dust had already turned to spits of northern rain, and later, Magdalene would remember how she had noticed for the wrong reasons that Mrs. Purcell's cabin was dark; how her past experience had mislead her to false impressions.

"Children conceived at midnight have wonderful, mysterious natures," Aurelia said, poking Magdalene in the rib before gathering her coat more tightly around her and opening the passenger side door.

"Then maybe you should have slept with him before dinner."

Aurelia tipped her head and laughed, her somber mood parted like sunshine through rain. She lifted herself heavily from the seat by bracing her arm on the frame of the jeep. She readjusted the book and cookies in her arms and waved her hand behind her after slamming the door. Magdalene watched her mother walk toward the cabin, head bent against the bits of rain that had turned to small grains of ice. Later, she would remember the unseasonable cold, the extraordinary forecast of snow in October in the foothills of Tucson, but now, she turned the radio back on, and backed out of the long drive and had traveled only partly down the switchback road when Mrs. Purcell's cabin exploded on the ridge above her like a dying sun, and in that blazing, canted light, time stopped. First, Aurelia was alive, sitting beside her in the jeep, talking about being breathed on by eucalyptus and moonlight, and then Magdalene was standing before a burning cabin with no knowledge of how she'd traveled from one place in time to the other. The events were not causally related, but disconnected across space, and on this different plane where she suddenly found herself, the habit of her mother's existence was in danger of being broken. She understood nothing else about this new place, not the properties of fire or smoke, not the heat on her skin, not the hands upon her, the shouting, the smells of smoke and water and burned hair, the screaming sirens that matched the wails coming from inside her chest. Then she was on another plane with fluorescent lighting and hospital beds, swatting like flies that swarmed her ears the explanations of uniformed strangers. There had been a gas leak in the propane burner. Perhaps Mrs. Purcell was already dead. It could have been after Aurelia entered the house and walked across the floor, when she removed her coat and the fibers crackled, igniting the dry, gassy air. They would never know for certain.

Her concept of 'father' would be forever after welded with destruction, not creation; death, not life.

* * *

The remains of their life fit into the two bags in the backseat of their rust-pocked jeep. The key in the ignition tried to turn the engine over and over, then quit. The unseasonable cold had lifted and the cry of a lone wolf echoed off the sun-vanished mountains in the still, hot air. The skin beneath the bandages on her arms itched. She had not returned to the hospital or changed the thin gauze in the two weeks since her mother's death and now she unwound the bandage of one arm. She yanked the gauze where it stuck to the palm-sized burn, and freely scratched the yellow scabbed skin until it shone with fresh pus and pain. She rewrapped the wound and winced pressing the gauze to her skin, repeated the process with her other arm, and when she was

244

through refreshing the sting to match the burn in her heart, she pushed the clutch to the floor, shifted into neutral, released the emergency break, and coasted down the steep drive, moving away from the house on the hill, remembering how he told her how she could remain, "At a reduced rate." How she told him she'd rather live in her jeep. She eased off the clutch, tapped the gas, and the jeep coughed and jerked to life. She steered down the road toward the diner where she would rescue the last of her mother's things. Beyond that, she had no idea where she was going, no plan, no future, no direction…

The brass bells jingled when she pushed through the diner's front door. Mr. Nimkar looked up from the cash register and the Ferrel twins sitting upon short, swivel stools at the counter, turned their identical, red-bearded faces toward her. Their thick, mitt-like hands dwarfed their cups of coffee, and heir blue hooded sweatshirts were covered with asphalt dust. She threw the house keys down and they skittered across the counter, stopping at Mr. Nimkar's greasy hand, but she kept her eyes on the twins who had always been kind to her mother, and had treated Magdalene with no less respect than anyone could expect to receive from decent human beings.

"It's not the same without her," and, "sorry about your Mom," the twins said, and she acknowledged their gestures with a nod, grateful for their presence, and briefly pressed their shoulders when she walked past them into the storeroom. She flipped on the fluorescent light. There, before the stacked cases of soda and canned goods, was a card table covered with a midnight blue tablecloth appliquéd with gold stars and silver moons. Upon this table, a clean white teacup, a glass decanter of loose tea, white paper doilies. Aurelia had read customers' leaves for $10 when she wasn't too busy waitressing tables or busing dishes or doing all she could to keep the diner running and Mr. Nimkar away. Magdalene stood before the table, smoothing the cloth with her hands, sliding her fingers around the rim of the cup when she felt Mr. Nimkar behind her. She grabbed the cup and the tea and the doilies then folded the tablecloth into a square and turned with loaded arms. Mr. Nimkar held an envelope in his hands. His nose was as oily as it had always been. She took a step backwards.

"I don't know what else you expected me to do," he said. She

watched him turn the envelope around and around in his hands
and in the antiseptic air she could smell his always too close
breath that always smelled like bologna and she brought the
tablecloth closer to her nose by hugging it closer to her chest.

"I never expected anything from you," she said.

His sneer was a dead smile, his brown eyes slippery.

"They pay for your school, they would pay for a dorm room."

"I've left school."

The Ferrel twins called out something and then the brass
bells on the front door jingled and the store was silent with their
leaving. She faced Mr. Nimkar for what seemed a long time. The
square fluorescent ceiling light hummed like a trapped insect.

"What are you going to do?" He asked.

She lowered her head and started past him. He took hold of
her arm. She shook him off and the clean white cup fell from her
arms and shattered on the floor. Neither one of them moved. He
shrugged and looked down at the envelope in his hands then held
it out to her as if he'd read instructions on the flap and told him
what to do.

"This was hers for the week. And some extra," he said.

When she didn't reach for it, he said, "Your pride, it will eat
you like a poison. Your mother—she knew this about you."

Her delicate face remained impassive and she did not let her
gaze stray from Mr. Nimkar's eyes, his hands.

"This is business, Magdalene. It has never supposed to be
personal."

She quickly shifted her bundle into one hand and grabbed the
envelope and stuffed it into the back pocket of her jeans and
brushed past him while words still oozed from his mouth. She set
her mother's things down on the counter and removed two cartons of cigarettes from a slot and reached for a lighter while staring at Mr. Nimkar framed in the storeroom light. She placed the
cigarettes upon her mother's things and shoved the lighter into
her front pocket and left the store, the brass bells ringing. The
night sky was black now and she stared at the stars, envying their
constantly burning state and thought of all the things that could
and would change, Mr. Nimkar's nose would always be oily and
his breath would always smell foul and the world would always be
divided into two groups of people: those who made things happen,

and those who allowed things to happen.

She set her mother's things on the passenger seat, left the door open and walked to the side of the store, her sandals cutting the pebbly dirt like knives. She stood behind the dumpster where she couldn't be seen and removed the envelope from her back pocket. Five $100 bills. She pulled the lighter from her pocket and held the flame below the edge of the envelope. Her hands shook. The flame jumped onto the paper, the bills, and she walked back to the diner and when the money was nearly all burnt and irrecoverable, she opened the door and threw it on the floor. She'd always thought there was time to make him pay for the lines etched in Aurelia's forehead but inaction had become a habit, and this one defiant act pitiful and small and quickly stamped out beneath Mr. Nimkar's heel. He wagged his head and turned his back, and she realized she'd made a mistake. Their house, his house, the house they'd always rented from him, freshly painted over for the new lives who didn't want to be re-minded of the lives that came before: a cigarette butt and thumb-print wasn't enough. She ran back to the jeep and started the ignition. The sound of metal scraped on metal as the ignition choked and died, choked and died, then finally caught. She wheeled out of the parking lot and hesitated at the road. She could see the lights of Tucson shattered across the valley like shards of clean white glass and in her hesitation, something was decided.

***

Coincidence: a remarkable concurrence of events or circum-stances without apparent causal connection; a correspondence of occurrence in nature or in time. It happens all the time for those awake to the possibility—or for those, perhaps, who require awakening. Like Feature. So-named by a blogo-rag on account of his ability to live entertainment-worthy stories that embarrassed his family. The name had evolved into print and stuck, at least among his friends, and now here he was: post bang-up from a mountain bar, and from Sue, who was as generous with herself as she was with the tequila. Sue or Cindy—he couldn't remember which, but it definitely wasn't 'Rebecca,' and neither did those long legs to her neck belong to his fiancée. He needed a story, but he couldn't even piece together what did happen. He banged his forehead on the pump over and over trying to clear his raging hang-over as his Mercedes filled with gas for the final journey down to the city, trying to fill those insanely dark spaces in his head with images of retained memory. Like that guy in the bar, the shots and back slaps and teeth constantly exposed in a stretched smile: had he been a photographer or a tourist with a camera? Not that it mattered. Either one could be equally dangerous, and without a story, he was a tequila shot away from losing more than Rebecca. His father, if asked, would sternly enact before the cameras the serious press releases crafted by his earnest staff. Meanwhile, behind the scenes, it was his mother who would banish his ass to some fucking Tupperware country like Albania.

Then she appeared, a girl with long bandaged arms. She scraped a plastic gas jug across the blacktop. She yanked the arm from the pump, and pressed the gas pump buttons like a travel agent on a keyboard searching for the fastest ticket out. The electronic pump finally clicked, and she pressed the nozzle into the gas can, folding over from the hips, as if she didn't have time for resistance from bone or muscle. She wore short , bristly hair that looked like it had been hacked off with a serrated knife; a birthmark on the side of her long neck matched the color of her hair. Her thin camisole shirt fell away from her body and her breasts were larger than he would have expected for such a slight frame. He smiled, alert now, a moment of clarity.

"Do you need some help? Out of gas?" he offered.

She jumped as if startled to learn she was not alone, even though he was standing maybe three feet away. Her pupils visibly widened as she focused on him with the surprised alarm of a feral animal. Then she dismissed him completely with the turn of her back, her hands fumbling with the plastic screw cap. She lifted the container and practically jogged away from him, her eyes averted, her arm out and body slightly tipped to balance the weight of the gas. Her bandages grew luminescent and ghostly blue in the neon the further she moved away. He was not used to being snubbed by women, and he felt his face flush with irritation. She wasn't that pretty.

"You're welcome for asking!" he yelled after her.
Little did he know: he'd just found his story.

***

Benjamin Bonner was too young to understand what Sara
meant when she tapped the side of his head and said, "What
makes us different and special is in here, not outside." His eyes
were his father's, green with thick lashes and brows resembling
thunderclouds over island seas, and he had his mother's dark
curls. But his right cheekbone was caved in, as if he'd been delivered wearing a baseball mitt, and his right eye was slightly lower.
As he grew older and his facial bones developed, the cheek would
fill out, giving him the slightly roguish look of a boxer who'd
taken too many hits in the ring. Girls would not find this unat-
tractive, but for now, the taunts of 'Bent' on the school playground caused him to move around in the world with his head
down, as if trying to grip an apple with his chin and right shoulder. By default, his gaze landed on his school books.

"It's what he intended for you," Sara would say, nodding at
the Jesus icon above the refrigerator, her voice as thick as the
furze of dust covering the plastic idol. Sara accepted her son's
face, as God's will, just Laundromats, daily hangovers. His Aunt
Lilly had her own theory. She told Ben his face had been hard-
bitten by grief. When Sara was pregnant with Ben, his father fell
off an eight-story scaffolding and smashed his head on the concrete below.

"The grief just ate her up inside," Aunt Lilly said over the
fried bologna and macaroni and cheese she made for him when
Sara worked overtime at the shoe factory, or didn't come home at
all. Aunt Lilly had lost an eyetooth when she was younger, but re-
sorted to superglue rather than face her fear of dentists. Years of
daily use had spread and hardened the glue like a cast across the
surrounding teeth giving her a paper mache smile and a slight lisp
when she read to Ben until the streetlights came on. An ashtray
balanced on her knee, she blew big, loopy smoke rings between
pages of Ivanhoe and The Three Musketeers. Dreaming about
knights and chivalry and shining armor, Ben thought himself
noble to have fed his mother's grief with half his face. But it

hadn't been enough; her grief hadn't been sated. Each morning before work, Sara wrapped white surgical tape around her fingers to prevent callouses, and gray electrical tape around her forearms for her tendonitis, before heading to the shoe factory to cover naked shoe heels with square pieces of Moroccan leather. He would pour his mother a shot of whiskey when she came home from work at the end of the day, which filled-in some of the lines on her face, but when Ben talked to her about school, her eyes remained unfocused and empty, even after she removed the earplugs she wore to stamp out the noise of the factory machines. He would unwrap the tape from her fingers and forearms. He would hold his breath until he saw that everything was still attached.

The taunts disappeared in high school, but so did he. Rather than slink invisibly along brick walls during lunch hours and free periods, he disappeared into bathroom stalls, a brown paper towel on his lap, eating crackers and spreadable cheese, his fingers salting the thin pages of his schoolbooks. The summer after junior year, he shot up to six foot two. When he returned to school, his shoulders grazed the walls of the bathroom stalls and the toilets seemed lower. He lunch slid from his knees to his lap when he opened a book. He stared at the ceiling, wondering where he could go now that he'd outgrown the stalls. He flushed the paper towel down the toilet and later that day, joined the basketball team, trading the cramped stall for the high-windowed space of the gym. He wasn't an athlete, but he felt like one when he pulled the uniform shirt over his head. All his lunch hours and free periods he spent dribbling, shooting, sweating. Frankie Sullivan, his coach, noticed his commitment, his perseverance, but when he released Ben from the bench, Ben shambled down the court trying to control the ball, a tangle of long limbs and loose angles.

"You've got tenacity and focus," Frankie told him, "a good frame." Besides being the basketball coach, Frankie was a chemistry teacher and a former Mr. Massachusetts. He had an ash-colored goatee, a solid gold eyetooth, and the jerky, lopsided walk of a man putting off a hip replacement.

"You need some muscle on those bones, though," Frankie said.

That Saturday morning, Frankie parked his car in front of a

gray shingle house on the rundown section of Washington Street just as the sun began to rise above the iron railroad bridge spanning the Merrimack River. A breeze swung a black and white "Tommy's Gym" sign on steel hinges. Hardened autumn leaves scraped the sidewalk. Ben followed Frankie down the stairs of reinforced concrete to a door with a six-paned window that had been painted black.

"This is where the big boy's play," Frankie said.

Ben stepped into a long room humid with sweat. Frankie led him to the showers and lockers in the back. Everywhere he looked there were men with skin-busting muscles, thick necks, popped tendons and veins. The mirrors were flecked with saliva, snot, blood. The thinly carpeted floor vibrated with slamming metal and bowel-deep, faced-clenched groans. Frankie gave him a leather belt with his name written in black marker on the suede inside—B. Bonner—and said, "It looks physical, but it's not. It's all up here, in your head." Ben recognized his mother's words and met Frankie's with a sinking in his stomach that felt like despair: it wasn't what was inside that was deficient, that needed building-up. He gave it a shot anyway and soon quit the basketball team. He worked out before school every morning on a strict schedule for the next two years. Doing dips with the mirror a foot away from his face, lifting himself on lateral bars, a chain attached to his leather belt, twenty pounds of iron strapped to the chain, he learned that both his mother and Frankie were right. His arms and shoulders quivered, a clean sweat soaked his hair and T-shirt. Shaking with fatigue he pushed himself further, worked beyond the burn of lactic acid and blood building to where goose bumps traveled up his chest and arms and the top of his head lifted off.

It became a habit to use his mind to push his body beyond its physical limits, to a transcendent place full of clarity, power, a place he took with him when he left the gym, when he left Massachusetts to attend college in Tucson on a full scholarship, when he got a part-time job at a gas station across the road from Magdalene Salgado McGregor. The first time she walked into the store while he was working, she bought a pack of cigarettes. The last time, she changed his life.

***

The smoldering remains of the former Salgado residence fueled the air of carnival excitement, lifting all the voices of the neighborhood as waves beneath wind, one dying as another rose. The young people, their restlessness propelled out of the typical boredom of their foothill life, actively loitered on the edges of the parking lot and the neon-blue glare of the gas station light, the stark florescence of the overheads illuminating the pumps. The boy-men leaned against shiny-painted cars or reclined on racing-striped hoods, trying to impress the young girls, who showed white teeth and smooth skin in clingy tops and tight jeans. Car stereos blasted and brown-bagged bottles were freely passed. The adults had brought the insides of their houses outside. The men smoked and played cribbage at two kitchen tables set beneath the mesquite tree. The light of their thick candles stubs set in pie plates threw spindly impressions of the branches upon the ground. The women congregated on frayed couches and folding chairs in semi-darkness around a bare mattress where a pile of children slept in their underwear. As the moon ascended over the hills opposite the ancient mountains, they remembered with self-satisfied voices the woman who had materialized from the high-altitude air with a blue-eyed child, no husband, and a perfect English tongue. They had lived apart from the neighborhood in their wood-framed, lavender-painted house on the hill. And on what: waitress pay? They clucked and snorted with low tongues and breath now that Aurelia was dead. A couple women made the sign of the cross. But no other end could be expected, they decided, for a woman who had paid Aurelia Salgado's price to live in a house aimed at the mountain tops.

***

Inside the gas station, Ben tried to overhear the local conversations, but he hadn't worked there long and they didn't trust him. He looked into their eyes when he took their money and gave back change, but they thanked him, and took their talk outside the store, sitting on plastic chairs that had once been for sale. They left him to pace behind the counter, to try not to look at the burned house across the street when his pacing returned him again and again to the plate-glass window. He tried to remember another time when he might have felt uneasy and nervous to this degree so that he might also remember how he had overcome these feelings. But what had happened would of course have no precedent in his experience. He'd always minded his own business, followed the rules.

"You're out."

A man held up two empty coffee pots from the burners aside the cappuccino and slushy machines. Ben turned from the window, alarmed that he hadn't been aware of anyone in the store. He told himself he'd have to get better at this as he moved from behind the counter, slid open a cabinet door below the coffee machine, pulled out two filters and prepackaged packets of coffee, and dumped the coffee into the filters. He poured water into the coffee pots, swirled it around, emptied them. He slid the filter back into the coffee machine and hit the brew button, said, "Three minutes."

He crumpled the empty coffee bags and shot them into the wastebasket. On the radio, Tom Petty sang, "You don't—have—to live like a refugee."

"You work last night?"

The man had followed him back to the counter, the heels of his cowboy boots clacking across the tiled floor. His black cowboy hat was pushed low on his brow and a sculpted nose rose from shadowed eyes and below that, a dark bushy mustache striated with white hair nearly that covered his lips when he wasn't talking.

"Who wants to know?"

The man flipped open his wallet and flashed a badge then closed it and slid it back into a pocket of is faded jean jacket. How was I to know, Ben thought; how was I to know.

"Yeah, I worked," he said. He drummed his forefingers on the counter to drown the thrumming in his chest.

"You know her?"

The detective pulled a picture from his front pocket and laid it down on the counter then put his hands back in his pockets and watched Ben. The picture had been taken when her hair was still a forest of dark curls. She was smiling. He couldn't believe she was the same person who had come in last night, gaunt, red-rimmed, hollow eyes, short choppy hair. The bandages wrapping her arms were dingy and frayed.

"You run out of gas?" he'd asked. She'd been looking out the window toward her house, her eyes hollow and large with a blue that blew him away ever since she first came into the store for a pack of cigarettes.

"I'll take three dollars and this," she said, referring to the plastic gas can with her chin. She tried a smile, but it failed and she swallowed hard. He wanted to touch the soft pockets below her collar bones that deepened when she reached for her wallet. He grazed her fingers while taking her money and she visibly stiffened. She back-pocketed the wallet with her change, scraping the plastic fuel can along the counter, not meeting his eyes. Then she was gone.

"No," Ben said. "I don't know her."

"You've never seen her before?"

"No, I've seen her. She lived across the road. I just didn't know her."

"How about last night—did you see her last night?"

The detective slid the picture off the counter and slipped it back into his side pocket and when he removed his hand again, it contained a stick of gum, and Ben thought: smooth. While the detective spoke he unwrapped the gum and casually popped it into his mouth. It was impossible to know how to play this, Ben thought. Had they found the plastic gas container she bought or did she burn it with the house? He should have asked her these questions. He should have been alert enough to know that he'd have to ask her these questions.

"I don't think she came in last night. I can't remember. It's a busy place."

The detective glanced around the empty store, dragging his eyes away from Ben's face as if it cost him great effort.

The detective punched a speed dial into his cell phone as he drove out of the gas station parking lot to the diner at the bottom of the dirt road.

"He knows where she is," he said.

He listened to the voice at the other end.

"Yes," he said, then clapped the phone flip shut.

He cut the ignition in the parking lot of the diner and walked in, setting the brass bells ringing. Heads turned from two of the red vinyl booths and one person at the counter. The detective stood with his hands in his pockets before a wire display set by the cash register. The diners returned to their plates of food. He removed a hand from his pocket and bounced a long finger off several packets of gum before selecting one.

"Go get the tray of glasses," Mr. Nimkar said to a waitress in a pale pink uniform, hustling her away from the register where she had been waiting to take the detective's money. Mr. Nimkar motioned outside with his eyes as he gave the detective change and the detective left the diner out the front door, Mr. Nimkar out the back, carrying a plastic bag of garbage. They met at the garbage bin. Mr. Nimkar tossed the bundle into the bin, startling a cat that leapt to the rim of the steel container, tail twitching, green eyes aglow. The cat dropped to the ground and bounded off into the night beyond the reach of the floodlight above the door.

The detective pulled a thick envelope from the inside pocket of his jean jacket, and handed it to Mr. Nimkar.

"No insurance claim," the detective said.

"Yes, but I can do nothing about the cops. They will investigate," Mr. Nimkar said, spreading the envelope and thumbing through the bills.

"That's not for you to worry about."

Mr. Nimkar shrugged, satisfied, and turned from the detective, shoving the envelope into the pocket of a stained white apron tied low beneath his paunch.

"She was supposed to stay in the house," the detective said.

Mr. Nimkar turned, his hand on the backdoor knob.

"I told her so. But what could I do: she's a proud girl. Perhaps, like her father?"

He pulled open the door and disappeared inside and flicked off the floodlight, plunging the detective in darkness. Cicadas snickered in tufts of desert grass.

The gas sloshed in the plastic jug when she shifted the jeep into gear. She'd left the engine running but didn't turn on the headlights. Focused on the driveway, and the house on the hill, she gunned the accelerator across the parking lot, the dirt road, and up the incline of the driveway. She hadn't screwed the cap on correctly. The dry light residue of gas coated her hands and bandages. The smell infused the jeep's interior. She cranked the emergency brake into place and cut the engine. From the rear-view mirror, she could have seen the Mercedes still parked alongside the pump, and Feature walking out of the store, absently inserting bills into his wallet, his eyes focused on the jeep at the top of the driveway across the street. She could have seen, Ben standing at the window, arms crossed across his body, chewing on a coffee stirrer. But Magdalene didn't look before she stepped down from the jeep crossed around its front, yanked open the passenger side door and lifted the gas tank from the floor where the spilled gas created inky blots on the worn gray carpeting.

She returned to her knapsack. She'd cleaned out the post office box when she closed it out, nearly two weeks worth of mail. She sorted through this now, found a newspaper circular, then shoved the remaining envelopes into her knapsack. She returned to the porch, and crumbled a sheet of the paper into a torch, lit it, and threw it onto the porch. She stepped back, mesmerized by the slow creep of the flame as it fanned out across the porch. She tripped over a thin pine root and fell back. She raised herself upon her elbows on her back and watched the flame jump onto the railings she used to climb as a child, envelope the porch swing, lick the roof. She could feel the burn on her body, but couldn't rise. She was clearly visible now. The heat excited her. She became conscious of the light and rose, stumbling backward then turning to run back to the jeep. She fumbled with the keys as a flame shot up through the roof of the porch and danced on the outer wall. The engine wouldn't turn over. She released the emergency break, intending, if she had any intentions, to back down the drive and then jump start once she positioned the car down the dirt road. But she couldn't keep her eyes off the flames, out it slowly consumed the house, and she glided backwards unconscious of the motion until she felt the jeep lurch backwards off a slope of the drive. She slammed on the breaks but the jeep was in a free fall off the small embankment. She gripped the steering wheel, trying to hold on, when the jeep crashed into a tree and came to rest, nestled in a crook of the embankment of the road and the drive. She uselessly tried to turn over the engine, knowing that if it did start she still wouldn't be able to unwedge the jeep from where it had come to rest. She reached over the back, grabbed her knapsack and suitcase, frantic now, and exited the jeep. The fire now roared, engulfing the small house like a dry piece of kindling, snapping, hissing, throwing off heat.

Ben is there. He grabs her things, they jog across the parking lot. Preserve that scene when he puts her beneath the cabinet. Feature watches the whole thing, disbelieving his eyes. He doesn't want to get involved. Later, when she goes to the attorney's office, he sees her in the waiting room. She looks nothing like the picture they have plastered on the evening news and with dark glasses on, she unrecognizable. But she recognizes him. He sees the flames as he travels down the hill. He can see it in his rear-view mirror. He slams on the breaks, disbelieving his eyes, he thinks about turning the car around in the middle of the road—if he does, he can tell what he saw, what he knows. But if he's there, he'll have to explain why he was on this remote mountain road, coming down from the mountains, at that time of the evening, and where was he the night before? He can't do that; he's got to come up with a story that explains his absence and it can't include being at this gas station.

Ben doesn't know who might have seen. He doesn't recall seeing anyone around from the neighborhood, but the houses have eyes and he can't be sure. They know everything, while knowing nothing. They don't trust the cops more than they don't trust him and he can't imagine.

Marina Pilar Gipps

Sometimes I slip away. Floating between persons and places,
I search the migratory waves of existence for words: musical
notes, brushstrokes, perhaps celluloid clips of memory–attempting
to portray more than the ordinary in this extraordinary world. As a
writer, I feel that bizarre turns on the street are worthy of investi-
gation—and that your ' typical' souls are not your usual suspects.
The following poems are from a collection, The Hackneyed Road
Narrows.

GREETING

Everyday another word

tugs on my shoulder.

I don't know if it's

hello or *goodbye.*

WHY MY POEM EXISTS

Nothing is more accessible than *a poem*.
Me and the lonely line that needs another.
Our quiet contemplation of the world without us
under a dim lamplight at dusk,
preparing to sleep for the inevitable dream.
We eat rice and beans to stay alive.
We are the only ones who befriend rats.
We are the patron saints of the homeless.
We live for the love of stanzas in little rooms,

huddled close as one line begets another,
the loneliness dissipating temporarily.
And so I am in this old house with no family—
only my poems who find me alien.

DRINKING THIS POEM
(for Vincent McGroary)

Truth, as we see it, is *fiction*.
Befriending bottle, wine spills,
letters from no one and from
someone—strewn;
i hold myself.

i cannot answer
your words for mine
are being taken
by this poem

right now

i feel blind
as the dog on the street,
blue night air of a dream.
It is cold, the dog emaciated.

Howling at a potential moon,
though no light
would show through.
i am this dog.
The voice enters me.

And the vision that was lost
is felt in the colors
of touch, of smell.
These tones, too,
overturning with time.

When the bottle is empty,
the pen is no longer fluid.
And the walls of the sky come to a close.

THERE'S SOMETHING SEXUAL ABOUT A YAWN.

It climaxes and goes nowhere
but into the thin air.

And I think the air keeps it,
and remembers it
when we don't.

Like the time I went driving
nowhere in a car
and didn't quite think,
until this week, about it.

When the car was gone,
and the ride-*over.*

THE SECRET LIFE OF PHILODENDRONS

*'All flowers talk to me and do hundreds of little living things
in the woods.'* —George Washington Carver, agricultural chemist

In the evening, you were told as a child,
to *keep plants out of your room.*
They would *suck up oxygen,*
the air that feeds you when all the sorry world
had closed her eyes to sleep.

You had become suspicious thereafter of evenings,
even those twinkling in their pinafores of stars—
for if you had not heard such lore

the peacefulness of bodies would have been more tolerable;
sitting up in your room, feeling for the vines of your open arms.

You were like that chaste philodendron attached to a lie detector,
violent in her suspicions; a reaction when an expert sought to
burn
one of her leaves. O dear god of botany,
show me the light of this life-sucking greenness:
a single thought reduced to the revelation of a microscope.

Listen to the sound-wave detectors,
the proof in the numerals of dreams—
green digits of the continuum speaking
of how the roots disembowel further
the blackness of the earth—

why a single impulse from your beloved philodendron
can activate a car two-and-a-half miles away;
the true reason you are wary of the well-kept garden,
its countless dead strewn in a basket.
Things grow, you say snipping with the prowess
of a hairdresser deep into the night.

And we are here with our silk parasols and feathered hats,
our canes of bone that ache.

AN URBAN MEMORY

The sheen of tile...
I glide to an abandoned barstool,
burgundy vinyl, the seat still warm.

Through a twilight window,
shadows pass anonymous greetings
as if trapped in glass. I reach into
my picked-over pockets for dimes
never fitting that stubborn juke I kick

wanting, waiting to hear
any love song...
dead people singing oldies.

A woman in a red dress looks ready
to deliver unwanted children
to wanted men, their pictures
on post office walls.

Together, we close our
soft shade eyelids, avoid
the rude awakening by sunlight.

WHORE

Don't kiss me, I've
kissed too many soldiers,
their hard male bodies.

Every town grows out of me now.
The naval bases are the borders of my skin,
stars and stripes within the scissors of my thighs.
I tell you no lies,
rock-beat radio
played to my breasts
homage of bad singers,
good soldiers of America,
spilling semen.
They come looking for my mouth,
expelling all the good vowels
of their continent.
Woman traveler of the farmlands,
food for the masses,
gory road before me,
I long to escape.

Everyone is looking for me,

afraid I am their daughter.
My face is not in the newspapers,
your younger brother's hands,
the safe brothels.
My skin is white like good money
to all the races
that scatter my parts to the wind.

I am your daughter,
the holy ghost
of witches burned in a char-house.
I am the living body
of the clenched and the breathless—
taking each morning like the end of the world.

DROWSE NOTE

No breasts to breed with.
No hair to pull
nor nipple to punish.
I open refrigerator doors
looking for answers in eggs.
Walk threadbare streets
feeling the funerals of handshakes.

Pray with these hands
to the bright invisible one
who created all this misery
with the wave of his own hands.
I tell him to take me
past black clouds and kerchief paper sails,
beyond tired lids opening the afternoon.

No sleeping to save you
when the bottle is empty
and your mouth is not working

with your shrink
to sing happy songs together
for dead polka dancers who wasted their lives
traveling the mid-west in mini-caravans.
God loves those who love themselves.

But who am I
to question the stare of paper,
the murderous pen, a red inked intention—
when I know in the darkest basement of every old house
are the shrunken bodies of sewing rooms
surrounded by mirrors— where you can get lost in yourself
just planning which shade of green you'll wear,
a torn, moldy shroud—
or which model you'll be.

DEATH LIKE A FINGER
(for Charlie Mehrhoff)

With photographs of an abandoned hotel in the mountains
where the dirt roads were speaking *'come follow'*.
This was no ordinary road my shaman friend knew,
this was the road of the blue truck traveling
to the ruins beyond the heliotropes.
In the mountains past the cottonwood clouds,
with the light behind them, wildflowers so high,
In the mountains where the blue truck pulled
to the side of the road where no police could interrupt
our quiet watch for spirits of gold diggers
the indians saw and were thought crazy.
'Did you see it? ' i asked, *'did you see*
something run that way? '
'South is death, ' the shaman told me, pointing—
'Was it a blonde boy? ' 'Yes, he ran from tree to tree.
How'd he get so high up? '

With the good demons upset in me, we drove a little further

past some ol' forty mobiles piled up on each other
like a chain of past lives or a reaction to apathy.
Shaman got out for an old archaeologist's look.

He reminded me of the flowers growing
in those car hoods where bullet holes
cut through all the tin and the flowers cut through
the beginning of a happy ending—
How i almost walked across the cars of death as i took
a photograph to commemorate them.
Shaman wiped the dust off his shoulders,
wishing himself in a desert when i told him—
'Charlie, let's leave.'

Driving away, a skull and crossbones marked our exit,
the mountains with the light behind them.
Look at the view behind you in the rearview mirror,' he said,
'My friend, if you dream about it, this is the place
where you'll never return.'

AT THE ALTAR

The burlap dress I once wore
carried potatoes.
And this day I had worn it for the church.
A special mass— the Irish priest
up at the lectern talking to himself.
I remember his eyes—

They grew large when he said *'Jesus'*
and small like a rat's when he mentioned
'the devil'' which was quite often.
The entire town paid more attention
when *'evil '* was mentioned...

Standing by the far back entrance,

I was looking straight ahead—
my parents' friends and enemies,
many were whispering.

So I walked down the aisle
as Father kept speaking—
the closer I walked, the louder he grew,
and the redder. All these people
were staring at my bare feet and pointing,
forgetting it was rude to point.

All this as I knelt in front of the altar,
bowed my head down on the ground,
with tears of feeling Him in my soul—
making the sermon end in the middle
as I waited...
for Father to anoint my forehead
just before I was taken away...

SOUVENIRS IN PASSING OF THE NIGHT

i

I sit in a kingdom asleep under streetlamps,
knowing a crucifixion is near.
In a dark dream, this rose exceeds,
a flame in the thorn of my mouth
swallowing nakedness under a sunny moon.
Through the nothings of beginnings I walk
attempting to overcome
the blackening salmon of my dreams.
The eyes are quiet this late summer
in this mortal ambush
where shadows are the dark forgotten.
In this wide night the expanse of a few lakes,
I smell the dead—they are sleeping.

ii

Tide runs my emotions like the moon hiding.
Fish swim through the runnels,
the long ripples along
waterlogged skin—
The body ages,
retires to the serene sea foam
in search of Venus.
The twilight wind turns old leaves
to young flesh.
Fish wings catch the light of stars.

iii

Stars fade as the beast in my chest.
My will is a doe, following
the poisoned snake, shedding his skin in the bushes—
on mornings, as I would be,
altering my miscellaneous self
as the tongue of water
creeps in between my toes,
pleading with the sinuous currents
of knowing
April melts the long hard edges of winter.
And branches loosen the debris of
that dangerously shiny moon.

iv

At sunrise, the long journey
comes to an end.
The detours of dreams
tell no more than
the sudden veerings of narrow valleys.
Black butterflies paint themselves
colorful to face the day.
The early dew of the rain of our dreams
turns crab grasses to peacock feathers.

I slip a wet pearl in my pocket
to remember.

BLACK TICKET

On a night of the deepest stillness,
a medicine cabinet had shown
the labyrinthian melancholy of stars.

In a victorian shadowbox, an evil juggler's head.
The light of cities trapped within bottles.
Poisonous abodes appearing to be hemlock;

Precious in their multitude of yeast-thriving
microbes held captive: bottle of Cephalexin:
'Juana B. Palacios, Take one, four times daily.'

She swallowed an unknown future.
The rash traveled around her waist.
'Cuando da la vuelta se muere.'*

Laid down to rest, no pills save her
from the leprosy that had become
her shrouded, final hours.

Closing the mirror of the cabinet,
a little breath sighs, a tiny death.
My eyes hold a continuous bridge.

Random objects cloistered in prisms of light,
a referent for the afterworld.
Prescription: long expired.

*upon completing its turn, one dies**

THE HACKNEYED ROAD NARROWS

The hackneyed road narrows.
Obsidian winged birds
fly by
Night wades the weary
horizon's unrest.

I begin again.
Must find a place.
A cat-bird
one lone dog-fish
beckoning distance
from cages.

I walk aware
of the love of man
and christ,
how murder is
seasonal change.

It is good to live
alone
willing to fly
distances
with sore winged
desire.

I would be
a bird,
rising to
the occasion,
spreading its wings
in the shape of
a cross.

For what little power
a man walks
listening to the leaves,

his dementia against death.
It takes so little
to be free.
So little
to lose a name
or an address,
walk the fires of grounds,
burning
small truths.

I shall
survive
this terrible road.
My bird shall
sing.

Richard Purinton

Words on Water: A Ferryman's Journal

The ferries we operate transport people, vehicles and goods across Death'sDoor, between Washington Island, Wisconsin and the Door Peninsula. Working around and on lake waters is a satisfying form of service, and the weather, seasons, people and experiences offer occasions for reflection and comment.

January 2, 2007

8 am. Light frost. The sun arises with clear blue skies. It's a morning with the feel of early fall, not early new year. There's not a snow bank in sight. The several days of heavy rain have long since soaked in and the pavement is dry. It's a great day—and a great drive to work—all of four minutes spent in my truck, barely enough time to let the coffee cool or the heater get warm. With the low gas warning light flashing, I pull off at the Hansen Amoco station.

Contractor and Islander baseball coach, Ted Jorgenson, on the other side of the pumps, and I exchanged greetings and information on the bowl games of the night before. Gas cap snapped in place, half tank 'fill' in my truck, and on to the ferry dock.

The drive is just 2 miles from home - from the golf course where home juts between the eighth green and number nine fairway—a drive I make twice or more a day, nearly every day of the year.

Like many mornings, I pass only one or two cars. Today, none, excepting Ted's truck at the filling station. Some days a deer or several turkeys might cross the road, but on this second day of January traffic is nil. The first ferry of the day is 8 am. And today's the last day of multiple trips before the scant winter ferry schedule takes hold until April 1st, with at least four round trips.

Not but a few years earlier, before the powerful Arni J. Richter ice breaker began winter service, we ran four or five round trips on the post-New Year's day to get the waiting crowd back to the mainland after a long holiday weekend.

It was an all day affair of back-to-back trips with the C.G. Richter and its 9-car capacity. Sometimes the crew squeezed an extra car or two, so that by the last trip only three or four cars were left to be loaded. With the C.G., if ice blocked the route—and there was ice on January 1st about 40 percent of the time—then trips took longer.

An altogether different scenario has played with the new Arni J. Richter. We make four trips, each one on schedule and unimpeded by ice. Customers and crew know where they stand, the days are organized and traffic flows without a hitch.

The ferry this 2nd of January, this first real work day of the New Year, is filled with people and cars heading across the Door, southward to homes in Green Bay, Chicago, Milwaukee. On the return trip the ferry's mostly empty, maybe a few retirees or island mainland shoppers or furnace repairmen coming to the island, to home or to work. Today school resumes, so the young families with children are already here, in school, at work and at home.

In the office, I write several letters. It's hard to get used to writing 2007 after 365 days of the '06. My calendar is still 2006, and mid-morning one Harley Davidson calendar is taken down for another, newer one. The 2007 version is tacked to my office bulleting board. Clean squares and a classic Harley Sportster replace a Road King and squares with notes and squiggles.

This is where I work, one eye on the clock, and my mind floating between the Federal Register proposal for Voyage Data Recorders, company end-of-year reports, and the tidying up of Christmas correspondence. I generally begin with, "The new year got off to a good start with big wins by the Packers and Badgers....," gloating a bit if my correspondent is not of Wisconsin roots. Share the smiles and hopes for the coming year with fellow fans.

This first day of work of the new year feels good. It's sunny, bright and the days ahead are going to be exciting.

January 3, 2007

A most frequently asked question by visitors: "What do people do here?"

By this they mean both the question and the implied answer, "I don't see many people or activities, so what is there for me to do here?" And, the more common, "How do people live and work here?"

The Island seems a mystery to many, including myself most days. How people find Washington Island, or how it finds them, must be as varied as any other community.

Some arrive for recreation and never care to leave, planning, scheming, even, for the day they will retire or change jobs. Or, fate will present them with an opportunity to live here. Marriage and divorce are also great motivators.

In my case, it was a combination of marriage to an island girl, Mary Jo, and her shared interest in returning to Wisconsin to live and raise our one-year-old old, Hoyt. I was on the down slope of a four-year enlistment in the U.S. Navy, and we lived in San Diego. Navy life, the ships, going to sea, the bustle of San Diego—all of that had great appeal for us both. But, we missed the seasons, the waters of Lake Michigan, too, and the familiarity with friends, family and places.

To the point here, what is it I do? We do? On Washington Island?

I had asked Arni Richter, my father-in-law, if I could work for him. This inquiry with about 16 months left to complete my Navy enlistment. I was a quartermaster, meaning I worked in ship navigation, bridge record keeping, was a wheelsman at times, maintained navigational charts and publications, etc. But prior to that, I had a love of sailing. Operating mechanically propelled vessels wasn't my greatest interest, but working on and around the water was. Mary Jo and I decided to move back to Wisconsin, to Washington Island, and I would begin work for Arni on the Ferry Line.

Now, some 32 years later, this is still what I do. Every day a check of the boats; an observation of the weather; then at day's end the line of autos with headlights on streaming past our home on Main Road as the last ferry of the day discharges its load and the crew ties up for the evening. This became my routine.

We have great times as a couple, and as a family, with our three children—now two of them married with children of their own. But I am always conscious of living on an island where what we do—ferrying people, cars and freight—is of the greatest importance to the island community. There are few activities in which my work is not brought to mind. Most of the time my thoughts are a relaxing reference to my work, but occasionally they include all of the stress, discontent and decision making inherent in any business environment.

So this morning, at my desk, in my office in the SW corner of the Ferry Terminal building, as sun streams in through the windows, the office phones are ringing with calls for making or changing reservations.

Bill Schutz, our office manager, is winding up the end of 2006 billing and income statements. Files and records of each of the hundreds of freight shipments and ticketing transactions and individual ferry trip records are boxed, to be filed away on a shelf.

Rich Ellefson, our operations and maintenance manager, is preparing pricing and equipment availability for a winter project on the Robert Noble: installation of a new ship's generator; 220v ship's service and new panels, lighting, shore ties, etc. It's a long list and a big job, but we have the right people, the time and the capability to accomplish this before winter is over. Actually, when I look outdoors, winter hasn't really yet begun!

My tasks these days are mostly office and administrative, with only occasional days spent outdoors or onboard the ferry as crew. Here is a sampling of my day's activities:

Letter to Carl Nolen, president of Capital Brewing Company, producer of Island Wheat Beer.

Register for on-line Random Drug Test program with employee names for our company DOT drug testing program.

Check the ads listing our interest in finding a new lessee at our Northport Restaurant. This one is a tough one, potentially!

Correspond with Ellen Hooker, biologist with the Wisconsin Division of Animal Health about cormorant disease on Pilot Island.

Review and edit—next to final edit—our Ferry Line 2007 brochure with schedule.

Send comment letter to the docket for Federal Register notice on Voyage Data Recorders—small black boxes our government is considering placing aboard passenger vessels. So far, our size vessels are not included, but in the future, who knows what ideas catch the fancy of the people in Washington, D.C.?

—and so on. Much of what I do seems peripheral, far away from the daily routine of putting people on the ferry and safely getting them across the Door. But the side tours can often take interesting turns and benefit (or detract from) our ability to provide service at a profit.

With traffic slowly declining these past three years, we're more conscious than ever of operating efficiently and profitably.

That's today's work outline. And, I may break that up with a hair cut at Jeanne Gunnlaugsson's hair shop, and with tree-cutting, chain sawing at Arni's home.

One thing about my day: its never dull, never too repetitive.

It's nearly 10 am when the Arni J. Richter, on time, rounds the tripod on its return trip. Today is the first day of our "winter ferry schedule", meaning just two round trips a day, one in the morning, one in the afternoon.

Mail, freight and traffic will discharge at our island dock in just a few minutes.

January 4, 2007

Record temperatures are predicted today across NE Wisconsin. Not even cold enough for frost last night.

An early, special ferry brought in two Liquid Propane tankers for Hansen Oil, to off load in the storage facility at Townline and Gunnlaugsson Roads, near Ray's home. Tomorrow, a special ferry is scheduled for a single, bulk gasoline tanker for Kieth Mann's CITGO station.

LP has been the fuel of choice for new construction and for retrofitting island homes with the new, compact, efficient gas furnaces. For years, a few homeowners used bottled gas for stoves, and maybe small cottage heating systems. Around 1990 the trend shifted to LP from wood or fuel oil or kerosene.

Storage capacity on the island took awhile to catch up with the local market demand, but over fifteen years time Hansen Oil put in three 10,000 gal. LP storage tanks.

Now, with the majority of heating units being gas-fired, storage is once more on the cusp...or...and this is the more likely scenario... . LP isn't being brought in until the demand is there to fill home tanks. Will this be the last LP incoming until April? The advent of the 104-ft. Arni J. Richter now makes possible the carriage of these bulk semi tankers in winter.

Do we want to carry such potentially hazardous cargo at times of the year when roads, docks and ferry decks may be icy? Not really. That is, we're not anxious to haul that sort of commodity in winter, but there is both the public service aspect and the emergency re-supply that is now possible.

In addition, we raised our rates for large trucks and LP+gas+ diesel commodities from December 21 through March 31st each year. The cost will be greater, the trip options fewer in winter, if the supplier doesn't stock up ahead of time. At least that is the notion. In addition, there is a very specific piece of ferry equipment being used. Granted there is no ice to be seen today anywhere on the horizon, but there will be, and there usually is this time of year. The cost of dock, ferry, ramps, and other supporting infrastructure, not to mention insurance and administrative overhead, requires a significant return in revenue for the service provided.

Human cargo may be the most precious, but it is also the most mobile, and flexible, and stable when conditions are rough or icy. Not so for large trucks.

The 'call' to load trucks with products such as LP is ours, and it's based on marine forecasts (we often use our website weather links at www.wisferry.com), and our seasoned judgment based on experiences of the past. Wind speed, direction, wave heights and temperature can each be a critical factor in deciding to haul those tankers or not.

The procedure is this: We tentatively put it on our dry-erase loading board for the following day after consulting with the trucking company and the weather forecast. At 4 am, as the truck driver heads to the Green Bay terminal to load, he calls to confirm. His call is answered by Hoyt (formerly by me) and he makes the final arrangement to meet at Northport with a ferry, usually around 7 am. If weather causes a cancellation, we reschedule for the next available day, and the driver loads his truck for a different customer instead.

That's the behind the scene on how the island gets LP, gas or diesel products.

I forgot to mention: all LP or gasoline loads must be special ferry transports without any passengers or other vehicles. Only the tankers and their drivers. Fuel oil, with a lower flammability rating, can be carried with a mixed load of passengers, vehicles and cargo.

January 5, 2007

An article I read in the Door County Advocate Marine column reminded me of Sir Ernest Shackleton, who died and was buried on South Georgia Island. A book I read in 7th grade about Shackleton had great impact on me, and gave me a notion of what adventure, tough conditions, and willful and prepared men can do.

The DCA ran a front page story, as they always do, with photos on the Jacksonport annual New Year's Day Polar Bear swim. Great theater. Good photo ops, lots of people. Is it a media event? If no one came to cover it—no cameras, no TV, no press, no onlookers—would it still be fun? Admirably, profits earned on concessions go to non-profit organizations, and the focus is to have fun, which people of all ages seem to do.

Washington Island has its own small gathering on January 1st. Jens Hansen, Bill Schutz, Paul Swanson and friends have sampled the waters of Washington Harbor's Schoolhouse Beach.

Bill's comment: "I think we're doing it the right way. They're (the Jacksonport dippers) only getting wet to the chest, or neck. We put our heads under!"

So, without cheering crowds or TV cameras, Bill, Jens and friends do their annual dip in cold lake waters, plus or minus 38 degrees no matter where you go this time of year. One island advantage is that the water at Schoolhouse is deep and clear. You can easily get your whole body wet, head to toe, just 25 feet off shore.

This was one island activity—one of many—this New Year's day.

At the Sportsman's Club (and there are sports women, too!)

anyone interested and capable of shooting clay birds can compete for a Loot Shoot, by age category, by gender, and for the "Champion of Champions". This tradition begins at 12 noon, an event begun at least 30 years ago by avid outdoorsman Dick VerHalen and his wife, Marilyn. Marilyn made up a pot of chili and towed the spread to their tennis court at the edge of their meadow, where dozens of islanders competed against the cold, clay birds flying through the air, and with joviality, each other.

January 6, 2007

Today I'm back in the office for a five-hour Saturday, after making three trips as part of crew yesterday. Once again, calm seas today and warm temperatures.

A funeral for Ann Greenfeldt brings members of an old island fishing family back for the burial at Schoolhouse Beach Cemetery.

For each of the featured individuals on their day of funeral service and interment, this is the last ferry ride.

Typically, Casperson Funeral Home of Sister Bay, with Greg Casperson accompanying the body and family for burial ceremonies, directs nearly every island funeral service. Casperson stockpiles concrete vaults in December for such winter eventualities, eliminating the difficulty of arranging for a heavy vault truck to cross to the island. So while the body, or ashes in urns, might arrive with the undertaker, the cement vault, if one is needed, is generally already on hand.

Undertaking is one service that is not available on the island, but we have been most fortunate to have a solid and reliable— and flexible—service in Sister Bay. Greg, his father Clyde, and Clyde's father before him, knew the faces and names of many island families. That familiarity alone is a measure of comfort to grieving families.

There are many interesting angles and stories regarding funerals. We laugh nervously when making light of grave matters.

Arni likes to tell the story of a casket slipping into the lake as he and his father, Carl, transferred a box with body from a rowing skiff to the open fantail of the fish tug-come-freight boat WELCOME. They had anchored off the ice banks near Europe

Bay, awaiting the delivery of the casket from Mr. Casperson, Clyde's father. From shore it was transferred to a small rowboat, and from there to the awaiting WELCOME. It was at that point when the box slipped from their grip. Imagine several hundred pounds of wooden casket and dead weight teetering between small skiff and fish tug, perhaps a small swell running from the previous night. The casket was partially submerged.

Mr. Casperson opened and reached into the retrieved box and "straightened up the gentleman's clothes and tie". No water had gotten in the casket. Arni raised anchor for the homeward trip to Detroit Harbor. One imagines the casket inside the small fish tug, jammed alongside the engine box, stove, mail and other assorted freight in the hold of the fish tug.

Clyde Casperson's undertaking services to islanders were well known. Years ago Ella Carlson was transported by ambulance through Sister Bay, having just been transferred from the island ambulance at NP after a winter ferry ride across the Door. Ella said to the ambulance crew, sensing this ferry ride might be her next-to-last, "Step on it when you go past Clyde's."

Ella's husband, Phil, was at one time Station Chief at Plum Island. One of his legs was nearly blown off when a booby-trapped rum runner, apprehended by Carlson's crew, blew up on him. Ella's father was also a light keeper on Plum and Pilot.

Sense of humor or sense of the future tinged with superstition? Ella was buried several weeks later at the island cemetery alongside her husband of many years.

January 7, 2007

Awoke before daybreak, fixed coffee and prepared for an early morning Sunday ride. It's a time when most people are sleeping in or relaxing in their homes.

A wet, damp frost covered the windshield. It hardly required a scraper. The wipers brushed the frost aside and the defroster/heater took over from there.

Up the road—that is, up town—just mile from home, a few car tracks appeared in the morning frost that covered the road. Only one led north, the direction we traveled. Ours was a nearly virginal passage this Sunday morning. The rest of the tracks headed south, perhaps to the Ferry Dock and the 8 am departure? No, that would be later. Perhaps the ferry crew's tracks, going to warm up the engines and get things ready for the morning run.

The sun appeared by 7:15, and the skies were clear. The island in these early minutes of morning was ours to enjoy, to visit with one another and drive wherever we chose. As often happens with us, sooner or later our drive brought us to the Ferry Dock. The 8am ferry had departed some 30 minutes earlier.

It's a great time to think and to enjoy each other's company in the truck as the day begins. We can talk at home, or not, but in the truck there is close companionship even when its not asked for. It's hard to run away from a question or dodge a topic, unless the radio interferes.

A drive, breakfast, church and a visit with Hoyt, Kirsten and Aidan will be a satisfying beginning to the day.

January 9, 2007

..."Do you haul the ferries out of water in winter?" we're sometimes asked.

The only time we haul them out of water is when they are dry docked, and then generally for special work or for a Coast Guard hull inspection, required every five years.

For typical winter lay up, all water systems are drained (or antifreeze added) and the hulls are allowed to freeze in the ice. Of course, this winter there is no ice yet, and so the ferries bob freely at the piers.

We expect a new generator to be delivered in a day or two. The existing 120v ship's service will be changed to 220v, and that will require new electrical panels and rewiring. The electrical panel order will require the longest lead time.

Once this job is accomplished, this ferry should be in good shape for many years, except for the replacement of the main engines, which are original equipment and were rebuilt two years ago.

Winter can be beautiful, and it can also be productive. Besides our ferry project, in various parts of the island carpenters and tradesmen are working, building new homes. Several of these homes, I'm told, are large post and beam construction, substantial second homes.

Marsten Anderson, Sister Bay, was just in and said, "Hello." He's looking at a masonry job out near Jackson Harbor. Bill Llwellyn had started the work, but he was tragically killed in an accident behind his home Christmas eve morning. A limb broke from a tree and struck him in the head. He was found on the ground, saw still idling alongside him. The emergency page for the Island Rescue Squad came in while church was in progress, and at least two island paramedics got up to leave for the call.

Bill was evidently unconscious for some time and could not be revived. He had recently retired to the island and lived in the former home of his parents, Jim and Vi, both deceased.

Jim owned and operated Jim's Up the Road for many years, also known as Nelsen's Hall.

Vi drove taxi, a service that was truly a service. For many hours each summer day, Vi would wait patiently in her taxi near the Ferry Dock for customers. Vi spent almost as many hours at the dock as any employee. She was upbeat, always smiling, and gave a tour loaded with local insight. Some of her customers requested her tour services year after year, like visiting yachtsman George Kress of Green Bay who sailed into Detroit Harbor every summer for decades aboard the Aria.

After Vi's passing, friends planted a small maple with an engraved plaque at the base near the ferry dock.

January 11, 2007

Blackbirds at daybreak, specks in treetops backlit by red morning sun that never sit still for long. They scatter, flying to the next grove of hardwoods like nervous, mindless insects. Grouping in a flock, they are independent flyers, yet part of the whole swooping black banner.

They remind me, this morning, somewhat of shoppers at Mann's Store, independent missions for cheese, bread, eggs, their carts blocking the narrow aisles by the fruit and vegetable section, the last turn just before the checkout. They are hard to avoid, their flocking. Their chattering is also hard to avoid, one or two aisles over, and at times you wish you weren't there to overhear. If you want gossip and news with your dinner, follow the flock.

January 12, 2007

UFDA MARBLES

This board game, generally for two or four players, uses a couple of card decks with jokers, a board with holes around the perimeter, and five marbles for each player. The object is to move from start gate to home gate before your opponent does the same. It's mostly card luck, with a little skill, and it moves quickly. There are other games with slightly different variations.

Barry and Grace Ann Carpenter brought it to the island, and taught it to fifty or so others over a several year period of time. This Friday evening at KK Fiske, we will participate in the first Ufda Marble Tourney. Actually, it's a social event, not a competition.

Kenny Koyen, ever the entrepreneur and magnet for media coverage, was the recent subject of Mark DeCarlo's "Taste of America" on the Travel Channel last Tuesday evening. Kenny took DeCarlo and his snappy humor out on the lake aboard the mighty Sea Diver, along with Kenny's son, Jesse. They lifted nets with enough whitefish to stock a pot for a fishboil. DeCarlo clowned while the kettle boiled. It was a quick look at a fishboil in its edited form, and an even hastier showing of a select crowd at KK tasting the results. One might have been unconvinced by DeCarlo's friendly enthusiasm for the whitefish boil as he seemed to have one foot already out the door, on to another community and another local American delicacy. He left with a new fedora on his head, a gift from Kenny.

But, who can fault even a small sandwich of air time between booyah in Brussels and liver mush in North Carolina? It was national publicity for the island and for Door County. Kenny, with his homespun appearance, multiple interests and skills, and a heart for his home on Washington Island. He has the ability to attract a camera lens. That is a commendable island success story, and it runs to his lawyer baskets, Island Wheat Beer, and the latest, Death's Door vodka.

January 13, 2007

Overcast has given way to sun and blue skies. Ice now covers of the harbor, since the last 24 hours. It's cold—typical January cold—but still very easy to get out and enjoy the fresh air and outdoors.

I heard the low, rumbling of the CAT engines as the Arni J. Richter slid up the channel toward the island docks. A large lumber truck filled the bow, supplies for contractors building a new island home. It also represents a competitive business opening with the local Lampert Yard, also known as Lampert's Home Center. There is a general effort to remain loyal to local businesses, but when a home owner or contractor can shave dollars from a project by ordering by the truckload, a reservation is made on the ferry. This is more commonplace with the advent of the Arni J. Richter as winter ferry, but it is evident other times of the year, too.

I was in a reverie of sorts, on the internet, reading about Sedona vortexes, an interest of Mary Jo's and a destination for us in April. (My wish is to ride a Harley through the mountainous landscapes; hers is to seek whatever is there for greater inner peace and knowledge. I think we will both succeed!)

But, as I was lost in thought on the descriptive text about vortexes, I drifted to the vortexes I've found special in my own back-yard.

The quiet of a deep swamp in November after being led in by tracks and the sight of white tails or birds

Immensity of the ice fields in February off the island's west side—the snaps, pops as fields grind and ice expands; the pinkish glow of the late afternoon sun, Door Bluff headlands 7 or more miles in the distance. The notion that I could set off on foot for Marinette, Cedar River, or Escanaba if I chose—it was commonly done by early islanders—or spend a week in a shack out on the ice miles off shore, fishing through the ice for a living.

The experience may be solitary, but the mind enfolds friends and voices from the past.

I think of my grand parents' farm—Richard and Emma Kalms, and the nine children raised there—with no electricity, miles of stone fences, and a kitchen wood stove for cooking and heat; the large stone at the base of the granary steps with a foot groove worn in over time from chores. I know it was much the same for island farmers, too, the toughness of the East Siders to tame swamp and rock-strewn fields by hand or with horse.

I can feel that strength and energy in certain locations when I'm patient and able to listen, and I'm guessing there is other energy out there, too from the early French explorers and trappers, and from the various native tribes who lived along the island shores.

A strong energy flows from the waters of Death's Door, for me, at least, positive, reassuring, and comforting. I once said to an island preacher, naively leaping to a marketing conclusion based on strong personal influences, that our job here, or at least one of our main tasks as residents and providers of services to island guests is to help put them in touch with their spirit.

Is this what a vortex is? Is that what Sedona is all about? I feel inadequate and unqualified to delve any deeper than that, and for most of us, the expression of one's interest in "recharging batteries" of life may be just that simple—no need to hear the tree or rock talk to us, but just enjoy the experience and create enough quiet to hear our own thoughts.

—more on that some other time!

'What's so special about the island?' is one of those frequently asked questions. There is no short or simple answer. It is the rock here, the tree there, the ice field or the bird. It's also the people, and the memory of humankind, the connection with the universe—and God.

There is no special Island connection to God, but maybe just an easier way to get to the core of being here than at other earthly locations. Connecting must be balanced with food, clothing, family harmony and a supportive, nurturing community.

That is not always easy to achieve or sustain. For a few, "isolation" overwhelms and the familiar—wherever and whatever that is—calls. And there is also the distasteful manipulation by a few, by government, by a society, even in so small a setting, so that life at times seems unbearable. There is a dark and unpleasant side to life in any community, no matter the pull of the vortex.

January 16, 2007

Sunrise brought clear skies and cold weather—actually the high pressure system brought the cold. It was just highlighted by the golden morning sun.

It inspired me to take several photos of the 8 am ferry as it loaded. Then I drove to the Potato Dock and took half a dozen more photos, all with my traditional Nikon F-2 film camera.

A couple of years ago my New Year's resolution was to take at least one photo a day. Some were to be intentional repeats of the same scene to show varied lighting, clouds and weather. Unfortunately, I didn't keep my resolution.

It is a satisfying notion, but it didn't succeed as an artistic endeavor. First a day, then several went by, and soon the goal was behind me. But, as much as possible, I continue to photograph, especially the ferries, with my inspiration the changing lighting and seasons.

I've managed to capture several powerful images of earth, water and sky, the contrast and variety is always stunning and memorable.

Photography is quick, relatively easy, and not a great expense, and I can often use the results for Ferry Line advertising. This too, can be a creative outlet, the truth and expression of ideas to win over the minds of customers, to communicate a feeling about a place or an activity.

January 17, 2007

Our coldest day of the winter thus far, 17 degrees F this morning, with a sharp 25+ MPH wind out of the NW. This changes the tactics used by our captains in a concerted effort to avoid taking on spray or solid water over the bow, or even by dipping the rail far enough in a trough to take slop on deck. There, in these cold temperatures, spray freezes to the steel decks almost instantly and begins to layer in ever greater thickness.

Aside from chipping the ice off with wooden mallets, or chisels, or if there is the luxury of time to allow it to melt or evaporate, the other option is to apply chemical products.

We found, thanks to conversation with Madeline Island Ferry Line folks, a limestone based product in either liquid or pellet form. It turns ice to slush, which can then be shoveled off the decks. It can also be applied while in port, pre-treating decks or steps prior to heading into seas.

But at this time of year, when winds and seas are common, its possible to baby the boat along, gently nudging into the larger swells rather than ramming, to avoid icing down, even with a route less than 4.5 nautical miles.

This Wednesday morning, our crew went over "light" with no traffic at 6:30 am and returned at 7:15 from Northport with a gasoline and an LP tanker—one each. Despite the avoidance of heavy seas, and the danger of rolling in the troughs with such a load, the decks became icy.

That first trip of the day was followed by the regular 8 am departure from the island, now 15 minutes behind, and then by a third round trip to return the empty tankers...

January 18, 2007

The beauty of a day like today is its consistently changing nature. First, clear and overcast. By mid-morning, large flakes of snow begin to fall, 2-3" of lake effect snow. Then, in the early afternoon, just as we were getting used to, and secretly hoping for more fluffy snow, there are gaps of blue skies and warming temperatures.

School isn't in session Friday, so there was a flurry of phone calls, a scramble to get the remaining spots on the ferry for the great exodus. Our vehicle will be among them as we head for Sturgeon Bay and Oshkosh, to do errands and to spend two nights with our four year old grandson while his parents travel to Iowa

For 'new' islanders, the act of leaving home has become known as going "off-island". I've never heard it said this way by the year around, rank and file islanders. A similar use by native

Door County people for their home territory is by the full name, Door County. Of late, it has become popular, with expanded use through books and articles, to refer to this place as simply, "Door." Examples of use remind me of the phrase, "I graduated high school in ———". I'm headed to Door. Welcome to Door. We're having a great time in Door, wish you were here, etc. etc.. It is distinctive, but admits to recent relocation.

On the other hand, we islanders have a few colloquialisms too. We Cross the Door, referring to that body of water, the passage known as Death's Door. Otherwise, it's nearly always THE Door. Then there is also the term 'Back Door', an island perspective that refers to the part of the Door less easily seen from Washington Island, that strait lying between Plum Island and Northport. The other part more familiar to us, between Plum and Detroit Islands, is the 'Front Door'.

Whether speaking or writing it, I live and work in Door County, and more specifically, on Washington Island. For folks on the island there is a tendency to refer to home as "The Island", and when they leave it to head south, they are going to "Door County" rather than the peninsula or the mainland. Callers in summer who are visiting Door County ask for directions to leave Door County and catch a ferry to the Island.

The separation by water creates differences in attitude, illusions of place. We're in Door County, part of the State of Wisconsin and the USA. For the most part, we're happy in our distanced relationship.

January 19, 2007

Mary Jo and I toss our bags in the Nissan along with seemingly ever-present bags of goods for the St. Vincent station in Green Bay, and head to the ferry and a weekend with our grandson, Atlas, in Oshkosh.

During the night there were 25 mph winds. We could hear it in the bare branched trees around our home on Main Road. The ferry captain chooses the south route, in the 'front door,' past the old Plum Island Coast Guard station buildings, past the red #2 nun marking the middle ground—mid-way between Plum and Detroit Islands—first toward Pilot, and then back around the south tip of Plum to Northport. The throttles are pulled back on several occasions, to let the steeper seas roll past without sending a cascade of water onto the foredeck, and to avoid slamming the bow. There are bright, blue skies above. It's a beautiful winter's day, despite the 18 degree temperature. We have a full load of vehicles, with numerous commercial vans, two box trucks (Mann's Store and Mann's Mercantile), and a contingency of islanders headed for points south.

The trip across takes slightly longer on the southern route, but not much longer. Despite the care of the captain, many auto windshields, especially those in the forward half of the car deck, are covered with frozen spray. The crew motions cars ahead, but many drivers can't see, and the crew assists with scrapers to clear the thin, hard film of ice. It reminded me of a trip on a Christmas morning when the ferry departed the island in ten degree temperatures, winds howling from the west, right on the nose as the ferry headed out the channel and toward Plum Island. There was no opportunity to slow, no choice in routes to avoid the seas. Seas were steep, and the spray flew, covering the entire car deck and the windows of the Robert Noble with a coating of ice. One crew member had to work with a scraper on the pilot house windows to keep an open hole through which to see the way. Under a slight lee of the reef on Plum Island, a decision was made to return to Washington Island and forgo the effort made. It was Christmas….someone would inevitably be disappointed, but the alternative wasn't a good one. I met the ferry as it pulled back in to the island, several inches of hardened spray on deck. Carol, my sister-in-law, was among those in her car, located in the first row about mid-way on the deck. Her windshield was so ice covered she hadn't realized, couldn't see, that the ferry had reversed course. The ferry had arrived back at the island dock, not Northport.

January 23, 2007

Winter Tuesdays used to be among my favorite days.
With only one round trip per day, and Tuesdays the only day

of the week during winter our island dentist, Dr. Tom Wilson, visited for office hours—I looked forward to his visit, as did Mary Jo and the rest of our family. Except for his first winter of island dentistry, Tom stayed with us at our home for his many winter time overnights. He and I seemed to hit it off: we both loved sports; we were both class of '65 high school graduates, Tom at Nicolet High, and myself at Sturgeon Bay.

Tom's understanding of island life, and his interest in his island patients made for great visits and memorable times. He and Gunilla, his Swedish-born wife whom Tom met when she was waitressing at Al's in Sister Bay in the late 60s, also visited with us socially from time to time. And, they also stayed with our children in 1979 when we left on a week's trip to Mexico. The day Mary Jo and I returned was the annual island Men's Day, a traditional day each February when snowmobilers and card players gathered at Fred Young's shed for fun and cards and a fish boil. Tom rode on the back of my sled.

The following morning, a Friday, the day the Wilsons left the island, the ferry C.G. Richter's transmission broke down at the southern end of Plum Island. The broken reduction gear, coupled with heavy ice of ten or more inches, resulted in a long wait for the Coast Guard ice breaker to appear on scene from Sturgeon Bay. In the late afternoon the cutter Acacia appeared off Pilot Island. By nine that evening, the cutter had broken a track from the south end of Plum Island nearly to the Potato Dock, where heavy weights were swung from a boom to smack the thick, hard ice. Then, under tow of the cutter, and with some forward only propulsion, the C.G. Richter and its compliment of passengers was escorted in toward the Potato Dock. Nearing ten o'clock that evening, with temperatures dropping to a minus 28 F (it would be the coldest night recorded that year and for many years afterward), I met the ferry, which was still several hundred yards off shore. By snowmobile I shuttled passengers to the beach and waiting cars and families on shore.

Tom and Gunilla weren't among them, however. A sailor on the Acacia had severe cramps, kidney stones it was feared, and the skipper asked if there was a doctor on board? Tom said he was only a dentist, but that didn't matter. He and Gunilla boarded the Jacob's ladder thrown over the side, and scrambled up to the warmth and good smells of the cutter's galley. Leaving the C.G. Richter, the Acacia then turned toward Northport to discharge the sick sailor, and Tom and Gunilla, before returning to finish their escort duties.

By midnight, Nathan Gunnlaugsson and Alvin Cornell had lines over to the old Potato Dock's rough pilings, unused since the early 70s when the potato boat car ferries (old Mackinac Straits railroad car ferries) were moored there. Then the Acacia sailed for home, and in the remaining hours of the night I slept in the pilot house aboard the ferry, tending the single-cylinder Nordberg generator from time to time, until the REA crew arrived later that next day to string wires from the nearest transformer to the ferry. Tom and Gunilla's car was one of nine left parked on the ferry deck, and it would remain there for two and a half weeks more until the ferry was repaired and the track to Northport was opened once again.

Actually, two more visits from the Acacia were required to open up the track sufficiently to where the ferry could make its own way safely. During the interim nineteen days, we ran snow-mobiles with U.S. Mail and freight over the ice, taking along an occasional passenger. That winter was a rare time when I snow mobiled over Plum Island, a short cut to Northport, and then only on a few limited trips.

But, back to Tom and our friendship.

We both enjoyed getting up early, putting on the coffee pot, and then riding around the island, shooting the breeze, commenting on new homes under construction. One of those early mornings, a year when there had been excellent brown trout fishing off the west side of the island, I took Tom on a tour by ice in the company pickup. I had to be at the island post office by 7:45 to pick up outgoing mail. I entered from shore to the ice near Figenschau Bay, then drove around Henning's Little Islands toward West Harbor. For reasons I can't explain today, I took a new and different route back to shore, dead center through the entrance of West Harbor where currents worked back and forth under the ice. In fact, earlier that weekend under a warming trend there had been an open hole, and now after refreezing the ice was only three inches thick.

But, of course, I wasn't aware of that as we drove along, chattering away on one topic or another. The bow of the Jeep pickup was pointed perfectly toward the inner harbor when the back wheels dropped. I barely had time to utter, "Oh s_ _ t" before the front dropped through. The force of water and ice cracked the windshield, and lake water was soon up to the bottom of the windshield and had begun to fill the cab.

Uncertain of my next move—I clumsily tried to open the door against ice and water pressure—I looked over at Tom. He had neatly rolled down his window and scrambled up onto solid ice, his Lands End canvas briefcase in tow. Following his example, with water now up to my knees in the cab, I rolled down my window. I grabbed the cardboard box from the seat between us that held outgoing Ferry Line mail and my 35 mm Nikon camera. I held it high out the window and slid it onto the dry truck roof. Then I pulled myself out the window, slipping into the icy water up to my armpits. But, at least I was standing on bottom.

My first thought after I rolled onto the solid flat ice was to photograph Dr. Tom, glowing with adrenaline, standing in front of the semi-submerged truck. It was our good fortune to be standing safely on the ice, not somewhere underneath it, and Tom's smile showed it. In fact, Tom hadn't even gotten his feet or clothing wet. His Land's End brief case that held his patient's records and sets of dentures in various stages of construction, was also dry and safe.

We hiked over to Herb and Marianna Gibson's, at West Harbor Resort, and they offered us hot coffee and use of their phone. I called the Ferry Dock and suggested someone else pick up the outgoing island mail (it wasn't even yet 7:45, but my 'wheels' were out of order) and then Herb drove Tom out to the ferry dock to catch the 8 am ferry, back home to Sister Bay. That was probably our most memorable morning, that and the fact it was also Valentine's Day. We each found our wives most appreciative for our well being that morning.

March 1, 2007

28 degrees—windy. Forecast: lots of snow and wind.
Winds prior to 8 am were moderate at 20 kts out of the east.

The morning ferry left on time.

About 9:30 am, time of departure from NP, the winds picked up sharply and it began to snow heavily. The AJR got away from NP OK, turned around in the slush ice inside the breakwall, and headed home.

By 11am, it was blowing a "gagger", as an old lake sailor would describe the stormy winds. We cancelled the PM trip.

Our afternoon was spent in the office lunchroom discussing various training topics, an opportune time to check in with everyone and to discuss safety issues. The mid-day weather was wild: white caps on a very short fetch of 200 feet, with swirling snow twisting its way across harbor ice further east of the ferry docks. Not making the trip becomes an easier call when the conditions are extreme, as they are now.

March 2, 2007

The temperature was 28 degrees. The atmosphere was clear but overcast. After the storm, we awake to near calm, and wet, wind driven snow has been stuck to the trunks of trees. Perhaps only 4-5" fell, but it was heavy and despite that it had blown into drifts. The ferry crew had plowed and shoveled and prepared the docks and ferry for the 8 am departure. Loaded and awaiting one more car, the crew noted the lake level had risen nearly one foot in the strong east winds. That level will ebb as the day progresses.

Arni will return home today from the hospital. He's received help and should be OK at home once again, perhaps less mobile than before.

Patches of blue appear over the line of cedars. Skis may slide swiftly through wooded trails, when snow shovels are rested.

March 3, 2007

22 degrees, Sunny, then overcast. Large snowflakes falling, then sunny once more.

The winds swing around to the NW, and with colder air temperatures and shift in direction ice will slide through the Door.

The ferry makes its trip without incident, but ice is deep, snow has filled in voids, and the going will be hard if more ice comes through the Door.

We depart on the 1pm ferry for Oshkosh to attend the Governor's Conference on Tourism 2007.

* * *

Snow lays in the ferry's route. Sticky and deep, it grabs the hull and the increased friction slows the ferry down. Hulls are meant for liquid water; liquid water is also essential for engine cooling, and for steerage. Snow on the water in deep bands grabs like dry cotton on skin.

Later, Saturday evening....when the ferry we rode on to NP broke through the Door ice field, it was apparent this snow covered ice was a test for breaking. We pushed hard, bow into ice, and we got only small progress for our efforts. Then Capt. Bill Jorgenson backed away and found an open lead and easier going.

The ferry crew encountered a different set of conditions on their attempted return.

A large field had moved into the Door while the crew reloaded autos and passengers at NP. Then, after nearly one hour and minimal progress, and no possibility of breaking through the ice fields, the crew turned back and headed for NP and safe harbor.

Passengers and their vehicles were unloaded, and they headed back down the highway once more to find food and lodging for the night.

Rich Ellefson, our Ops Mgr. on board as part of the crew, Jim Hanson, and Capt. Bill Jorgenson, skipper, found rest at a motel in Ellison Bay once the ferry was secured.

Meanwhile on the island, Hoyt fielded a variety of non-stop calls at the Ferry Office. Calls from an inquiring public; calls from passengers' family members and from family members of the crew; calls from the crew; contact with the U.S. Coast Guard.

The ferry crew would try it again Sunday morning, but with the assistance of a CG ice cutter.

When a call for assistance is made, Coast Guard Sector Sault Ste. Marie determines what vessel "assets" may be used. The Mobile Bay out of Sturgeon Bay was undergoing repairs at their homeport, so the Biscayne Bay, a sister vessel, would be dispatched from St. Ignace, a seven-hour sail to Death's Door.

March 3, 2007 (continued)

The Biscayne Bay's skipper, despite recommendations from Hoyt, entered Green Bay waters through the Rock Island passage, not the Death's Door Passage, and the cutter immediately encountered ice. By the time the cutter had made Denny's Bluff at the midpoint on Washington Island's west side, their progress was measured by only a few yards per buck (each time they rammed the ice).

This choice had clearly proved to be the wrong course, directly into stacked and layered bay ice, in addition to being the long way around. It was already mid-to-late morning when the Biscayne Bay reversed course and exited through Rock Island Passage to the open lake. From there they sailed south to Pilot Island and Death's Door, where the loaded, overdue ferry awaited.

One good thing was that the main part of the Door Passage (the Back Door) was clear of ice. Unfortunately, the Front Door between Plum and the Detroit Harbor entrance had filled with a field of very heavy ice, ice that shoved to the bottom in certain areas. The Biscayne Bay took hours to make a track from the south end of Plum to the tripod, where, nearing shore, both heavy ice and sufficient water for navigation ran thin.

For a good share of this five-hour exercise, the AJR broke ice alongside the Biscayne Bay, practicing "team-icebreaking", to make better progress in the heavy going. By mid afternoon, the AJR was secure at the island dock, homeport, and the crew reloaded for another run.

The evening TV news at 10 pm from Green Bay carried coverage, with footage taken from the NP Pier of the AJR, its crew, and the USCG Biscayne Bay in the background. Rich and Bill, two ferry captains, were right-on with their remarks.

March 18, 2007

Mid-20s overnight; frost in morning; beautiful, sunny day once again.

Rich Ellefson says its great maple syrup weather: cold nights but warm sunshine during the day to get the sap moving.

This is a matter of hydraulics, according to the experts. Hard to understand the workings of sap in the spring, but on a good day each maple tree tap can yield a half gallon of sap.

Rich, his wife, Kerstin, and two young boys, Mack and Jed, collect the sap in buckets and store it in large drums. Then Grampa Dick Ellefson, back from Florida early this year, keeps an eye on the fire. It takes many hours to boil down a batch, and that translates into lots of firewood.

The first batch is usually the clearest, the lightest, and therefore, the most highly prized.

* * *

I got up at 5:15 this morning and worked in basement at a carving project, St. John's cross from the Stav church.

A quick visit to see Aidan before his nap on my way home from church. His smiles are infectious, and he looks different, older with his new teeth in his smile, rather than just gums. He's putting out more sounds, and most of them are recognizable for the objects or activities he intends to describe.

* * *

A print of an Icelandic family sitting in their one-room farm house comes to mind. There are at least three generations along with some farm animals. This sketch depicts a scene by candle-light, perhaps in the 1800s or a time earlier than that. The focus is on the one person reading aloud to the others.

Iceland is, or was, the nation with the highest literary rate of any nation in the world. True, not a large population, but it is quite rural with many miles between towns and villages and even between farms. The emphasis on learning to read was great despite distances and isolated farms.

I like to think not all learning of importance takes place at major cities or universities. They are centers for learning, teaching, for research and experimentation, but basic reading and writing can take place almost anywhere. Truth has no bounds best describes this, and in some cases, the opportunities to retreat to silence and inner thought might actually encourage original ideas and concepts.

Photograph, Richard Purinton

Notes on Contributors

Julie C. Eger's work as a massage therapist has fed her belly and warmed her home. Her passion for writing feeds her soul. She lives in a state of wild divine in the heart of Wisconsin. She is responsible for having raised two sons. She is a member of the Wisconsin Regional Writers Association. In 2005 she won first place in the article category, third place in the essay category, and second place in the 2004 nostalgia category of the Jade Ring Contest. Her work has appeared in *Peninsula Pulse, Siftings, Country Today*, and the *Waushara Argus*. Her poetry has been accepted for publication in *Hummingbird. The Secrets of Arbishaw County* is her first novel.

Vicki Elberfeld lives with her brother in a small house on a quiet suburban street near Chicago. A student of literature, linguistics, dance, speech, and theater, she remains grateful to her teachers, including the prototype for *Neurotic Woman's* professor. Vicki has worked as a tutor, teacher, waitress, maid, dancer, and storyteller. She agrees, "It's never too late to have a happy childhood" and loves telling stories to children over 30.

Hatto Fischer was born in 1945 near the Starnberger Lake in Bavaria, Germany, and emigrated to Ottawa, Canada, with his parents and sister in 1957, where he later studied economics and political science at Carleton University before continuing his studies in philosophy and sociology at the London School of Economics (1969–70). After further studies of philosophy at the Philosophical Seminar in Heidelberg, he wrote his Ph.D. on "articulation problems of workers and the tradition of the German Trade Union" in Berlin. Since 1988 he has been living mostly in Athens, Greece. As a writer and coordinator of European projects, including the Article 10—ERDF project CIED (Cultural Innovation and Economic Development), he has explored the field of articulation in many facets. After being advisor for the Green party at the European Parliament to the Committee of Culture, Media, Sports, Education and Youth, he produced a study on the potential of Internet Radio to further the European Debate. He is coordinator of the Non-Profit Urban Society POIEIN KAI PRATTEN ("to create and to do") in Athens (www.poieinkai

prattein.org) and is undertaking two studies for the city of Volos as part of the Interreg III B HERMES project, one on successful cultural planning strategies and the other on the use of multimedia in museums. Equally in the HERMES project he worked 2003–06 as editor and contributor to heritageradio network (www.heritageradio. net). Together with Takuya Kaneda and Thomas Economacos he is currently organizing workshops for and exhibitions of the Kids' Guernica peace murals (www.kids-guernica.org). Also with Spyros Mercouris he is advising the Network of European Cultural Capital Cities and preparing with him the symposium "The Productivity of Culture" to be held in Athens October 2007.

Debra Fitzgerald: I live in Door County, Wisconsin via Massachusetts, New Jersey, Colorado, Missouri and Illinois. My favorite word is 'yet.'

I pay the mortgage on my 1850s farmhouse as a staff reporter for a newspaper, the Door County Advocate. I thought I wrote for readers, yet both state and national judges have awarded me 19 times during the four years I've been with the paper. I get a small section of wall above my desk in the newsroom to display these atta-girl plaques. I'd appear a lot less conceited if they'd give me a bigger wall.

I have an MFA in creative writing, a cigarette habit, and an addiction to men who emit trace elements of outlaw. None of them have done me in yet.

I've featured one 'interesting' person for the Chicago Tribune. The others, who are not real, have been condemned to the unpublished realm of my computer. They live on within their fictional constraints in about 50 short stories, and a collection called, "How I Killed Jack." This doesn't include the novels. The novels.

I've assistant-taught a graduate class of creative writing students in Slovenia, and once, had an ill-conceived notion that teaching a semester of "business writing" for a Wisconsin technical college would employ my under-utilized skills. Yet it did pay for a trip to Mexico.

Once, during a glorious fit of lit-crit fever, I wrote an essay entitled, "Translating Ideas: What Scientists Can Teach Fiction Writers About Metaphor." I received the acceptance letter almost a year later and popped a bottle of Moet & Chandon when the piece was published in the March/April, 2003 issue of AWP. Yet, while reading the piece, I thought, 'who wrote this schlock'...

Jude Genereaux lives in Wisconsin's great white north, relishing life in the rural Midwest and recent retirement. "After a lifetime spent in the 9 to 5 world, the freedom to focus all of my energy on home, family and writing, is a blessing greatly treasured." Her work has been included in "Hummingbird," "Nature of Door," "WFOP Calendars," "Selections of WI Academy AS&L" and a number of small press and newspapers.

Marina Pilar Gipps, born 1966 in Chicago, the daughter of an Argentine mother and British father, was awarded a Master of Arts degree from the English/Writing program at the University of New Hampshire—where she worked with Charles Simic in an independent study. Prior to her studies in New Hampshire, she attended the summer MFA Writing and Poetics program at The Naropa Institute in Boulder, Colorado—where she studied with Allen Ginsberg. Her poetry has appeared in *Abraxas, Bombay Gin, Exquisite Corpse, Rambunctious Review, Potato Eyes, Poetry Motel, Tray Full of Lab Mice, Willow Springs*—among other publications.

Bruce Hodder is an English poet and prose writer, literary and music critic, born in Ipswich, Suffolk in 1964. He has been published in a number of small-circulation print magazines in the U.K. and the U.S., as well as on the internet. "Death Row Dog" is one of the many nicknames of the author, including "the Beat Brit Bard," coined by American poet t.k.splake. Hodder may be best known as the author of the blog 'Suffolk Punch' (www.bluefredpress.blogspot.com), which continues to attract a growing audience worldwide. He is also the founder of Blue Fred Press, a minor post-Beat/alternative press in the U.K.

Catherine Hovis, DeKalb, IL. Wife, mother, grandmother, MFA student @ Columbia College Chicago (Fall 2003 to present) CEO Hearing Help Express. Writing workshops: The Clearing, Ellison Bay, WI; Stonecoast, conducted by USM in Maine; Solstice Summer Conference @ Pine Manor College, MA; and Writer's in Paradise at Eckerd College, FL.

Laurie Kahn is dedicated to the art of psychotherapy, both practice andteaching. She is a writer, a feminist, and the mother of three children (a spoken-word-poet, a political activist and an aspiring scientist.) Her essays and articles appear in *Oy to Joy*

(JRC press) *From There to Here* (JRC press), *The Reconstructionist Journal*, and *The Journal of Trauma Practice*. She lives in Evanston, Illinois with her husband, dog, and occasional children.

Bobbie Krinsky, of Madison, Wisconsin, is a studio silversmith turned poet, photographer and memoirist. She is a founding member of Westwing Studios, the Dane County Home's (now Badger Prairie Health Care Center's) in-house artists. Their extraordinary story is the springboard for *Voices: Elegy for an Asylum*—a collection of photo-essays, stories and poetry about the events and recollections that capture the spirit of people (real and imagined) who lived and worked at the County Home.

Recent awards, publications and photography exhibits include: *The Light Project* finalist, Green Bay Symphony Orchestra, 2007; Wisconsin Fellowship of Poets Triad Contest—2000, 2006; *Madison 150 Photo Contest,* 2006; WFOP Calendars; *How Art Heals*, Red Gym, UW, Madison, WI, 2006; *The Asylum Project*, Overture Center, Madison, WI, 2006; *Epidemic Peace Imagery:* Traveling Exhibit; *Elegy For An Asylum:* Photographs and Prose—Dane County Home, 1864–2004, from 2004 to 2005 Wisconsin Press Women's *Impressions/Expressions,* Literary And Visual Arts; Bames & Noble's Writers' Place readings from *Elegy For An Asylum*.

Ralph Murre has been an architect and mariner, a farm boy and city kid, an art student and motorcycle racer, and is a poet and dreamer who lives near Jacksonport, Wisconsin. His writing has appeared in a number of journals and reviews, both in print and on-line. His book of poetry, from Cross + Roads Press, is *Crude Red Boat*. He says he attempts to get lost in the woods or at sea, but so far, has always returned.

Becky Post is retired from teaching music and Russian in the public schools of La Crosse, Wisconsin, and has taught English and music in Dubna, Russia. She has had poems published in *Wisconsin Poets' Calendars* and in *Free Verse* and has had several articles published. She writes fiction, poetry and music and is working on a new novel, part of which takes place in Russia. She works as a substitute teacher and musician.

Richard Purinton was born and raised in Sturgeon Bay, Wisconsin. A graduate of Sturgeon Bay HS, 1965; UW Madison BA

Journalism, 1970; 4 years US Navy; 33 years with Washington Island Ferry Line, Inc. He lives and works on Washington Island and on/in/around the ferries on a daily basis, as captain, and now as company president. Married to Mary Jo Richter, daughter of Arni and Mary Richter. Home is on Main Road. Three children, two grandchildren. Son, Hoyt, is also a ferry captain and is company Vice President.

Purinton authored and self-published *Over and Back* in 1990; a booklet on Harry F. Purinton, *An Artist in the 30s*. He is contributing editor of the *Foghorn*, national monthly publication of the Passenger Vessel Association, and the editor of the *Ferry Line's Passenger Cabin News*.

Jim Roseberry lives in Madison, Wisconsin where he has been writing this, his first book. He grew up in California and received his undergraduate degree from UC-Berkeley in 1968. He was drafted in January,1969 and spent a year in Vietnam from July, 1969 to July, 1970.

Bonnie T. Summers' work has appeared in *After Hours—A Journal of Chicago Writing and Art*, the *Journal of Religion and Abuse*, Woman Made Gallery's *Her Mark 2007 Datebook*, *Moon Journal Magazine*, Door County's *Peninsula Pulse*, *Pietisten* and online at ChicagoPoetry.com. She is the 2006 Nonfiction winner of the Guild Complex Prose Series for her essay, "Red." She was awarded a 2004 Individual Artist Grant in nonfiction from the Money for Women/Barbara Deming Memorial Fund for her memoir-in-progress. She is indebted to Jerry Perlmutter, PhD, the originator of Integrative Somatic Psychotherapy and founder of the Midwest Institute for Somatic Psychotherapy (www.misp-org.com), for walking right into the fires of healing and transformation with her.

Kristin Thacher grew in up in the hills of West Virginia and now lives off the grid in the mountains of northern New Mexico. She is a potter and a poet.

Tibor alone is enough. I was born in France to working class parents of Ruthenian and Romanian heritage and educated sporadically in various European countries and Canada. A failed life, I have come to celebrate that. Make it my work to remain unknown. My kind lives either isolated or in transit with no destination. There is enough biography in the world. Enough trafficking in fame for comfort's sake. Let art speak for itself. For me.

Dorothy Terry, chronicler of the *Fantastical Travels of TSE*, is a Chicago area poet. Her poetry has been published in *The Thing about Second Chances*, Polyphony Press, Chicago; *InPrint*, Persiflage Press, Chicago, and *Zocalo,* Oaxaca, Mexico; and *InPrint*, Newberry Library, Chicago. She was selected as an annual Newberry reader in 2004, representing Brooke Bergan's workshop. She also has served on the Editorial Board of a upcoming anthology by Persiflage Press, and is currently completing three books: *Snapshots*, a book of short form poetry; *Under Mt. Alban*, poems of Oaxaca, Mexico; and *The Last Trumpet*—A poetic drama about the Great Flood of Orleans, circa 2005 A.D., including the activities of the Devil Himself as well as the famous Baron Samedi.

George E. Wamser, 53 this year, feels as though he has "turned the corner towards fall in life, but isn't quite ready for the fox farm yet!" His weekly online electronic column, *North Country E-Tales (gewamser@yahoo.com),* appeared by subscription five years ago and concerned the pleasures, adventure, humor and drama, subjects big and small essential to a North Country Lifestyle, and has carried a tiny but loyal readership all that time.

It was an experiment in journalism over the then new internet media long before anybody even thought about "blogging". It has grown and changed over time, adding original art and photography. The whole idea of the column was to keep Wisconsin expatriots all over America and beyond, hungry for news from home. His audience has extended from Alaska to Iraq, Milwaukee to California. He always elicits comments and criticism from his readers.

Other than living in Oconto County, full or part time all his life, George wants you to know that he has no particular qualification to write anything for anybody, and that he is simply a blue collar worker, a printer by trade, who is extremely interested in nature, and human nature. He is keenly aware of the great environmental changes going on in the North Country over the last forty years, and is extremely concerned about how much of the resources will remain for future generations.

He lives in Oconto, Wisconsin with his Native American wife, Wanda, where they built their own cabin; *The Good Medicine Lodge* on Sunrise Lake near Mountain 20 years ago.

He serves strong coffee and good campfires as an incentive for good conversation. He is a person who takes full advantage of the recreational possibilities the North Country has to offer, including backpacking remote areas of the Nicolet National Forest. His love for all this—earth, air, fire, and water—is equaled only by the love he feels for both family and friends.

"Simply said...one life up here ain't enough!"

Robert M. Zoschke was born in Oak Park, Illinois. He has spent most of his life living in and around Chicago, where he was an award-winning advertising copywriter before taking to the road. His short stories, poetry and essays have been published in literary journals, newspapers and on the web. He currently resides in a shack of writer's solitude in Door County, Wisconsin.

Cross+Roads Press List

#1. AN EVENING ON MILDRED STREET, poetry, Mariann Ritzer
#2. THE THOUGHT MUSEUM, poetry, Paul Schroeder
#3. I WANT TO TALK ABOUT YOU, poetry, Dave Etter
#4. EYE DEA, The Autobiography of An Invisible Artist, Bill Stipe
#5. A FIRE ON THE WATERS OF DOUBT, poetry, Pedro D. Villarreal
#6. I THOUGHT YOU WERE THE PICTURE, Artist's Journal, Emmett Johns
#7. ONCE I LOVED HIM MADLY, short fictions, Mariann Ritzer
#8. FINDING THE LOST WOMAN, A Poet's Journal, DyAnne Korda
#9. THE JAMES DEAN JACKET STORY and Other Stories, Don Skiles
#10. THE LAST HOUSEWIFE IN AMERICA, poetry, Donna Balfe
#11. BLUE ISLAND, poetry, Phillip Bryant
#12. TANGLETOWN, poetry, Mike Koehler
#13. Ben Zen, THE OX OF PARADOX, poetry, Tom Montag
#14. WHITE SHOULDERS, poetry, Jackie Langetieg
#15. BACK BEAT, poetry/prose, Albert DeGenova and Charles Rossiter
#16. PRACTICE, The Here & Now, poetry/prose, Edith Nash
#17. BLACK BODY PARTS, poetry, Monique Semoné Ferrell
#18. OUR LADY OF SEVEN SORROWS and Other Stories, prose, D. L. Snyder
#19. THE BLUFF, prose, Sue Wentz
#20. A BUTTERFLY SLEEPS ON THE TEMPLE BELL, prose/poetry, Don Olsen
#21. A BLESSING OF TREES, poetry, Alice D'Alessio
#22. CIGARETTE LOVE SONGS AND NICOTINE KISSES, poetry, Emily Rose
#23. BREATH TAKING, poetry, Susan O'Leary
#24. THE FATHER POEMS, poetry, David Pichaske
#25. THE RAIN BARREL, prose/poetry, Frances May
#26. A GLEAM ACROSS THE WAVE, biography, Arthur and Evelyn Knudsen
#27. SALUD, selected writings, Curt Johnson
#28. CRUDE RED BOAT, poetry, Ralph Murre
#29. OTHER VOICES: Works in Progress, anthology, Norbert Blei, editor

Broadsides

Broadside Beat #1: LITTLE BITS OF TRUTH, Women in the Beat, Susan O'Leary
Broadside Beat #2: ON EROTIC WRITING, Mariann Ritzer
Broadside Beat #3: OBSCURITY, Don Skiles
Broadside Beat #4: SMOKEY THE BEAR SUTRA, Gary Snyder
Broadside Beat #5: CALL AND ANSWER, Robert Bly
Broadside Beat #6: CROW, Chris Halla